THIRTY YEARS
OF LYNCHING
IN THE
UNITED STATES

1889-1918

Published by the

National Association for the Advancement of Colored People
National Office
70 Fifth Avenue, New York

APRIL, 1919

WITH A NEW INTRODUCTION BY
Paul Finkelman
*John Hope Franklin Visiting Professor of American Legal History
at Duke Law School
and the President William McKinley Distinguished Professor of Law
and Public Policy at Albany Law School*

THE LAWBOOK EXCHANGE, LTD.
Clark, New Jersey

ISBN 9781584779650

Lawbook Exchange edition 2012

The quality of this reprint is equivalent to the quality of the original work.

THE LAWBOOK EXCHANGE, LTD.
33 Terminal Avenue
Clark, New Jersey 07066-1321

*Please see our website for a selection of our other publications
and fine facsimile reprints of classic works of legal history:*
www.lawbookexchange.com

Library of Congress Cataloging-in-Publication Data

National Association for the Advancement of Colored People.
 Thirty years of lynching in the United States, 1889-1918 / National
Association for the Advancement of Colored People ; with a new
introduction by Paul Finkelman.
    p. cm.
 Includes bibliographical references and index.
 Reprint of the 1919 ed.
 ISBN 978-1-58477-965-0 (hbk. : alk. paper) -- ISBN 1-58477-965-9
(hbk. : alk. paper)
 1. Lynching--United States. I. Title.
 HV6457.N3 2012
 364.1'34--dc23
                              2012032964

Printed in the United States of America on acid-free paper

Introduction

Paul Finkelman*

The term "lynching" probably stems from a Revolutionary era Virginia militia officer, Charles Lynch, who summarily executed loyalists as well as some blacks. Out of this experience came the term "lynch's law." Before 1820 the term "lynch law" was generally applied to any extra-legal violence, in the name of "law" and "justice," including whippings or other punishments. By the 1830s this term had morphed into "lynching," and was clearly part of everyday language. The first use of the word "lynching" in a published book seems to be in *Col. Crockett's Exploits and Adventures in Texas*, written by Davy Crockett and published in 1836. It appears in newspapers a year later. By this time the term was almost always applied to incidents where the victims were killed, usually by hanging, but sometimes by shootings, and occasionally by being burnt alive. Victims were often tortured before they were finally killed.

Lynchings are often thought of as mob violence, although this is not entirely correct. Often lynchings were conducted by carefully chosen citizens and were organized. In 1893 for example, about 10,000 people attended the lynching of Henry Smith, a black man, in Paris, Texas. Citizens built a scaffolding in preparation for the lynching that was carefully orchestrated and involved horrifying torture of the victim before he was burned alive. This was not mob violence but an organized ritual killing. On the other hand, some lynchings were spontaneous outbursts of mob violence. Still others —the classic lynching of a horse thief in the West—involved aggrieved citizens acting as prosecutors, jurors, judges, and then executioners in a swift exercise of what lynchers would have called frontier justice.

---

* Paul Finkelman is currently the John Hope Franklin Visiting Professor of American Legal History at Duke Law School. He is also the President William McKinley Distinguished Professor of Law and Public Policy at Albany Law School.

During the Civil War there were lynchings in the United States and the Confederacy. In the South white Unionists—opponents of secession—were lynched in a number of places. In New York City about 100 blacks were lynched during anti-draft riots in July 1863. After the War thousands of blacks were lynched in the South by the Ku Klux Klan and other white terrorist organizations. In 1871 anti-Chinese riots in Los Angeles led to somewhere between 20 and about 80 deaths. Some of these were killed in gunfights as the Chinese tried to defend themselves from the white mob, but a number were hanged—lynched—by the mob.

By 1880 lynching had significantly diminished in most of the United States. But in the South a new wave of lynchings was about to begin. Over the next forty years more than 5,000 people—mostly southern blacks—would be lynched. Starting in the mid-1880s the *Chicago Tribune* and the Tuskegee Institute began to keep records—as best they could—of these lynchings. In 1912 the newly formed National Association for the Advancement of Colored People (the NAACP) began to monitor and record all known lynching. In 1918 the NAACP published the book reprinted here.

Thirty Years of Lynching provides information on the lynchings of 3,224 people between 1889 and 1918. As the book notes, this is most certainly an undercount. The NAACP had evidence of 181 other lynchings but it did not include them in this volume because the organization was "unable, due to imperfections in the available data" to give the name, date, place, or alleged offense of the victim. In addition, it is likely that hundreds of other people—blacks in the deep South, Mexican-Americans in the Southwest, Chinese in the West, and some Indians—were also lynched but there were no reports of these events. Particularly in the deep South some blacks simply disappeared without a trace. They might have moved north or west, but many were simply murdered and their bodies never found. This was a quiet kind of lynching.

Significantly, the NAACP report also did not count the many blacks killed by mobs of whites in race riots during this period. From the end of the Civil War through the 1930s a "race riot" involved mobs of whites invading black neighborhoods, or just attacking any blacks they saw. In 1906 dozens of blacks were killed in the Atlanta race riot and perhaps hundreds were injured. In 1898 as many as 100 blacks were killed in a similar riot in Wilmington, North Carolina. Although the victims of lethal violence by whites, these riots were not categorized as lynchings, despite the cold-blooded murders of blacks by rioting whites.

The NAACP, organized in 1909, focused on fighting segregation, discrimination, and racism by educating the public and through litigation. Lynching had been a major concern of African-Americans since the end of the Civil War. While many whites were lynched—especially in the West and before 1900—the overwhelming majority of lynching victims were black. Most lynchings took place in the South, where until World War I, more than 90% of all blacks lived. Some southern governors and public leaders tried to stop lynching, with some modest success. From 1899 to 1918 there were only six lynching in Maryland and 27 in Virginia. This contrasts with more than 250 lynchings in Georgia, more than 240 Mississippi, and more than 150 in both Texas and Louisiana in this period. *Thirty Years of Lynching* was published to help bring an end to lynching. NAACP leaders believed that a public examination of lynching would help put pressure on southern leaders to put a stop to this peculiar and horrifying American form of injustice.

By 1918 lynching was in fact on the decline. Between 1889 and 1893 more than 840 people were lynched but from 1914 to 1918 the number had been reduced to 325. In the 1920s, after the publication of this book, lynchings would continue to decline. But in the immediate post-World War I period huge race riots in Chicago, East St. Louis, Tulsa and elsewhere left hundreds of blacks dead, as murderous white mobs invaded black neighborhoods, indiscriminately killing African Americans, destroying property, and sometimes torching whole sections of a city. In the late 1920s and early 1930s lynching would decline more rapidly.

From Reconstruction onward, lynching served as a severe and violent form of social control. In the South, the Ku Klux Klan, other white terrorist organizations, local law enforcement personnel, and mobs murdered blacks for alleged crimes or for no crimes at all. In the last quarter of the nineteenth century many lynchings were politically motivated. Blacks who ran for office, worked in politics, voted, testified in court, reported crimes, or even tried to establish schools for their children, were victims of lynchings. These murders sent a powerful message to all southern blacks: involvement in public life could be lethal. By 1900 almost all southern blacks had been disenfranchised. Lynching was still a form of control designed to keep blacks "in their place," discourage black entrepreneurship, limit black education, suppress any possible black political activity, and discourage blacks from asserting any rights. One lynching could send a huge message to everyone in the county, city, or section of a state about the importance of giving complete deference to whites.

The book reprinted here is one of the most comprehensive studies of lynching in U.S. history. The NAACP data shows that most lynchings were not about interracial sex – the great paranoia of the southern white Americans. Many blacks were lynched because they had allegedly committed murders. However, many of these "murderers" were never tried and the evidence against those lynches was speculative at best. But other blacks were lynched for no apparent reason, or for some minor transgression of social and racial rules—as understood by whites—such as "inflammatory language," "insulting remarks to a white woman," "being disreputable," or just "race prejudice." This last cause—racial prejudice—was indeed at the root of almost all lynchings of African-Americans.

The great value of this book in the struggle against lynching was its incredible detail and the sheer volume of reported incidents. Since the rise of white terrorism after the Civil War, blacks and their white allies had complained about lynchings. But, those who were indifferent to civil rights, or even hostile to black rights, were often skeptical of these claims. Newspaper reports were scattered. Many lynchings in the South were ignored by the northern press, or given just a few lines, here and there. Many northerners also accepted southern white claims that lynchings were in response to black sexual attacks on white women. Thus, in effect some whites in the North, like almost all whites in the South, argued that these lynchings were justified and even necessary.

Thirty Years of Lynching was the answer to these skeptics and those northern whites who accepted southern justifications for what was in fact lawless and lethal violence. Each event was documented—with names, dates, places, and even the alleged reason for the lynching. The sheer number of the recorded lynchings, state-by-state, year-by-year, showed how pervasive this violence was. The details of the documentation, which allowed skeptics to check local, regional, or national papers for the days following a lynching, provided strong evidence of how much lynching was taking place, and how violent the South had become. The sheer volume of the lynchings was numbing, and compiled in one place provided enormous evidence of the crimes against blacks in the South.

The listing of the "reasons" for lynchings also undermined the southern justifications for the crime. Most victims had not attacked white women. The largest category of victims were those who had allegedly committed murders. While some were lynched after they were convicted in a trial, most had not been tried or given any due process. Many were undoubtedly completely innocent of their alleged crime. Significantly, many victims of lynchings had done nothing that northerners would consider a crime. Reasons for lynchings included "being troublesome," "gambling," and "incendiarism." In Texas, in 1901 a "quarrel over profit sharing" that led to the lynching of five blacks. These "causes" of lynchings underscored the brutality of the white South towards blacks. One black in Texas was lynched for "writing a letter to a white woman." In the South this was considered, quite literally a "hanging offence" but in the North all people would have understood it was not a crime at all.

The barbarity of lynching was made clear by the reasons for the killings contained in this volume. In Madison County, Texas, in 1895, a man, listed only as "A Negro," was lynched even though the record showed he was "Guilty of no Offense." Two lynching in West Virginia in 1902 underscore the arbitrary nature of these killings. Mr. T. Williams (his first name was unknown) was lynched for "alleged conjuring"—the unproved allegation of something that few people in America would recognize as wrong, and that no jurisdiction in the nation considered criminal. A few months later, Peter Jackson was lynched because of "mistaken identity." A man in South Carolina was lynched for "refusing to pay a note," and another for "frightening women." In Tennessee men were lynched for "insults," "giving evidence," "drunkenness," and "bad reputation." In 1908 Gilbert Thompson was lynched in Georgia for rape, but later authorities determined he was innocent.

But, guilty or innocent, charged with a capital offence, or a minor crime, or no crime at all, the South continued to create what the singer Billie Holliday called "strange fruit"—the bodies of black men hanging from trees and lampposts. Lynching, after all, was only partially caused by a perverted sense of justice and the demand for community action in the face of real or perceived crimes. More importantly, lynching was a tool of racial repression.

While this book was valuable as evidence in the struggle against lynching in the twentieth century, in our own time it remains the single most comprehensive source available for studying lynching. The data here is a gold mine for students and scholars who want to understand this crime and its place in American history. Making this important volume available to general readers and scholars allows all Americans the opportunity to reexamine an older culture of racism, violence, and lawlessness that sadly still exists in some parts of the nation.

Durham, N.C.
August 2012

THIRTY YEARS
OF LYNCHING

IN THE

UNITED STATES

1889-1918

✿

Published by the

National Association for the Advancement of Colored People

National Office
70 Fifth Avenue, New York

APRIL, 1919

Price - One Dollar

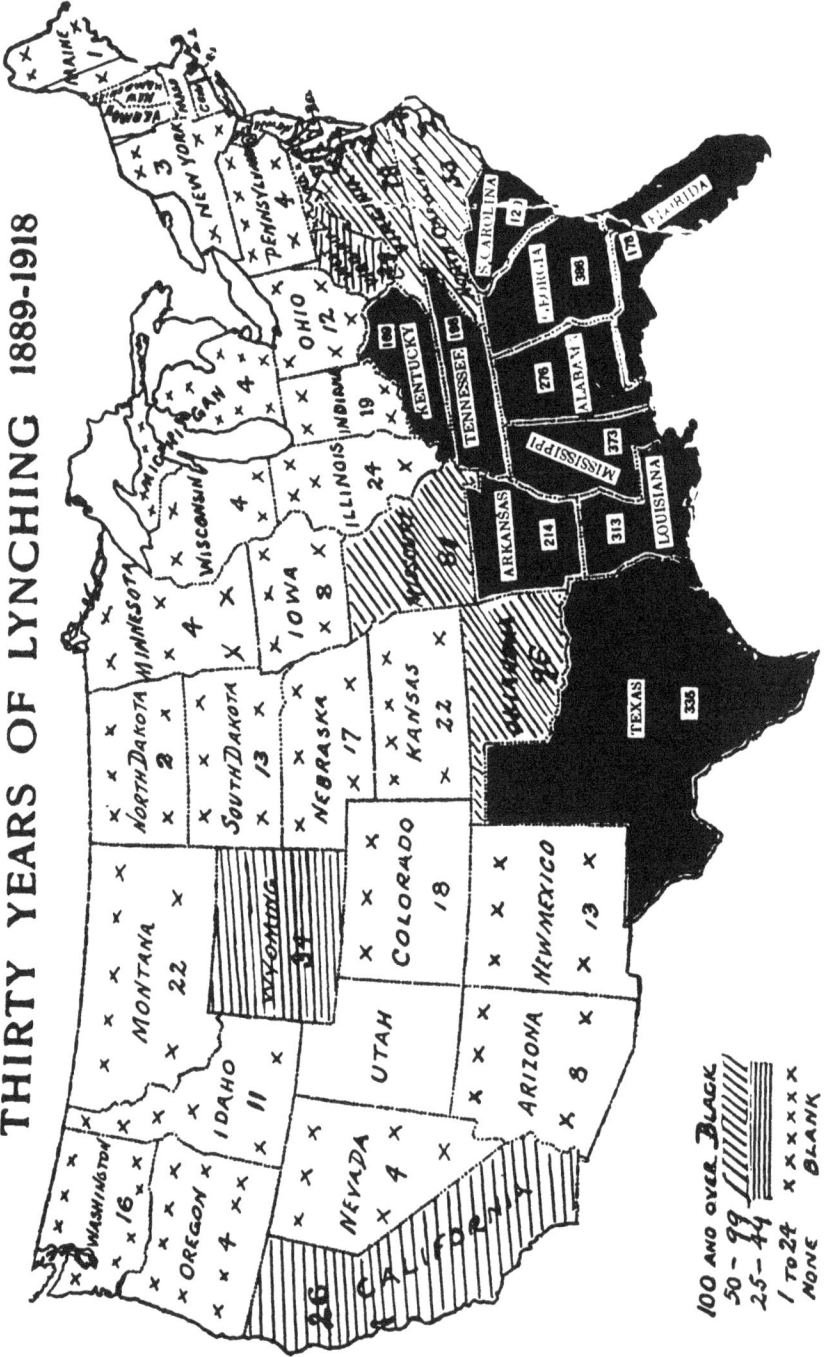

THIRTY YEARS OF LYNCHING 1889-1918

MAINE 1

NEW HAMPSHIRE

VERMONT

NEW YORK 3

PENNSYLVANIA 4

S. CAROLINA

FLORIDA 120

GEORGIA 386

N. CAROLINA

OHIO 12

MICHIGAN 4

WISCONSIN 4

ILLINOIS 24

INDIANA 19

KENTUCKY 168

TENNESSEE 196

ALABAMA 276

MISSISSIPPI 373

LOUISIANA 313

ARKANSAS 214

IOWA 8

MINNESOTA 4

NORTH DAKOTA 2

SOUTH DAKOTA 13

NEBRASKA 17

KANSAS 22

MISSOURI 81

OKLAHOMA 95

TEXAS 335

MONTANA 22

WYOMING 34

COLORADO 18

NEW MEXICO 13

IDAHO 11

UTAH

ARIZONA 8

NEVADA 4

CALIFORNIA 26

WASHINGTON 16

OREGON 4

100 AND OVER — BLACK
50 – 99
25 – 49
1 TO 24 — x x x x x
NONE — BLANK

CONTENTS

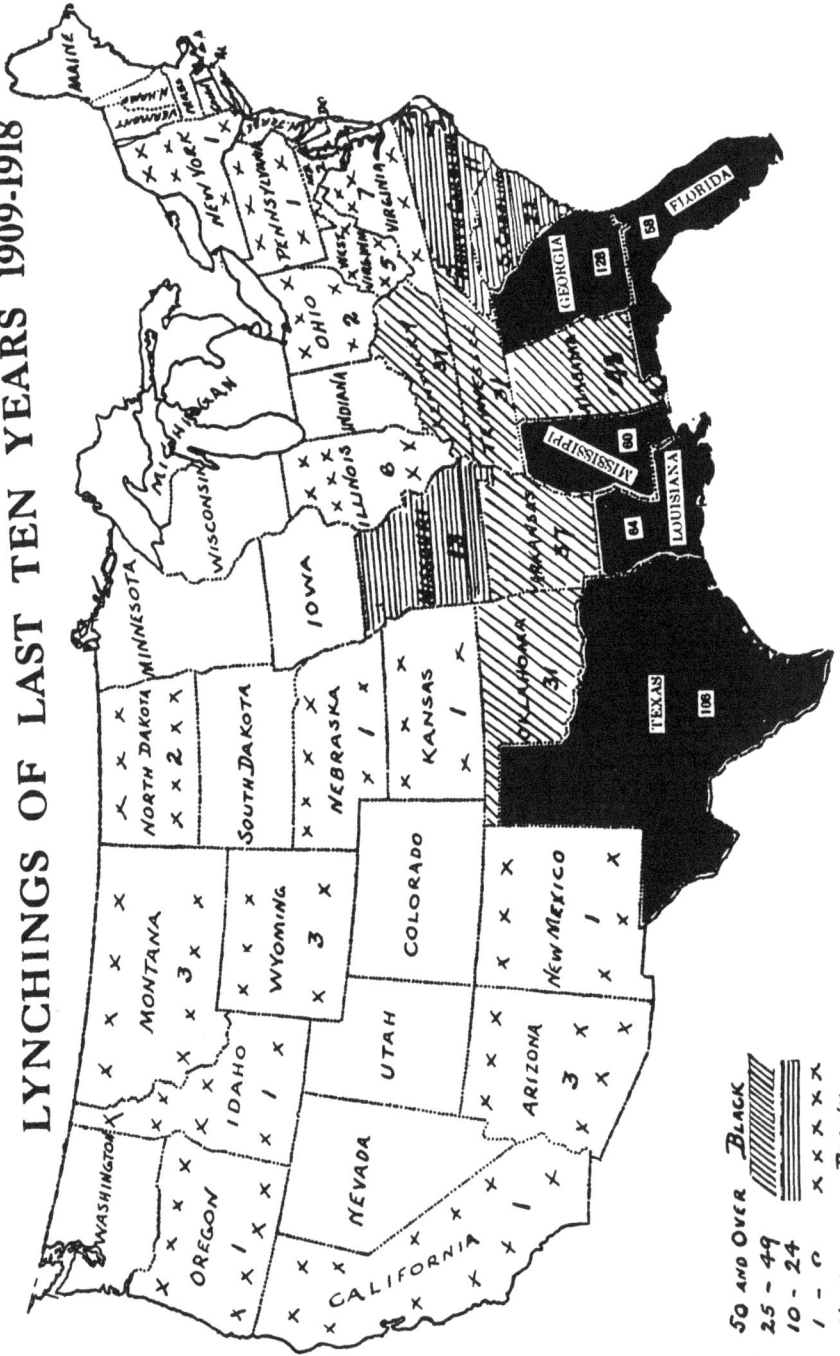

LYNCHINGS OF LAST TEN YEARS 1909-1918

Legend:

- 50 AND OVER — BLACK
- 25 - 49
- 10 - 24
- 1 - 9 — xxxxx
- NON — BLANK

State values:

- MAINE
- NEW YORK — 1
- PENNSYLVANIA — 1
- WEST VIRGINIA — 7
- VIRGINIA — 5
- OHIO — 2
- INDIANA
- ILLINOIS — 6
- MICHIGAN
- WISCONSIN
- IOWA
- MINNESOTA
- NORTH DAKOTA — 2
- SOUTH DAKOTA
- NEBRASKA — 1
- KANSAS — 1
- MONTANA — 3
- WYOMING — 3
- COLORADO
- NEW MEXICO — 1
- WASHINGTON
- IDAHO — 1
- OREGON — 1
- NEVADA
- UTAH
- ARIZONA — 3
- CALIFORNIA — 1
- FLORIDA — 83
- GEORGIA — 128
- MISSISSIPPI — 90
- LOUISIANA — 64
- TEXAS — 106
- OKLAHOMA — 31
- ARKANSAS — 31
- MISSOURI — 4
- TENNESSEE — 31
- KENTUCKY — 11

FOREWORD

Until the recent outbreaks in Germany, where, under revolutionary conditions, a few lynchings have taken place, the United States has for long been the only advanced nation whose government has tolerated lynching. The facts are well known to students of public affairs. It is high time that they became the common property, since they are the common shame, of all Americans.

The National Association for the Advancement of Colored People, within the limits of its financial resources, has been carrying on an educational and publicity campaign in the public press, through its own pamphlet publications and the columns of *The Crisis*, and through public meetings, to bring home to the American people their responsibility for the persistence of this monstrous blot upon America's honor. Lynching has had, and to some degree still has, its apologists, who have alleged one and another excuse for it in given cases. But, none of the several pleas which has been made to explain or excuse it can stand the light of reason or find the slightest real justification in a nation governed by law, which has found ample means to cope with lawlessness whenever and wherever the public authorities have taken seriously their oaths of office.

On July 26, 1918, when the nation was at war with the Central Powers, President Wilson appealed to "the governors of all the states, the law officers of every community and, above all, the men and women of every community in the United States, all who revere America and wish to keep her name without stain or reproach, (to) cooperate, not passively merely, but actively and watchfully, to make an end of this disgraceful evil," saying, "It cannot live where the community does not countenance it."

Despite President Wilson's earnest appeal, made under such extraordinary circumstances, lynchings continued during the remaining period of the war with unabated fury. Sixty-three Negroes, five of them women, and four white men fell victims to mob ruthlessness during 1918 and in no case was any member of the mobs convicted in any court and in only two instances were trials held. In both of these instances the mob members were acquitted. One case was that of the lynchers of the white man, Robert P. Praeger, in Illinois, the other that of the lynchers of a Negro, Will Bird, in Alabama.

The present publication, "Thirty Years of Lynching in the United States, 1889–1918," sums up the facts for this period. It is believed that more persons have been lynched than those whose names are given in Appendix II following. Only such cases have been included as were authenticated by such evidence as was given credence by a recognized newspaper or confirmed by a responsible investigator.

In presenting this material we have refrained from editorial comment, restricting our text to a brief summary of the facts which are more fully illustrated in the tables printed in Appendix I. In addition to the two appendices named, and to the summary of the facts disclosed in the tables, we have included a short summary of the actual happenings in the cases of one hundred persons lynched, as taken from press accounts and, in a few cases, from the reports of our own investigators. These data appear under the heading, *The Story of One Hundred Lynchings*.

Acknowledgment is made to Miss Martha Gruening and to Miss Helen Boardman, who assisted her, for work done in examining the files of leading newspapers and other records for a period of thirty years and in compiling data from which *The Story of One Hundred Lynchings* has been taken.

JOHN R. SHILLADY, *Secretary.*
National Association for the Advancement
of Colored People.

SUMMATION OF THE FACTS DISCLOSED IN TABLES

More or less accurate records of lynchings have been kept by the Chicago *Tribune*, Tuskegee Institute and, since 1912, *The Crisis* and the National Association for the Advancement of Colored People. These records go back to 1885. In the present study of the subject, we have confined ourselves to the story of the past thirty years, from 1889 to 1918, inclusive. During these years 3,224 persons have been killed by lynching mobs.* Seven hundred and two white persons and 2,522 Negroes have been victims.† Of the whites lynched, 691 have been men and 11 women; of the colored, 2,472 were men and 50 were women. For the whole period, 78.2 per cent. of the victims were Negroes and 21.8 per cent. white persons.

DISTRIBUTION OF THE LYNCHINGS

For the thirty years' period as a whole, the North has had 219 victims, the South, 2,834, the West, 156, and Alaska and unknown localities, 15 victims. An examination of Table No. 3 will show that the eight South Atlantic States are responsible for 862 of the total of 2,834 for the South as a whole; the four East South Central States have had 1,014 victims, and the four West South Central States 958. Georgia leads in this unholy ascendancy with 386 victims, followed closely by Mississippi with 373 victims, Texas with 335, Louisiana with 313, Alabama with 276, Arkansas with 214, Tennessee with 196, Florida with 178 and Kentucky with 169. The nine states above named are those

---

* A total of 181 persons has been eliminated from the total number of persons lynched (43 white, 138 colored), as shown in annual summaries in *The Crisis*. (See following foot-note.)

† *The Crisis*, annual summaries of the number of persons lynched for the thirty years' period, show a total of 745 white persons and 2,650 colored. *The Crisis'* figures are based, for the years prior to 1912, upon Chicago *Tribune* figures. Forty-three white persons and 138 colored have not been included in the present study because we have been unable, due to imperfections in the available data, to record the name of person lynched and the date, place and alleged cause of the lynching. Had these eliminated persons been included, concerning whose lynching there is strong probability, our total would have been 3,405.

which, for the thirty years' period, have each a percentage of the total number of lynchings in excess of five per cent.

Fifty colored women and 11 white women were lynched in 14 states. Thirteen of the 14 states in which women fell victims to mobs were Southern states, Nebraska being the only state outside the South which lynched women.

Comparing the northern, southern and western states by five years' periods (see Table No. 5), the following is noted:

NUMBER OF PERSONS LYNCHED

Geographical Division	1889– 1893	1894– 1898	1899– 1903	1904– 1908	1909– 1913	1914– 1918
The North........	66	73	44	9	15	12
The South........	690	661	474	362	343	304
The West.........	76	34	24	9	4	9

This summation shows that while in all sections of the country there has been a progressive decrease in the number of lynchings at each of the five years' periods, this decrease in the North and West has far outrun the decrease in the South. The North and West together have lynched 21 persons during the last five years' period, whereas during the same time 304 persons were lynched in the South.

Georgia began the first five years' period with 61 lynchings and ended the last five years' period with exactly the same number. This number, by the way, was the lowest, with one exception, which Georgia reached during the thirty years. Alabama, on the contrary, began with 84, a number one-third greater than Georgia's, which had been reduced during the last five years' period to 19. Mississippi began with 91 for the first period and ended with 28 in the latter five years' period. Georgia and Texas alone, of all the states, have made no proportionate decrease in the number of lynchings during the thirty years' period. Texas shows an increase during the last five years over her record for three preceding five years' periods.

In considering these facts it should be borne in mind that the number of lynchings has steadily been decreasing. When, therefore, Georgia and Texas show no decrease in the former state and only a small decrease in the latter state, it means that relative to the country as a whole, lynchings have been on the increase in these two states.

DECREASE IN LYNCHING DURING PAST THIRTY YEARS

Table No. 8 shows the percentage of decrease in the number of persons lynched during each five years' period. Comparing the five years, 1914–1918, with the five years, 1889–1893, the table shows a decrease of 61.3 per cent. in the total number of persons lynched. The percentage of decrease in the number of whites lynched was 77.6 and of colored, 54.4. Since 1903 the number of whites lynched has been decreasing steadily. The increase for the period 1914–1918 to 61 white persons lynched is largely accounted for by the fact that in 1915, 43 whites were lynched. Twenty-seven of these were Mexicans who were lynched in the state of Texas. Many citizens of Texas look upon Mexicans in somewhat the same way as they look upon Negroes (alas for democracy), so that the lynching of this number of Mexicans would not be regarded by them in the same light as would the lynching of so many white Texans or other white citizens of the United States.

Except in 1915 and in 1909 and 1910, the number of whites lynched in any year since 1903 has been less than ten. The percentage of whites lynched in the first ten years' period of our study was 30 per cent; in the second ten years' period, 12.4 per cent, and in the third ten years' period, 15 per cent.

ALLEGED OFFENSES WHICH APPEAR AS "CAUSES" FOR THE LYNCHINGS

Table No. 6 sums up the known facts regarding the alleged offenses committed by the men and women lynched. It is to be remembered that the alleged offenses given are pretty loose descriptions of the crimes charged against the mob victims, where actual crime was committed. Of the whites lynched, nearly 46 per cent were accused of murder; a little more than 18 per cent were accused of what have been classified as miscellaneous crimes, *i.e.*, all crimes not otherwise classified; 17.4 per cent were said to have committed crimes against property; 8.7 per cent crimes against the person, other than rape, "attacks upon women," and murder; while 8.4 per cent were accused of rape and "attacks upon women."

Among colored victims, 35.8 per cent were accused of murder; 28.4 per cent of rape and "attacks upon women" (19 per cent of rape and 9.4 per cent of "attacks upon women"); 17.8 per cent of crimes against the person (other than those already mentioned) and against property; 12 per cent were charged with miscellaneous crimes and in 5.6 per cent of cases no crime at all was charged. The 5.6 per cent. classified under "Absence of Crime" does not include a number of cases in which crime was alleged but in which it was afterwards shown conclusively that no crime had been committed. Further, it may fairly be pointed out that in a number of cases where Negroes have been lynched for rape and "attacks upon white women," the alleged attacks rest upon no stronger evidence than "entering the room of a woman" or brushing against her. In such cases as these latter the victims and their friends have often asserted that there was no intention on the part of the victim to attack a white woman or to commit rape. In many cases, of course, the evidence points to *bona fide* attacks upon women.

An examination of Table No. 7 shows that the decreases in succeeding five years' periods in the number of victims charged with rape and "attacks upon women" have been more pronounced than for any other alleged cause. The percentage of Negroes lynched for alleged rape and attacks upon white women (compared with the total number of Negroes lynched for all causes) in the several five years' periods is shown in the following summary:

1889–1893	1894–1898	1899–1903	1904–1908	1909–1913	1914–1918
31.8	30.7	28.1	27	28	19.8

It is apparent that lynchings of Negroes for other causes than the so-called "one crime" have for the whole period been a large majority of all lynchings and that for the past five years, less than one in five of the colored victims have been accused of rape or "attacks upon women" (rape, 11 per cent; attacks upon women, 8.8 per cent; total, 19.8 per cent).

THE STORY OF ONE HUNDRED LYNCHINGS*

To give concreteness and to make vivid the facts of lynching in the United States, we give below in chronological order an account of one hundred lynchings which have occurred in the period from 1894 to 1918. These "stories," as they are technically described in newspaper parlance, have been taken from press accounts and, in a few cases, from the reports of investigations made by the National Association for the Advancement of Colored People. Covering twenty-five years of American history, these accounts serve to present a characteristic picture of the lynching sport, as it was picturesquely defined by Henry Watterson.

The last of the "stories" describes one of the rare events in connection with lynchings, that of the conviction of members of a mob involved in such affairs. In this case no lynching was consummated, it having been prevented by the prompt and public-spirited action of the mayor of the city (Winston-Salem, North Carolina), and members of the "Home Guard" and Federal troops who defended the jail against a mob.

ALABAMA, 1894

Three Negroes, Tom Black, Johnson Williams and Tony Johnston, were lynched at Tuscumbia, Alabama. They were in the local jail, awaiting trial on the charge of having burnt a barn. A mob of two hundred masked men entered the jail, after having enticed away the jailer with a false message, took the keys from the jailer's wife and secured the three prisoners. They were carried to a near-by bridge. Here a rope was placed around the neck of each victim, the other end being tied to the timbers of the bridge, and they were compelled to jump.

New York *Tribune*, April 23, 1894.

TENNESSEE, 1894

Six Negroes, Daniel Hawkins, Robert Haines, Warner Miller, Edward Hale, John Hayes and Glenn White, were taken from the custody of detective W. S. Richardson and shot to death at Millington, Tennessee, September 1st.

---

* One hundred *persons* lynched, not one hundred occasions on which lynchings occurred.

They were charged with barn burning but none of them had been tried. The prisoners, who were handcuffed together in a wagon, were ambushed and shot as Richardson was driving them down a ravine.   He had been led into the ambush by being told that the bridge he wished to cross had been washed away.

The Coroner's jury reported that the Negroes came to their death "at the hands of parties unknown."

New York Tribune, Sept. 2, 1894.

TEXAS, 1895

News has been received of the lynching of a Negro in this part of Madison County on Tuesday night.   He was accused of riding his horse over a little white girl and inflicting serious injuries on her.   Later developments go to show that the mob got hold of the wrong negro.   The guilty one made his escape.

Chicago Tribune, November 22, 1895.

TEXAS, 1897

Robert Henson Hilliard, a Negro, for a murder to which he confessed and for alleged rape, was burned to death by a mob at Tyler, Texas.   Hilliard confessed the murder but stated that he killed his victim because he had unwittingly frightened her and feared that he would be killed.

A report of the crime and its punishment was written by an eye-witness and printed by a local publishing house.   It ended as follows:

"Note: Hilliard's power of endurance was the most wonderful thing on record.   His lower limbs burned off before he became unconscious and his body looked to be burned to the hollow.   Was it decreed by an avenging God as well as an avenging people that his sufferings should be prolonged beyond the ordinary endurance of mortals?

The End

"We have sixteen large views under powerful magnifying lenses now on exhibition.   These views are true to life and show the Negro's attack, the scuffle, the murder, the body as found, etc.   With eight views of the trial and burning.   For place of exhibit see street bills.   Don't fail to see this."

BRECKENRIDGE-SCRUGGS CO.

No indictments were found against any of the mob's members.

GEORGIA, 1899

Sam Hose, a Negro farm laborer, was accused of murdering his employer in a quarrel over wages.   He escaped.   Several days later, while he was being hunted unsuccessfully, the charge was added that he raped his employer's wife.   He confessed the murder, but refused, even under duress, to confess the other crime.

The following account of the lynching is taken from the New York *Tribune* for April 24, 1899:

"In the presence of nearly 2,000 people, who sent aloft yells of defiance and shouts of joy, Sam Hose (a Negro who committed two of the basest acts known to crime) was burned at the stake in a public road, one and a half miles from here. Before the torch was applied to the pyre, the Negro was deprived of his ears, fingers and other portions of his body with surprising fortitude. Before the body was cool, it was cut to pieces, the bones were crushed into small bits and even the tree upon which the wretch met his fate was torn up and disposed of as souvenirs.

"The Negro's heart was cut in several pieces, as was also his liver. Those unable to obtain the ghastly relics directly, paid more fortunate possessors extravagant sums for them. Small pieces of bone went for 25 cents and a bit of the liver, crisply cooked, for 10 cents."

No indictments were ever found against any of the lynchers.

LOUISIANA, 1899

A peculiarly horrible affair occurred two days ago at Lindsay, near Jackson, La. Mitchell Curry, hearing that someone was in his cornfield, took two Negroes and went to drive away the intruder. There had been an attempted assault on a white woman by a Negro, Val Bages, and by some unexplained course of reasoning, Mitchell Curry, on seeing a large Negro in the field, became convinced that the man was the criminal.

The fellow took flight, was followed, and finally climbed a magnolia tree. The tree was surrounded and the Negro ordered to remain where he was while one of the pursuers was sent for rope to hang him. Presently, however, the man deliberately slid down out of the tree, and halfway down he was shot to death. On examination of the body the man's clothing marked No. 43, was found to be that worn at the State Insane Asylum in the neighboring town of Jackson. On investigation it was learned that the insane occupant had escaped a few days before and the helpless fellow, wandering at large, had suffered death for a crime he had not committed.

Special despatch to New York *Tribune*, July 27, 1899.

FLORIDA, 1901

Will Wright and Sam Williams, charged with being implicated in a murder, were lynched without trial in jail at Dade City, by a mob of thirty or more men. Sheriff Griffin refused to give up the keys and they broke down the outer door. Unable to break down the steel doors of the cells, they opened fire through the steel bars, shooting both the Negroes to death.

The Coroner's jury found that they came to their death at the hands of "parties unknown."

New York *Tribune*, February 7, 1901.

TENNESSEE, 1901

Ballie Crutchfield, a colored woman, was lynched by a mob at Rome, Tennessee, because her brother stole a purse.

The mob took Crutchfield from the custody of the sheriff, and started with him for the place of execution, when he broke from them and escaped.

"This," says the despatch, "so enraged the mob, that they suspected Crutchfield's sister of being implicated in the theft and last night's work was the culmination of that suspicion."

The Coroner's jury found the usual verdict that the woman came to her death at the hands of parties unknown.

New York *Tribune*, March 16, 1901.

LOUISIANA, 1901

Louis Thomas, at Girard, La., a Negro, broke into a local store and stole six bottles of soda-pop. He was later found by a white man named Brown, disposing of its contents, and on being accused of theft, struck his accuser. Brown procured a rifle and shot the Negro twice through the body, but as neither wound proved fatal, a mob of white men took the Negro from the house where he lay wounded and strung him up.

New York *Tribune*, July 16, 1901.

GEORGIA, 1903

Griffin, Ga.—William Fambro, a Negro, was shot to death on the outskirts of this city late last night by a mob of white men, who fired on his house. Fambro's wife, who was in the house, escaped injury. The Negro some time ago was arrested on the charge of insulting a white woman and was tried and sentenced to a term in the county chain gang. His fine afterwards was paid by his employer. Over a thousand shots were sent into the building before the mob retired.

Special to the Chicago *Tribune*, February 24, 1903.

DELAWARE, 1903

George White, a Negro, accused of rape and murder, was taken out of jail at Wilmington, Del., dragged to the scene of his alleged crime and forced to confess. He was tied to a stake, burned and riddled with bullets, even as he was being burned. The Chamber of Commerce of Wilmington, which met a few days later, refused to pass a resolution condemning the lynching but passed one against forest fires.

New York *Tribune*, June 23, 24, 1903.

GEORGIA, 1903

A mob, formed near Liberty County, pursued through seven counties a Negro supposed to be Ed Claus, who had assaulted Susie Johnson, a young white woman, and lynched him, hanging him and shooting him full of holes. After he was lynched it was found he was not Claus.

New York *Tribune*, July 27, 1903.

MISSISSIPPI, 1904

Luther Holbert, a Doddsville Negro, and his wife were burned at the stake for the murder of James Eastland, a white planter, and John Carr, a Negro. The planter was killed in a quarrel which arose when he came to Carr's cabin, where he found Holbert, and ordered him to leave the plantation. Carr and a Negro, named Winters, were also killed.

Holbert and his wife fled the plantation but were brought back and burned at the stake in the presence of a thousand people. Two innocent Negros had been shot previous to this by a posse looking for Holbert, because one of them, who resembled Holbert, refused to surrender when ordered to do so. There is nothing in the story to indicate that Holbert's wife had any part in the crime.

New York *Tribune*, February 8, 1904.

ALABAMA, 1904

For murdering and robbing a peddler, Horace Maples, a Negro, was hung and then shot full of holes at Huntsville, September 7th. The mob secured his release from jail by building a fire in the hallway in the jail, the jailer surrendering the prisoner finally because there seemed no other way of saving the other prisoners from asphyxiation.

Ray Stannard Baker, "Following the Color Line."

GEORGIA, 1904

For the brutal murder of a white family (the Hodges family) at Statesboro', Georgia, two Negroes, Paul Reed and Will Cato, were burned alive in the presence of a large crowd. They had been duly convicted and sentenced, when the mob broke into the courtroom and carried them away, in spite of the plea of a brother of the murdered man, who was present in the court, that the law be allowed to take its course. None of the lynchers were ever indicted.

Ray Stannard Baker, "Following the Color Line,"
Chicago *Tribune*, December 31, 1904.

GEORGIA, 1904

Because of the race prejudice growing out of the Hodges murder by Reed and Cato and their lynching, Albert Roger and his son were lynched at Statesboro', Ga., August 17, for being Negroes. A number of other Negroes were whipped for no other offense.

> Ray Stannard Baker's "Following the Color Line,"
> Chicago *Tribune*, December 31, 1904.

GEORGIA, 1904

On account of the race riots which grew out of the above murder (Hodges) and lynching, McBride, a respectable Negro of Portal, Ga., was beaten, kicked and shot to death for trying to defend his wife, who was confined with a baby, three days old, from a whipping at the hands of a crowd of white men.

> Ray Stannard Baker, "Following the Color Line,"
> Chicago *Tribune*, December 31, 1904.

GEORGIA, 1905

At Watkinsville, Georgia, a masked mob entered the jail at 2 A.M. and took out nine prisoners, one white man and eight Negroes. Eight were shot to death and one, a Negro, escaped only by shamming death. The mob overpowered the town marshall and the jailer, carried the men out and tied them to fence posts by their necks and then fired five volleys into their bodies. Only one of the prisoners had been convicted. This was Rich Allen, a Negro, under sentence of death for the murder of another Negro. All the others were awaiting trial, the various charges against them being murder, larceny and attempted rape. The mob had announced its intention of clearing the jail, but one Negro, charged with gambling on the misdemeanor side of the jail, escaped their notice.

> New York *Tribune*, June 30, 1905.

LOUISIANA, 1906

For the crime of killing a white man's cow, William Carr, a Negro, was killed at Planquemines, Louisiana. The lynching was conducted in a most orderly manner, Carr being taken from the Sheriff without resistance by a mob of thirty masked men, hurried to the nearest railroad bridge and hanged without ceremony.

> Despatch to New York *Tribune*, March 18, 1906.

TENNESSEE, 1906

Ed Johnson, a Negro, convicted of rape and sentenced to be hanged, was granted an appeal by the Supreme Court of the United States. Johnson was in jail at Chattanooga, Tennessee. A mob broke down the jail door, took him out and hanged him.

New York *Tribune*, March 20, 1906.

SOUTH CAROLINA, 1906

For attempting to enter a house and frightening a child who was alone in it, Willie Spain, a young Negro at St. George, S. C., was taken from jail and hung to a tree. The mob then shot five hundred bullets into his body.

New York *Tribune*, August 24, 1906.

ARKANSAS, 1910

Pine Bluff, Ark., March 25.—Resenting alleged improper conduct on the part of Judge Jones, a Negro, and a young white woman, a mob of forty men gathered at the county jail here tonight, overpowered the jailer and his deputies, and hanged the Negro.

Special to the Chicago *Tribune*, March 26, 1910.

KENTUCKY, 1911

Shelbyville, Ky., January 15, 1911

(Special)

Just at sunrise this morning two local Negroes took the hemp cure for propensity to insult white women. So effective was it that the mob who administered it decided to hold one more clinic. At this session an aged Negro paid the penalty for beheading a Negro woman.

An unusual feature of the lynching was that the two young Negroes who were strung up for insulting white girls, both broke the rope by which they were suspended. Each made a dash for safety and was riddled with bullets, although one of the bodies has not yet been discovered, and the suspicion is that he crawled to some underbrush to die. The mob numbered only twenty men, all masked.

Before they went to the Shelby County jail, the lynchers raided a blacksmith shop and obtained sledge hammers and bolt cutters and other tools. On account of the smallness of the mob and the conduct of its members, entrance was gained to the jail office before the deputies on watch realized that a lynching was to be attempted. The officials were covered with a dozen rifles and ordered to give up the keys to the cells, but this they refused to do, and the lynchers did not insist. Instead, they began battering down the cell doors with the sledges and the bolt cutters. When they had taken Wade Patterson and Jim West from their cells, some one suggested that they might as well hang old Gene Marshall, a Negro awaiting death sentence. All three Negroes pleaded for their lives but the lynchers paid no attention to them. The lynching was devoid of the minor brutalities that frequently mark such occasions. There was no abuse of the prisoners. The mob was made of quiet, determined men whose mission was to execute but not to torture. The prisoners were led in silence to the Chesapeake and Ohio bridge over the Emminance Pike. . . . The two Negroes were to have been arraigned tomorrow.

Special to the Chicago *Tribune*, January 16, 1911.

OKLAHOMA, 1911

At Okemah, Oklahoma, Laura Nelson, a colored woman, accused of murdering a deputy sheriff who had discovered stolen goods in her house, was lynched together with her son, a boy about fifteen. The woman and her son were taken from the jail, dragged about six miles to the Canadian River, and hanged from a bridge. The woman was raped by members of the mob before she was hanged.

The Crisis, July, 1911.

FLORIDA, 1911

At Lake City, Fla., a Negro named Norris quarreled with a white man, apparently over a trivial matter, the result being a murderous assault on the Negro by the white man. The matter came up before a justice of the peace and the Negro was exonerated.

Later, the white man accompanied by several other white men, came to the Negro's house and reopened the quarrel. In the shooting affray that followed one white man was killed and another wounded. Norris and his associates awaited the coming of the sheriff and surrendered to him. Six of them were arrested and sent to Lake City for safe-keeping. A party of lynchers gained admission to the jail by means of a forged telegram and secured the Negroes under pretext of taking them to Jacksonville for greater protection. They then took them to the outskirts of the town and shot them to death.

Investigation by the National Association for the Advancement of Colored People.

SOUTH CAROLINA, 1911

Will Jackson was lynched at Honeapath, S. C., for an alleged attack on a white child. He was hanged to a tree by his feet and his body riddled with bullets. His fingers were cut off for souvenirs. The mob was led by Joshua W. Ashleigh, a local member of the State Legislature, and his son, while Victor B. Chesire, editor of a local newspaper, *The Intelligencer*, after taking part in the lynching, got out a special edition telling about it in the following words: "*The Intelligencer* man went out to see the fun without the least objection to being a party to help lynch the brute." The then Governor of the State, Cole Blease, absolutely refused to use the power of his office to bring the lynchers to justice, and the Coroner's jury found that the Negro came to his death "at the hands of parties unknown."

The Crisis, December, 1911.

GEORGIA, 1911

Two colored men, Allen and Watts, were lynched in Monroe, Georgia, one for an alleged attack on a white woman, the other for "loitering in a suspicious manner." Judge Chas. H. Brand ordered Allen brought to Monroe for trial although it was known that the citizens had organized a mob to lynch him. The Judge was offered troops by the Governor to protect the prisoner but refused. Allen was sent to Monroe in charge of two officers. The train was stopped and he was taken off and shot. The mob then proceeded to Monroe where they stormed the jail, took out Watts and hanged and shot him. The same Judge had refused to ask for troops on a previous occasion, saying that he "would not imperil the life of one man to save the lives of a hundred Negroes."

No indictments were found against the lynchers.

The Crisis, August, 1911.

PENNSYLVANIA, 1911

For shooting and killing a constable in a fight, the details of which were not known, Zach Walker, a Negro of Coatesville, Pennsylvania, was taken from the hospital, where he lay wounded as a result of the fight, dragged through the streets on the cot to which he was chained and burned alive.

The bedstead was broken in half, and the man, still chained to the lower half, was dragged half a mile along the ground, thrown upon a pile of wood, drenched with oil and burned alive.

Other human beings, to the number of several hundred, looked on in approval. When Walker, with superhuman strength, burst his bonds and tried to escape, they drove him back with pitchforks and fence rails and held him there until his body was burnt to ashes. Those who could get fragments of his charred bones, took them off as souvenirs.

Albert Jay Nock in the *American Magazine*, February, 1913.

All attempts to indict members of the mob failed. They were given an ovation by their fellow-citizens when they returned from the Grand Jury.

GEORGIA, 1911

T. W. Walker, a colored man of Washington, Ga., killed C. S. Hollinshead, a wealthy planter of the same place. It was stated that there was no apparent cause for the crime, but a Northern colored paper published the charge that Walker killed Hollinshead for attacking his wife and an Atlanta paper reprinted it. A crowd of white men tried to lynch Walker, who had been sentenced to death, but were so drunk that he succeeded in escaping. He was caught and resentenced to instant execution. Before he could be taken from the court room, a brother of Hollinshead shot and severely wounded him. He was then taken out and hanged, the court announcing that the brother would not be prosecuted. The only arrest made in connection with the affair was that of the Negro editor who published the charge against Hollinshead.

The Crisis, January, 1912.

TENNESSEE, 1911

Ben Pettigrew, a successful Negro farmer, and his two daughters, were on their way to Savannah, Tenn., taking a load of seed cotton to a cotton gin there. They were ambushed by four white men who shot the father, hanged the daughters and then drove the load of cotton under the tree from which their bodies dangled and set fire to it.

The case is remarkable, because two of the murderers, friendless, ignorant white boys, were ultimately hanged for their part in it.

The Crisis, January, 1912.

LOUISIANA, 1912

At Yellowpine, La., Ernest Allums, a colored boy of nineteen, was whipped for insulting women. The accounts vary as to the manner in which they were insulted, one report saying that he wrote "suggestive letters" and another that the insults were sent over the telephone. He was ordered to leave town but refused and was lynched.

The Crisis, June, 1912.

WEST VIRGINIA, 1912

In Bluefield, W. Va., September 4, 1912, Robert Johnson was lynched for attempted rape. When he was accused he gave an alibi and proved every statement that he made. He was taken before the girl who had been attacked and she failed to identify him. She had previously described very minutely the clothes her assailant wore. When she failed to identify Johnson in the clothes he had, the Bluefield police dressed him to fit the description and again took him before her. This time she screamed on seeing him, "That's the man." Her father had also failed to identify him but now he declared himself positive that he recognized Johnson as the guilty man. Thereupon Johnson was dragged out by a mob, protesting his innocence, and after being severely abused, was hung to a telegraph pole. Later his innocence was conclusively established.

"The Lynching of Robert Johnson," James Oppenheim in *The Independent*, October 10, 1912.

GEORGIA, 1912

Anne Bostwick, a Negro servant woman subject to violent fits of insanity, who stabbed her mistress to death in one of them, was lynched at Pinehurst, Ga., June 24th. According to the Coroner's jury "she came to her death at the hands of parties unknown." A special correspondent to the Cincinnati *Inquirer*, however, writes:

"Great crowds attended and saw the shot-riddled body of the Negress cut from the tree. Sheriff Bennett has made no arrests and none are expected. The truth is that there is general rejoicing over the lynching of the Negress and the lynchers are known to everybody. The Negress was lynched from an auto. The machine in which she was sitting was driven under a tree, a rope placed about her neck and the other end tied to a limb of the tree. The machine was started at high speed and the Negress left hanging. Her body was then shot to pieces. Her eyes were shot out and such a fusillade directed at her waist that she was cut in two."

The same paper says of the verdict:

"The verdict was rendered in the face of the fact that the automobiles in which the lynching party pursued the slayer and the sheriff are known to be owned by some of the most prominent citizens of Cordele, Vienna and Pinehurst."

The Macon *Telegraph* said as to the woman's sanity:

"While living here (Fort Valley) the lynched Negress was tried by a jury and found a fit subject for the lunatic asylum but owing to the crowded condition of that institution she could not be received. In her rational moments she was a good reliable servant, but became violent at times."

The Crisis, August, 1912.

GEORGIA, 1912

At Jackson, Georgia, Henry Etheridge was lynched April 26 for being active in securing recruits for a colony to Africa. Race prejudice is also given as the cause.

The Crisis, June, 1912.
Chicago *Tribune*, December 31, 1912.

TEXAS, 1912

Dan Davis, a Negro, was burned at the stake at Tyler, Texas, for the crime of attempted rape, May 25, 1912.

There was some disappointment in the crowd and criticism of those who had bossed the arrangements, because the fire was so slow in reaching the Negro. It was really only ten minutes after the fire was started that smoking shoe soles and twitching of the Negro's feet indicated that his lower extremities were burning, but the time seemed much longer. The spectators had waited so long to see him tortured that they begrudged the ten minutes before his suffering really began.

The Negro had uttered but few words. When he was led to where he was to be burned he said quite calmly, "I wish some of you gentlemen would be

Christian enough to cut my throat," but nobody responded. When the fire started, he screamed "Lord, have mercy on my soul," and that was the last word he spoke, though he was conscious for fully twenty minutes after that. His exhibition of nerve aroused the admiration even of his torturers.

A slight hitch in the proceedings occurred when the Negro was about half burned. His clothing had been stripped off and burned to ashes by the flames and his black body hung nude in the gray dawn light. The flesh had been burned from his legs as high as the knees when it was seen that the wood supply was running short. None of the men or boys were willing to miss an incident of the torture. All feared something of more than usual interest might happen, and it would be embarrassing to admit later on not having seen it on account of being absent after more wood.

Something had to be done, however, and a few men from the edge of the crowd, ran after more dry-goods boxes, and by reason of this "public service" gained standing room in the inner circle after having delivered the fuel. Meanwhile the crowd jeered the dying man and uttered shocking comments suggestive of a cannibalistic spirit. Some danced and sang to testify to their enjoyment of the occasion.

Special correspondence of the St. Louis *Post-Despatch*.
The Crisis, June, September, 1912.

MISSISSIPPI, 1914

Sam Petty, a Negro, accused of having killed a deputy sheriff, Chas. W. (Kirkland), was lynched at Leland, Miss.

Petty, wanted on a trivial charge, killed Kirkland with a shot-gun when the officer entered a cabin late today, in which the Negro had taken refuge. Petty was captured by a posse, bound and placed in an oil-soaked, dry-goods box and the match applied. A moment later, the man, his clothing aflame, broke from his fastenings and started to run, but before he could gain headway, was shot dead.

The body was put in the box, fresh inflammables were piled about it and within half an hour it was burnt to ashes.

Associated Press Despatch, February 24, 1914.

LOUISIANA, 1914

K. McKnight, T. Lewis and M. Suden were lynched without trial because they were accused of murdering a postmaster. One of them, an old man, bore an excellent reputation in the neighborhood. There was no evidence against him and even under duress he refused to confess to the crime. He was burnt at the stake in the presence of a large crowd, which included a local theatrical troupe.

The Crisis, January, February, 1915.

The conviction is irresistible that the old man who was burned to death had nothing whatever to do with the crime. If he had been guilty, the torture to which he was subjected would have forced a confession and the wonder is that he did not confess, anyhow, in the agony of his roasting flesh, as many innocent victims have done in the vain hope of escaping torture. In all probability the guilty murderers of the village postmaster are at large, while the blood of innocents rests upon the hands of those who took it upon themselves to discharge the functions of the law.

Editorial, Houston, Texas, *Post.*

OKLAHOMA, 1914

Marie Scott of Wagoner County, a seventeen-year-old Negro girl, was lynched by a mob of white men because her brother killed one of two white men who had assaulted her. She was alone in the house when the men entered, but her screams brought her brother to the rescue. In the fight that ensued one of the white men was killed. The next day the mob came to lynch her brother, but as he had escaped, lynched the girl instead. No one has ever been indicted for this crime.

The Crisis, June, 1914.

GEORGIA, 1915

The Aftermath

A Georgia sheriff was murdered something over a year ago. Naturally, there was intense excitement (in Worth County) where the crime was committed and of the six Negroes who were arrested, five were promptly hanged by a mob. The sixth one, Jim Keith, chanced to be rescued from the lynchers, much to their indignation. He was put on trial and convited of complicity in the murder, but not of actual participation in it, and he was sentenced to imprisonment for life. Recently some new facts came to light and in the second trial that was accorded to Keith, because of their importance, not only was he cleared by the jury of having any hand at all in the killing, but it was also proved that the five Negroes who were lynched were equally guiltless.

From an editorial in the New York *Times*, February 12, 1917.

NORTH CAROLINA, 1916

Joseph Black was hanged at Kingston, N. C., because his son was accused of attacking a white child. He was arrested and taken out of the reach of mob violence by the officer, so the mob lynched the father instead.

The Crisis, May, 1916.

TEXAS, 1916

Jesse Washington, a defective Negro boy, of about nineteen, unable to read and write, was employed as farm hand in Robinson, a small town near Waco, Texas. One day, the wife of his employer found fault with him, whereupon he struck her on the head with a hammer and killed her. There is some, but not conclusive, evidence that he raped her. He was arrested, tried, found guilty and sentenced to death by hanging within ten days of the commission of the crime. As the sentence was pronounced, a mob of fifteen hundred white men, who feared the law's delays, broke into the court-room and seized the prisoner. He was dragged through the streets, stabbed, mutilated and finally burned to death in the presence of a crowd of 15,000 men, women and children. The Mayor and Chief of Police of Waco also witnessed the lynching.

After death what was left of his body was dragged through the streets and parts of it sold as souvenirs. His teeth brought $5 apiece and the chain that had bound him 25 cents a link. No one was ever indicted for participating in the lynching.

> Investigation by the National Association for the Advancement of Colored People.

FLORIDA, 1916

Boisy Long, a Negro farmer of Newberry, Fla., was accused by some white farmers of hog stealing. The sheriff came to arrest Long at two o'clock in the morning. With him was another white man, who was supposed to be the owner of the hogs in question, and to have sworn out the warrant. What occurred in the house is not known, but both the white men were shot, the sheriff dying of the wound.

Long escaped, so that when the Newberry people came to get him they took his wife, Stella Long, and a friend of hers, Mrs. Dennis, on the ground that they refused to give information. It is said that they were tortured to get the information.

The citizens of Newberry and Gainesville continued to look for Long. They did not find him but they met James Dennis, and shot him. James Dennis's brother went into Newberry to buy a coffin and they threw him in jail. Then they met Josh Baskin, a neighbor of the Longs and Dennises, and a preacher. They hanged him. Then they went to the jail, brought out the three Negroes already in jail and hanged them. Mary Dennis was the mother of two children and was pregnant. Stella Long had four children.

Boisy Long has been captured and indicted for shooting the sheriff and the other white man. None of the lynchers has been indicted.

> Investigation by the National Association for the Advancement of Colored People.

SOUTH CAROLINA, 1916

Anthony Crawford, a wealthy Negro farmer of Abbeville, S. C., came into town to sell a load of cotton and cotton seed. He got into a dispute with a white storekeeper over the price of the cotton seed and cursed him. He was arrested for disorderly conduct and released on $15 bail. A mob, enraged at this miscarriage of justice, pursued him into a cotton gin and in self-defense, he struck the leader with a hammer, crushing his skull but not fatally injuring him. The mob then dragged him out, beat, kicked, stabbed and partially blinded him. He was rescued with some difficulty by the sheriff and removed to the county jail. The same afternoon the mob broke into the jail, dragged him out through the streets to the fair grounds, hung him to a tree and riddled his body with bullets. Not one of the lynchers was ever indicted.

> Roy Nash, *Independent*, Dec. 11, 1916, Investigation by the National Association for the Advancement of Colored People.

TENNESSEE, 1917

On April 30, Antoinette Rappal, a sixteen-year-old white girl, living on the outskirts of Memphis, disappeared on her way to school. On May third her body was found in a river, her head severed from it. On May 6 a Negro woodchopper, Ell Person, was arrested on suspicion. Under third degree methods he confessed to the crime of murder. The Grand Jury of Shelby County immediately indicted him for murder in the first degree.

The prisoner was taken secretly to the State penitentiary at Nashville. It was known that he would be brought back for trial to Memphis. Each incoming train was searched, and arrangements were made for a lynching.

On May 15 the sheriff disappeared from Memphis. He returned on May 18, announcing that he was informed that several mobs were between Arlington and Memphis. The men were reported to be drinking. "I didn't want to hurt anybody and I didn't want to get hurt," he said, "so I went South into Mississippi."

The press did nothing to quell the mob spirit, and on May 21 announced that Ell Person would be brought to Memphis that night. Thousands of persons on foot and in automobiles went to the place that had been prepared for the lynching.

With a knowledge of these conditions, Person was brought back from Nashville, guarded only by two deputies. Without difficulty he was taken from the train, placed in an automobile, and driven to the spot prepared for his death.

The Memphis *Press* reported the lynching in full. We give a few of its statements.

"Fifteen thousand of them—men, women, even little children, and in their midst the black-clothed figure of Antoinette Rappal's mother—cheered as they poured the gasoline on the axe fiend and struck the match.

"They fought and screamed and crowded to get a glimpse of him, and the mob closed in and struggled about the fire as the flames flared high and the smoke rolled about their heads. Two of them hacked off his ears as he burned; another tried to cut off a toe but they stopped him.

"The Negro lay in the flames, his hands crossed on his chest. If he spoke no one ever heard him over the shouts of the crowd. He died quickly, though fifteen minutes later excitable persons still shouted that he lived when they saw the charred remains move as does meat on a hot frying pan.

" 'They burned him too quick! They burned him too quick!" was the complaint on all sides."

> Investigation of the burning of Ell Person at Memphis, by James Weldon Johnson. Published by the National Association for the Advancement of Colored People

TENNESSEE, 1918

Jim McIlherron, was prosperous in a small way. He was a Negro who resented the slights and insults of white men. He went armed and the sheriff feared him. On February 8 he got into a quarrel with three young white men who insulted him. Threats were made and McIlherron fired six shots, killing two of the men.

He fled to the home of a colored clergyman who aided him to escape, and was afterwards shot and killed by a mob. McIlherron was captured and full arrangements made for a lynching. Men, women and children started into the town of Estill Springs from a radius of fifty miles. A spot was chosen for the burning. McIlherron was chained to a hickory tree while the mob howled about him. A fire was built a few feet away and the torture began. Bars of iron were heated and the mob amused itself by putting them close to the victim, at first without touching him. One bar he grasped and as it was jerked from his grasp all the inside of his hand came with it. Then the real torturing began, lasting for twenty minutes.

During that time, while his flesh was slowly roasting, the Negro never lost his nerve. He cursed those who tortured him and almost to the last breath derided the attempts of the mob to break his spirit.

> Walter F. White, in *The Crisis*, May, 1918.

GEORGIA, 1918

Hampton Smith, a white farmer, had the reputation of ill treating his Negro employees. Among those whom he abused was Sidney Johnson, a Negro peon, whose fine of thirty dollars he had paid when he was up before the court for gaming. After having been beaten and abused, the Negro shot and killed Smith as he sat in his window at home. He also shot and wounded Smith's wife.

For this murder a mob of white men of Georgia for a week, May 17 to 24, engaged in a hunt for the guilty man, and in the meantime lynched the following innocent persons: Will Head, Will Thompson, Hayes Turner, Mary Turner, his wife, for loudly proclaiming her husband's innocence, Chime Riley and four unidentified Negroes. Mary Turner was pregnant and was hung by her feet. Gasoline was thrown on her clothing and it was set on fire. Her body was cut open and her infant fell to the ground with a little cry, to be crushed to death by the heel of one of the white men present. The mother's body was then riddled with bullets. The murderer, Sidney Johnson, was at length located in a house at Valdosta.

The house was surrounded by a posse headed by the Chief of Police and Johnson, who was known to be armed, fired until his shot gave out, wounding the Chief. The house was entered and Johnson found dead. His body was mutilated. After the lynching more than 500 Negroes left the vicinity of Valdosta, leaving hundreds of acres of untilled land behind them.

> *The Lynchings of May, 1918, in Brooks and Lowndes Counties,*
> *Georgia,* by Walter F. White. Published by the National
> Association for the Advancement of Colored People.

MISSISSIPPI, 1918

On Friday night, December 20, 1918, four Negroes, Andrew Clark, age 15; Major Clark, age 20; Maggie Howze, age 20; and Alma Howze, age 16, were taken from the little jail at Shubuta and lynched on a bridge over the Chickasawha River. They were suspected of having murdered a Dr. E. L. Johnston, a dentist.

An investigation disclosed the following facts: That Dr. Johnston was living in illicit relations with Maggie Howze and Alma Howze. That Major Clark, a youth working on Johnston's plantation wished to marry Maggie. That Dr. Johnston went to Clark and told him to leave his woman alone. That this led to a quarrel, made the more bitter when it was found that Maggie was to have a child by Dr. Johnston; and that the younger sister was also pregnant, said to be by Dr. Johnston.

Shortly after this Johnston was mysteriously murdered. There were two theories as to his death; one that he was killed by Clark, the other that he was killed by a white man who had accused him of seducing a white woman. It was generally admitted that Johnston was a loose character.

Alma Howze was so near to motherhood when lynched that it was said by an eye-witness at her burial on the second day following, that the movements of her unborn child could be detected.

> Investigation by the National Association for the Advancement
> of Colored People.

NORTH CAROLINA, 1918

Mob Leaders Go To Prison

Realizing that if a lyncher is permitted to remain unpunished the decency of the community is greatly endangered, Judge B. F. Long of the Superior Court sentenced fifteen white men, indicted for participation in a riot in Winston-Salem, Nov. 17, to serve from fourteen months to six years in prison. The men were found guilty of attempting to lynch Russell High, a prisoner in the city jail.

The fifteen men were a part of a mob that for a night and morning terrorized Winston-Salem, and in their efforts to lynch a black man, innocent of the crime of assault for which he had been arrested on suspicion, put life and property in peril and incidentally killed four people, one a little white girl. The Mayor of the city acted with promptitude and courage, calling out the Home Guards and the fire department which played water on the mob. Nearly every policeman was hurt. The Governor rushed troops from Camp Green at Charlotte. For many days cannon guarded the streets. "We don't mean to be sentimental on this matter," a prominent business man is quoted as saying, "but we aren't going to have our city's good name spoilt by a lynching."

Condensed from reports of the North Carolina press.

APPENDIX I

Analyses of Number of Persons Lynched

TABLE NO. 1

NUMBER OF WHITE AND COLORED PERSONS LYNCHED IN UNITED STATES, 1889-1918*

Years	Total	White	Colored
1889	175	80	95
1890	91	3	88
1891	194	67	127
1892	226	71	155
1893	153	39	114
1894	182	54	128
1895	178	68	110
1896	125	46	79
1897	162	38	124
1898	127	24	103
1899	109	22	87
1900	101	12	89
1901	135	27	108
1902	94	10	84
1903	104	17	87
1904	86	7	79
1905	65	5	60
1906	68	4	64
1907	62	3	59
1908	100	8	92
1909	89	14	75
1910	90	10	80
1911	71	8	63
1912	64	3	61
1913	48	1	47
1914	54	5	49
1915	96	43	53
1916	58	7	51
1917	50	2	48
1918	67	4	63
	3,224	702	2,522

* Victims of the Atlanta, Ga. (1906), and East St. Louis, Ill. (1917), riots have been excluded from this and subsequent tables.

TABLE No. 2

NUMBER OF PERSONS LYNCHED, BY FIVE YEARS' PERIODS AND BY COLOR AND SEX, 1889–1918

Years	Grand Total	WHITE				NEGRO			
		Total	Male	Female	Per Cent. White	Total	Male	Female	Per Cent. Negro
1889-1893	839	260	258	2	32.2	579	571	8	67.8
1894-1898	774	230	221	9	29.7	544	529	15	70.3
1899-1903	543	88	88	0	16.2	455	451	4	83.8
1904-1908	381	27	27	0	7.0	354	348	6	93.0
1909-1913	362	36	36	0	10.2	326	320	6	89.8
1914-1918	325	61	61	0	18.8	264	253	11	81.2
Total	3,224	702	691	11	21.8	2,522	2,472	50	78.2

TABLE No. 3

NUMBER OF PERSONS LYNCHED, BY GEOGRAPHICAL DIVISIONS
AND STATES AND BY COLOR, 1889-1918*

Section and Division	Total No.	White	Per Cent.	Negro	Per Cent.
UNITED STATES......	3,224	702	21.8	2,522	78.2
THE NORTH.........	219	118	54.4	101	45.6
New England..........	1	1	100.0	0	0
Maine.............	1	1	100.0	0	0
New Hampshire.....	0	0	0	0	0
Vermont...........	0	0	0	0	0
Massachusetts.......	0	0	0	0	0
Rhode Island.......	0	0	0	0	0
Connecticut........	0	0	0	0	0
Middle Atlantic........	8	4	50.0	4	50.0
New York.........	3	2	66.6	1	33.4
New Jersey........	1	1	100.0	0	0
Pennsylvania.......	4	1	25.0	3	75.0
East North Central......	63	33	53.1	30	46.9
Ohio..............	12	4	33.4	8	66.6
Indiana...........	19	10	55.0	9	45.0
Illinois.............	24	12	50.0	12	50.0
Michigan..........	4	3	75.0	1	25.0
Wisconsin..........	4	4	100.0	0	0
West North Central.....	147	80	54.7	67	45.3
Minnesota.........	4	4	100.0	0	0
Iowa..............	8	5	62.5	3	37.5
Missouri...........	81	30	37.0	51	63.0
North Dakota.......	2	2	100.0	0	0
South Dakota.......	13	13	100.0	0	0
Nebraska..........	17	15	90.0	2	10.0
Kansas............	22	11	50.0	11	50.0
THE SOUTH	2,834	425	15.0	2,409	85.0
South Atlantic..........	862	78	9.1	784	90.9
Delaware..........	1	0	0	1	100.0
Maryland..........	17	2	11.7	15	88.3

* Of the total number of lynchings for the thirty years' period, 6.9 per cent occurred in the Northern States, 87.8 per cent in the Southern States and 4.8 per cent in the Western States, while 15 lynchings are recorded in Alaska and "places unknown", 4 of these latter having occurred in Alaska. Individual States having a percentage of the total number of lynchings in excess of 5 per cent are: Georgia, 12.1 per cent; Mississippi, 11.6 per cent; Texas, 10.5 per cent; Louisiana, 9.6 per cent; Alabama, 8.9 per cent; Arkansas, 6.9 per cent; Tennessee, 5.9 per cent; Florida, 5.5 per cent; Kentucky, 5.2 per cent.

TABLE No. 3—Continued

Section and Division	Total No.	White	Per Cent.	Negro	Per Cent.
South Atlantic—Cont.					
Virginia............	78	11	15.1	67	84.9
West Virginia.......	29	7	24.0	22	76.0
North Carolina......	53	12	22.6	41	77.4
South Carolina......	120	3	2.5	117	97.5
Georgia............	386	26	6.7	360	93.3
Florida............	178	17	9.6	161	90.4
District of Columbia.....	0	0	0	0	0
East South Central......	1,014	134	13.3	880	86.7
Kentucky..........	169	45	26.7	124	73.3
Tennessee..........	196	34	17.7	162	82.3
Alabama...........	276	32	11.6	244	88.4
Mississippi.........	373	23	6.1	350	93.9
West South Central.....	958	213	21.7	745	78.3
Arkansas...........	214	32	15.1	182	84.9
Louisiana..........	313	49	15.8	264	84.3
Oklahoma..........	96	60	62.8	36	37.2
Texas.............	335	72	21.9	263	78.1
THE WEST	156	144	92.3	12	7.7
Mountain.............	110	101	91.8	9	8.2
Montana...........	22	22	100.0	0	0
Idaho.............	11	11	100.0	0	0
Wyoming..........	34	29	85.3	5	14.7
Colorado...........	18	16	88.8	2	12.2
New Mexico........	13	11	84.6	2	15.4
Arizona............	8	8	100.0	0	0
Utah..............	0	0	0	0	0
Nevada............	4	4	100.0	0	0
Pacific.................	46	43	93.5	3	6.5
Washington........	16	16	100.0	0	0
Oregon............	4	3	75.0	1	25.0
California..........	26	24	92.3	2	7.7
ALASKA and UNKNOWN	15	15	100.0	0	0
Alaska.................	4	4	100.0	0	0
Places Unknown........	11	11	100.0	0	0

TABLE NO. 4

WOMEN AND GIRLS LYNCHED, BY STATES, 1889-1918*

	Total	White	Colored
UNITED STATES...................	61	11	50
Alabama........................	...	...	7
Arkansas.......................	..	..	5
Florida.........................	..	..	2
Georgia........................	..	..	5
Kentucky.......................	..	1	3
Louisiana.......................	..	1	4
Mississippi......................	..	1	11
Nebraska.......................	..	1	..
North Carolina..................	..	1	..
Oklahoma.......................	..	..	2
South Carolina..................	..	..	4
Tennessee......................	..	2	1
Texas..........................	..	3	6
Virginia........................	..	1	..

*The percentage of women lynched to the total number, is 1.5.

TABLE No. 5

NUMBER OF PERSONS LYNCHED, BY STATES AND BY FIVE
YEAR PERIODS, 1889-1918

Section and Division	Total	1889–1893	1894–1898	1899–1903	1904–1908	1909–1913	1914–1918
UNITED STATES	**3,224**	**839**	**774**	**543**	**381**	**362**	**325**
THE NORTH	**219**	**66**	**73**	**44**	**9**	**15**	**12**
New England	**1**	**0**	**0**	**0**	**1**	**0**	**0**
Maine	1	0	0	0	1	0	0
New Hampshire	0	0	0	0	0	0	0
Vermont	0	0	0	0	0	0	0
Massachusetts	0	0	0	0	0	0	0
Rhode Island	0	0	0	0	0	0	0
Connecticut	0	0	0	0	0	0	0
Middle Atlantic	**8**	**2**	**2**	**2**	**0**	**1**	**1**
New York	3	1	1	0	0	0	1
New Jersey	1	0	0	1	0	0	0
Pennsylvania	4	1	1	1	0	1	0
East North Central	**63**	**20**	**20**	**12**	**3**	**5**	**3**
Ohio	12	4	5	0	1	2	0
Indiana	19	7	7	5	0	0	0
Illinois	24	4	7	5	2	3	3
Michigan	4	3	0	1	0	0	0
Wisconsin	4	2	1	1	0	0	0
West North Central	**147**	**44**	**51**	**30**	**5**	**9**	**8**
Minnesota	4	2	2	0	0	0	0
Iowa	8	3	3	1	1	0	0
Missouri	81	18	26	20	4	6	7
North Dakota	2	0	0	0	0	2	0
South Dakota	13	4	8	1	0	0	0
Nebraska	17	9	7	0	0	1	0
Kansas	22	8	5	8	0	0	1
THE SOUTH	**2,834**	**690**	**661**	**474**	**362**	**343**	**304**
South Atlantic	**862**	**180**	**182**	**164**	**103**	**132**	**101**
Delaware	1	0	0	1	0	0	0
Maryland	17	3	7	1	4	2	0
Virginia	78	35	16	14	6	3	4
West Virginia	29	11	4	9	0	4	1

TABLE No. 5—Continued

Section and Division	Total	1889–1893	1894–1898	1899–1903	1904–1908	1909–1913	1914–1918
South Alantic—Cont.							
North Carolina....	53	16	8	10	8	3	8
South Carolina....	120	28	36	19	15	14	8
Georgia..........	386	61	69	73	55	67	61
Florida..........	178	26	42	37	15	39	19
District of Columbia.	0	0	0	0	0	0	0
East South Central..	1,014	276	247	173	142	94	82
Kentucky.........	169	41	52	20	19	13	24
Tennessee........	196	60	55	32	18	20	11
Alabama.........	276	84	79	36	29	29	19
Mississippi.......	373	91	61	85	76	32	28
West South Central.	958	234	232	138	116	117	121
Arkansas.........	214	64	47	34	32	21	16
Louisiana........	313	83	73	61	32	31	33
Oklahoma........	96	16	40	4	5	19	12
Texas...........	335	71	72	39	47	46	60
THE WEST	156	76	34	24	9	4	9
Mountain..........	110	58	19	16	6	4	7
Montana.........	22	12	1	6	0	2	1
Idaho...........	11	9	0	0	1	1	0
Wyoming.........	34	24	2	4	1	1	2
Colorado........	18	1	12	4	1	0	0
New Mexico......	13	9	1	0	2	0	1
Arizona..........	8	3	1	1	0	0	3
Utah............	0	0	0	0	0	0	0
Nevada..........	4	0	2	1	1	0	0
Pacific..............	46	18	15	8	3	0	2
Washington.......	16	8	7	1	0	0	0
Oregon..........	4	1	1	1	0	0	1
California........	26	9	7	6	3	0	1
ALASKA and UNKNOWN	15	7	6	1	1	0	0
Alaska.............	4	0	4	0	0	0	0
Places Unknown....	11	7	2	1	1	0	0

TABLE NO. 6

NUMBER OF PERSONS LYNCHED, BY OFFENSES CHARGED
AND BY COLOR, 1889-1918*

	Mur-der	Rape	Attacks upon Women *	Other Crimes Against the Person	Crimes Against Prop-erty	Miscel-laneous Crimes	Absence of Crime †	Total
Total......	1,219	523	250	315	331	438	148	3,224
White......	319	46	13	62	121	135	6	702
Per cent. of total whites lynched....	45.7	6.6	1.8	8.7	17.4	18.1	1.4	100.0
Negro......	900	477	237	253	210	303	142	2,522
Per cent. of total Negroes lynched....	35.8	19.0	9.4	9.5	8.3	12.0	5.6	100.0

* This classification includes all cases in which press accounts state that attacks upon women were made, but in which it was not clear whether rape was alleged to have been consummated or attempted.
† Under this heading are listed such causes as "testifying against whites," "suing whites," "wrong man lynched," "race prejudice," "defending himself against attack," etc.

TABLE NO. 7

NUMBER OF PERSONS LYNCHED, BY OFFENSES CHARGED AND BY FIVE YEARS' PERIODS, 1889-1918

		1889–1893	1894–1898	1899–1903	1904–1908	1909–1913	1914–1918	Total
Murder	Total	288	286	198	145	180	122	1,219
	White	104	93	55	14	16	37	319
	Negro	184	193	143	131	164	85	900
Rape	Total	167	128	75	69	55	29	523
	White	16	15	6	4	4	1	46
	Negro	151	113	69	65	51	28	477
Attacks Upon Women	Total	37	57	61	33	39	23	250
	White	4	3	2	2	1	1	13
	Negro	33	54	59	31	38	22	237
Other Crimes Against the Person	Total	43	56	78	56	23	59	315
	White	16	27	7	2	6	4	62
	Negro	27	29	71	54	17	55	253
Crimes Against Property	Total	108	123	46	19	16	19	331
	White	66	34	10	1	2	8	121
	Negro	42	89	36	18	14	11	210
Miscellaneous Crimes	Total	162	84	50	36	40	66	438
	White	51	57	6	4	7	10	135
	Negro	111	27	44	32	33	56	303
Absence of Crime*	Total	34	40	35	23	9	7	148
	White	3	1	2	0	0	0	6
	Negro	31	39	33	23	9	7	142

* See foot-note, Table No. 6.

TABLE No. 8

PERCENTAGE OF DECREASE DURING EACH FIVE YEARS'
PERIOD, 1889-1918.

1889-1893=100 PER CENT.

Years	Total Number	Per Cent. Decrease	WHITE		NEGRO	
			Total Number	Per Cent. Decrease	Total Number	Per Cent. Decrease
1889-1893......	839	0	260	0	579	0
1894-1898......	774	7.8	230	14.1	544	4.7
1899-1903......	543	35.2	88	67.1	455	20.3
1904-1908......	381	54.6	27	89.5	354	38.0
1909-1913......	362	57.2	36	85.8	326	43.6
1914-1918......	325	61.3	61	77.6	264	54.4

PERSONS
LYNCHED.
1889-1918

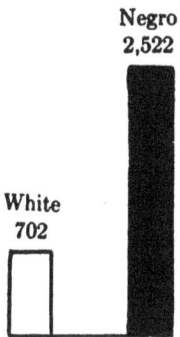

Negro
2,522

White
702

PERSONS LYNCHED, 1889-1918
BY GEOGRAPHICAL DIVISION

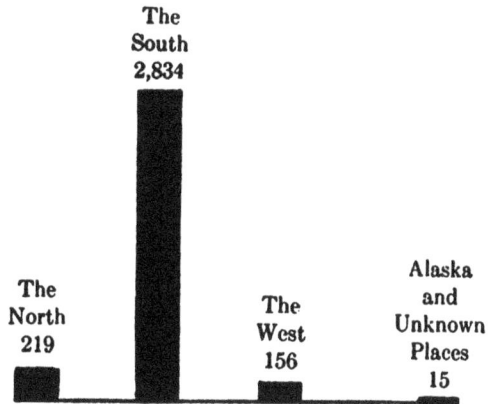

The
South
2,834

The
North
219

The
West
156

Alaska
and
Unknown
Places
15

PERSONS LYNCHED BY FIVE-YEAR PERIODS

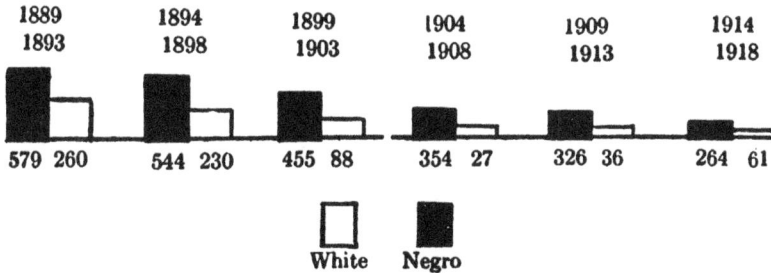

1889 1893	1894 1898	1899 1903	1904 1908	1909 1913	1914 1918
579 260	544 230	455 88	354 27	326 36	264 61

White   Negro

ALLEGED CAUSES (NEGRO VICTIMS)

1889-1918

Total Lynched...2522

Murder.....900

Rape.......477

Attacks Upon Women*.....237

Crimes Against the Person 253

Crimes Against Property....210

For Miscellaneous Crimes 303

No Crime...142

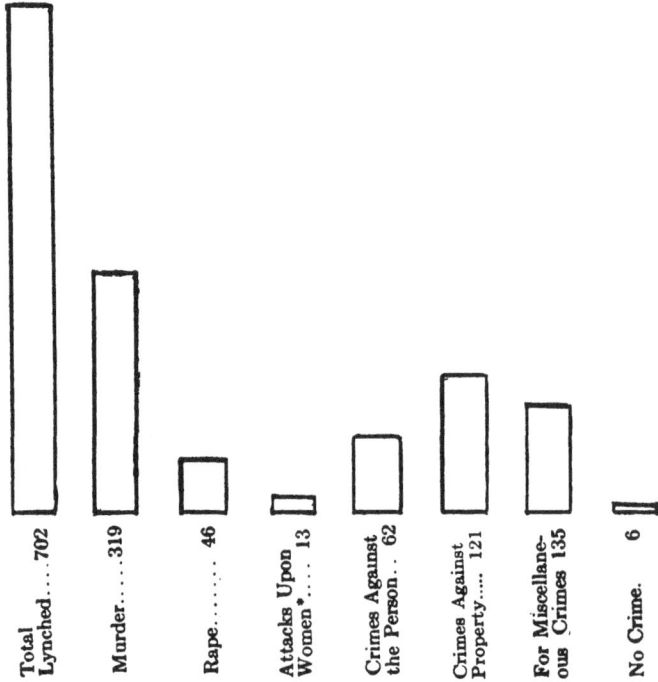

*See foot-note *, Table No. 6, Appendix I.

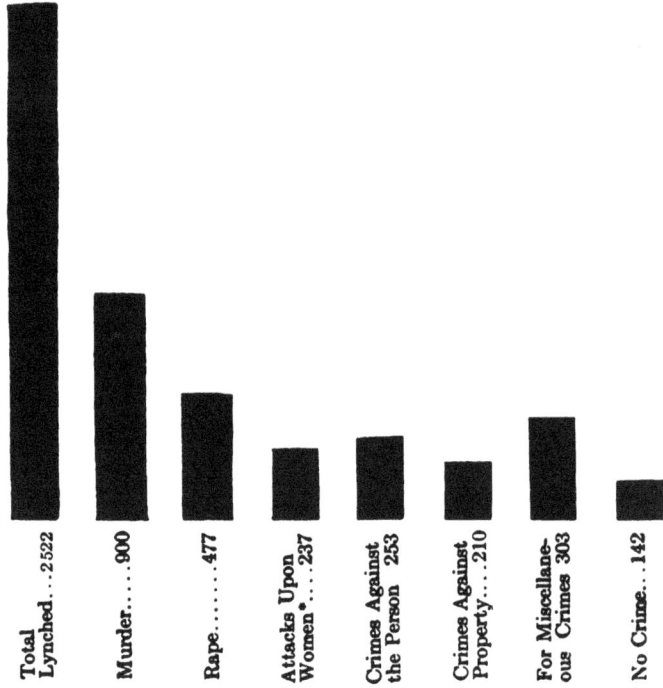

ALLEGED CAUSES (WHITE VICTIMS)

1889-1918

Total Lynched....702

Murder.....319

Rape........ 46

Attacks Upon Women*..... 13

Crimes Against the Person.. 62

Crimes Against Property..... 121

For Miscellaneous Crimes 135

No Crime.   6

*See foot-note *, Table No. 6, Appendix I

PERSONS LYNCHED, 1889-1918
BY STATES.*

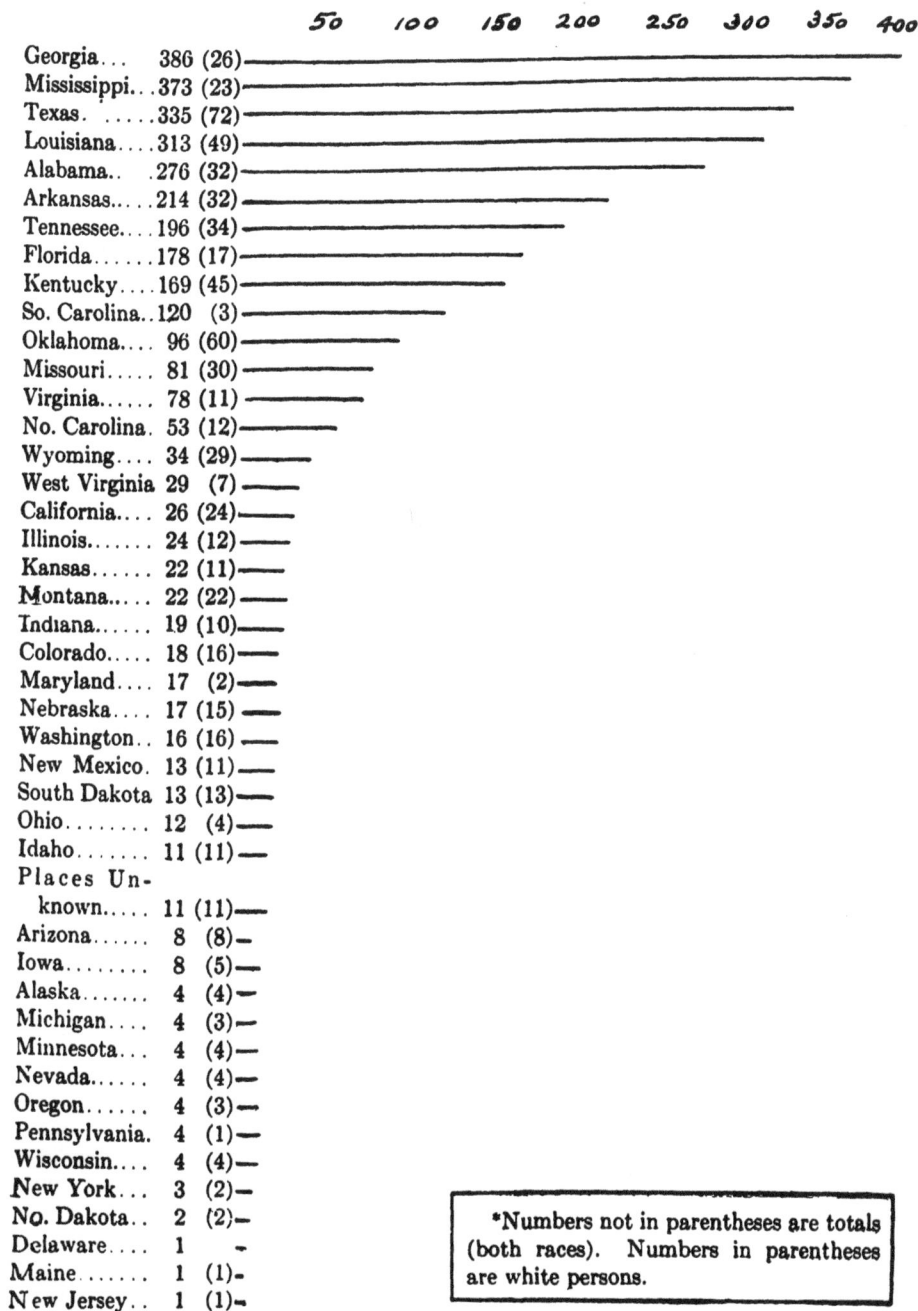

	50	100	150	200	250	300	350	400

State	Total	(White)
Georgia...	386	(26)
Mississippi...	373	(23)
Texas.	335	(72)
Louisiana....	313	(49)
Alabama..	.276	(32)
Arkansas.....	214	(32)
Tennessee....	196	(34)
Florida......	178	(17)
Kentucky....	169	(45)
So. Carolina..	120	(3)
Oklahoma....	96	(60)
Missouri.....	81	(30)
Virginia......	78	(11)
No. Carolina.	53	(12)
Wyoming....	34	(29)
West Virginia	29	(7)
California....	26	(24)
Illinois......	24	(12)
Kansas......	22	(11)
Montana.....	22	(22)
Indiana......	19	(10)
Colorado.....	18	(16)
Maryland....	17	(2)
Nebraska....	17	(15)
Washington..	16	(16)
New Mexico.	13	(11)
South Dakota	13	(13)
Ohio........	12	(4)
Idaho.......	11	(11)
Places Un-known.....	11	(11)
Arizona......	8	(8)
Iowa........	8	(5)
Alaska.......	4	(4)
Michigan....	4	(3)
Minnesota...	4	(4)
Nevada......	4	(4)
Oregon......	4	(3)
Pennsylvania.	4	(1)
Wisconsin....	4	(4)
New York...	3	(2)
No. Dakota..	2	(2)
Delaware....	1	
Maine.......	1	(1)
New Jersey..	1	(1)

*Numbers not in parentheses are totals (both races). Numbers in parentheses are white persons.

APPENDIX II

Chronological List of Persons Lynched in United States, 1889 to 1918, inclusive, arranged by States*

Negroes are listed in **bold faced** type.
Whites are listed in light faced type.

ALABAMA

1889

Jan.	15	**MEADOWS, GEORGE**	Pratt Mines, Jefferson Co.	Rape
May	22	**DICKSON, NOAH**	Walnut Grove, Etowah Co.	Rape
Sept.	2	**TWO UNKNOWN NEGROES** (2)	Montevallo, Shelby Co.	Murder
"	27	**STEELE, JOHN**	Birmingham, Jefferson Co.	Murder
Oct.	4	STARK	Locality undetermined	Supposed murder
Dec.	27	**WILSON, BUD**	Tuscaloosa, Tuscaloosa Co.	Attempted rape

1890

Mar.	22	**MOSELEY, ROBERT**	Huntsville, Madison Co.	Rape
"	31	**GRIFFIN, FRANK**	Stanton, Chilton Co.	Rape
Apr.	2	**UNKNOWN**	Brantley, Crenshaw Co.	Murder
July	13	**JONES, JOHN**	Anniston, Calhoun Co.	Robbery
"	25	**UNKNOWN NEGRO**	Riverton, Colbert Co.	Miscegenation
Aug.	12	**COOK, ISAAC**	Montgomery, Montgomery Co.	Desperado

1891

Apr.	2	**GROHAN, ZACHIOLI**	Whistler, Mobile Co.	Rape
"	15	**ELLIOTT, ROXIE** (woman)	Centerville, Bibb Co.	
"	25	**RANDALL**	Winfield, Marion Co.	Robbery and murder
July	6	**BROWN, ROBERT**	Locality undetermined	Rape
"	6	**BROWN CALVIN**	Locality undetermined	Rape
"	26	**UNDERWOOD, JESSE**	Tuscumbia, Colbert Co.	Rape
Aug.	1	**WILLIAMS, ELLA**	Henry Co.	Incendiarism
"	1	**WILLIAMS, WILLIAM**	Henry Co.	Incendiarism
"	1	**LOWE, WILLIS**	Henry Co.	Incendiarism
"	1	**LOWE, ELIZA**	Henry Co.	Incendiarism
"	21	**PORTER, RAY**	Clanton, Chilton Co.	Cause not given
Sept.	3	*SIMS, JAMES*	Choctaw Co.	Murder
"	29	**TWO UNKNOWN NEGROES**	Georgiana, Butler Co.	Murder
Oct.	1	**BROWN, JOHN**	Childersburg, Talladega Co.	Testifying against whites
"	15	**WRIGHT, SAM**	Helena, Shelby Co.	Rape
Dec.	22	*MILLER, JESSE*	Bibb Co.	Outlaw
"	26	*SIMS, ROBERT*	Choctaw Co.	Outlaw
"	26	*FOUR SAVAGE BROTHERS*	Choctaw Co.	Outlaw
"	27	*SIMS, JOHN*	Choctaw Co.	Outlaw
"	27	*SIMS, MOSELY*	Choctaw Co.	Outlaw

1892

Jan.	18	*HINTON, HENRY*	Choctaw Co.	Outlaw
Feb.	13	**TWO NEGROES**	Sylvan, Tuscaloosa Co.	Incendiarism
"	14	**WEBB, WILEY**	Selma, Dallas Co.	Rape
Mar.	10	**UNKNOWN NEGRO**	Macon Co.	Assault
Apr.	1	*MULLENS, JOHN*	Locality undetermined	Murder
"	19	**WILLIAMS, JERRY**	Inverness, Bullock Co.	Murder
"	19	**DAVIS, GEORGE**	Inverness, Bullock Co.	Murder
"	19	**WILLIAMS, WILLIAM**	Inverness, Bullock Co.	Murder
"	19	**ROBERTS, ALBERT**	Inverness, Bullock Co.	Murder
May	8	**HOES, GEORGE**	Butler, Choctaw Co.	Rape
"	16	**ROWDER, BERRY**	Childersburg, Talladega Co.	Robbery
"	16	**ROWDER, JAMES**	Childersburg, Talladega Co.	Robbery
"	16	**CANTOR WILLIAM**	Childersburg, Talladega Co.	Robbery
June	23	*CHAMBLERS', CHRISTOPHER*	Red Creek Bay, Locality Undetermined	Attempted murder

*On page 104, for convenience, we print separately the list of persons lynched for 1918, as the list for the preceding years had been set up before the 1918 list had been authenticated.

ALABAMA—Continued

July	5	UNKNOWN NEGRO	Jasper, Walker Co.	Attempted rape
"	8	PRATER, EDWARD	Clay Co.	Rape
Oct.	13	JONES, BURRELL	Monroeville, Monroe Co.	Murder
"	13	JONES, MOSES	Monroeville, Monroe Co.	Murder
"	13	TWO NEGROES	Monroeville, Monroe Co.	Murder
"	30	PARKER, ALLEN	New Monroesville, Monroe Co.	Incendiarism
Dec.	30	*HOPP, JAMES*	Greenville, Butler Co.	Murder
"	30	*KELLY, CHARLES*	Greenville, Butler Co.	Murder

1893

Jan.	19	WILLIAMS, JAMES	Pickens Co.	Rape
Apr.	14	ONLU, ED	Eufala, Barbour Co.	Murder
June	24	EDWARDS, DAN	Selma, Dallas Co.	Rape
"	27	MURPHY, ERNEST	Daleville, Dale Co.	Rape
July	17	UNKNOWN NEGRO	Brierfield, Bibb Co.	Murder
Aug.	13	*CHAMBERS, KURT*	Coffeyville, Clarke Co.	Desperado
"	13	*JAMES, LEE*	Coffeyville, Clarke Co.	Desperado
Sept.	6	UNKNOWN NEGRO	Centerville, Bibb Co.	Rape
"	15	HULL, PAUL	Carrolton, Pickens Co.	Arson
"	15	ARCHER PAUL	Carrolton, Pickens Co.	Arson
"	15	FAIR, EMMA	Carrolton, Pickens Co.	Arson
Dec.	8	MINTY, BENJAMIN	Berlin, Dallas Co.	Alleged murder
"	8	GIOHEN, JOSEPH	Berlin, Dallas Co.	Alleged murder
"	8	WILKINS, ROBERT	Berlin, Dallas Co.	Alleged murder
"	10	TWO NEGROES	Locality undetermined	Murder
"	12	FOUR NEGROES	Near Selma, Dallas Co.	Attempted robbery
"	28	SEGARS, MACK	Brantley, Crenshaw Co.	Unknown offense

1894

Feb.	17	*HENDRICKS*	Stanton, Chilton Co.	Murder
"	17	*GEORGE, W.*	Stanton, Chilton Co.	Murder
"	17	*SEDDON, A.*	Stanton, Chilton Co.	Murder
"	26	*DOUGLAS, T.*	Locality undetermined	Murder
Mar.	29	JACKSON, OLIVER	Montgomery, Montgomery Co.	Murder
Apr.	2	ENGLISH, HOLLAND	Bakerhill, Barbour Co.	Murder
"	5	TWO NEGROES	Near Selma, Dallas Co.	Alleged murder
"	14	LEWIS, WILLIAM	Lamison	Murder
"	22	BLACK, THOMAS	Tuscumbia, Colbert Co.	Barn burning
"	22	WILLIAMS, JOHN	Tuscumbia, Colbert Co.	Barn burning
"	22	JOHNSON, TONY	Tuscumbia, Colbert Co.	Barn burning
July	19	BROWNLEE, JOHN	Oxford, Calhoun Co.	Political cause
Nov.	14	MOSELEY, ROBERT	Dolimite, Jefferson Co.	Rape
Dec.	11	*BRONSON, GEORGE*	Clarke Co.	Murder
"	11	*SMITH, CHARLES*	Clarke Co.	Murder
"	11	*BROWN, LEE*	Clarke Co.	Murder

1895

Mar.	19	DAWSON, DANIEL	Tyler, Dallas Co.	Alleged arson
"	19	HOLMAN, ROBERT	Tyler, Dallas Co.	Alleged arson
"	19	HOLMAN, JOSEPH	Tyler, Dallas Co.	Alleged arson
Apr.	15	DUNEGAN, MANUEL	Chilton Co.	To prevent evidence
Apr.	21	COLLEY, ZEB	Greenville, Butler Co.	Alleged murder
"	21	RATTLER, JOHN	Greenville, Butler Co.	Alleged murder
"	21	DEANE, MARY	Greenville, Butler Co.	Alleged murder
"	21	GREEN, MARTHA	Greenville, Butler Co.	Alleged murder
"	21	GREEN, ALICE	Greenville, Butler Co.	Alleged murder
May	5	*HAMES, ANDY*	Stevenson, Jackson Co.	Murder
"	19	SHIVERS, JERIDO	Coffee Co.	Rape
"	31	FREEMAN, JAMES	Columbus City, Marshall Co.	Rape
June	5	POWELL, JAMES	Locality undetermined	Attempted rape
"	13	ALEXANDER, J. M.	Tuskegee, Macon Co.	Protecting negro
"	26	BROWNE, THOMAS	Point Clear, Baldwin Co.	Burglary
Oct.	5	McGRADY, TOBE	Perote, Bullock Co.	Rape
"	22	*HENDERSON, JOHN*	Vinegar Bend, Washington Co.	Attempted rape

1896

Feb.	10	*LEEDS, JAMES*	Seddon, Saint Clair Co.	Attempted assault
"	17	*WILSON, ROBERT*	Montgomery, Montgomery Co.	Murder
Apr.	12	ADAMS, REDDRICK	Seale, Russell Co.	Murder
May	9	*WILLIAMS, EDEN*	Manitua, Green Co.	Incest
June	20	ORR, LEON	Locality undetermined	Rape
"	24	WESTMORELAND, WILLIAM	Montgomery, Montgomery Co.	Murder
Aug.	1	MORELEY, ISADORE	Near Selma, Dallas Co.	Attempted murder
"	1	HUNTER, WILLIAM	Near Selma, Dallas Co.	Attempted murder
Sept.	27	FITCH, JOHN	Locality undetermined	Attempted rape

ALABAMA—Continued

Oct.	10	ANDERSON, JAMES	Taylor Ferry, Houston or Madison..........Alleged murder
Oct.	10	CYAT, HENRY	Locality undetermined..........Alleged murder
"	12	UNKNOWN NEGRO	Locality undetermined..........Murder
"	14	UNKNOWN NEGRO	Toadvine..........Murder
"	21	*HOLLINSHEAD*	Washington Co..........Turning State's evidence
Dec.	7	WARDLEY, WILLIAM	Irondale, Jefferson Co..........Passing counterfeit money
"	22	JAMES, JOSEPH	Woodstock, Bibb Co..........Rape

1897

Jan.	31	JACKSON, JAMES	Bibb Co..........Murder
Mar.	18	BEARD, ANDY	Kennedy, Lamar Co..........Elopement with white girl
"	20	SMITH, JOHN	Scottsboro, Jackson Co..........Rape
"	26	MARRITT, JOHN	Pickens Co..........Assault
May	12	WHITE, MOLLY	Jefferson, Marengo Co..........Murder
"	12	FRANKS, AMANDA	Jefferson, Marengo Co..........Murder
"	13	NANCE, JAMES	Jefferson, Marengo Co..........Murder
June	1	HAYDEN, JOHN	Lamar Co..........Mistaken for another
July	9	THOMAS, JAMES	Blossburg, Jefferson Co..........Refusing to give evidence
July	16	TERRILL	Elba, Coffee Co..........Murder
"	20	DANIEL, JAMES	Goose Co..........Attempted rape
"	21	SPEAKS, JAMES	Riverton, Colbert Co..........Rape
Aug.	30	PHARR, JACK	Claiborne, Monroe Co..........Robbery
Sept.	2	UNKNOWN NEGRO	Excel, Monroe Co..........Murderous assault
Nov.	29	ABRAMS, HENRY	Near Montgomery, Montmery Co..........Murder
Dec.	16	BONNER, LOUIS	Kennedy, Lamar Co..........For giving evidence, by white caps
"	16	BONNER, JOHN	Kennedy, Lamar Co..........For giving evidence, by white caps
"	17	BEARD, BUD	Carrolton, Pickens Co..........Rape

1898

Feb.	20	KELLOG, JOHN	Blanche, Cherokee Co..........Attempted rape
Mar.	21	CALLOWAY, JOHN	Calhoun Co..........Paying attention to white girl
June	17	JACKSON, SOLOMON	Wetumpka, Elmore Co..........Murder
"	17	SPIER, LOUIS	Wetumpka, Elmore Co..........Murder
"	17	THOMPSON, JESSE	Wetumpka, Elmore Co..........Murder
"	17	REESE, CAMP	Wetumpka, Elmore Co..........Murder
"	17	JACKSON, WILLIAM	Wetumpka, Elmore Co..........Murder
July	12	JOHNSON, SIDNEY	Coaling, Tuscaloosa Co..........Rape
Sept.	13	ANDERSON, ALBERT	Locality undetermined..........Murder
Oct.	2	ANDERSON, JOHN	Lafayette, Chambers Co..........Murder
Oct.	23	UNKNOWN NEGRO	Lafayette, Chambers Co..........Murder

1899

Jan.	5	McGREGOR, MARSAL	Banks, Pike Co..........Suspected arson
June	7	*HILL, WILLIAM*	Bibb Co..........Accomplice in murder
Aug.	17	HUNT, CHARLES	Brantley, Crenshaw..........Attempted rape
"	21	*LONIN, PETER*	Electric, Elmore Co..........Murder
"	21	*SON OF PETER LONIN*	Electric, Elmore Co..........Murder
Nov.	2	SLOSS, ALBERT	Near Courtland, Lawrence Co..........Attempted rape

1900

Mar.	18	HUMPHRIES, CHARLES	Lee County..........Attempted rape
May	7	UNKNOWN NEGRO	Geneva, Geneva Co..........Rape
Oct.	2	TOWNSEND, WINFIELD	Eclectic, Elmore Co..........Attempted rape
"	30	ABERNATHY	Duke, Calhoun Co..........Assault

1901

Jan.	3	McADAMS, LOUIS	Wilsonville, Shelby Co..........Murderous assault
Mar.	6	DAVIS, BUD	Moulton, Lawrence Co..........Unknown offense
May	6	MAYES, ED	Selma, Dallas Co..........Sheltering a murderer
"	6	MAYES, "DIC"	Selma, Dallas Co..........Sheltering a murderer
"	6	DAWSON, ROBERT	Selma, Dallas Co..........Sheltering a murderer

ALABAMA—Continued

May 11...WILLIAMS, WILLIAM	South Side	Theft
" 11...UNKNOWN NEGRO	Leeds, Jefferson Co.	Mistaken identity
" 30...REEVES, FRANK	Butler Co.	Attempted rape
June 16...HARRIS, GEORGE	Limestone Co.	Arson
July 15...HERMAN, ALEXANDER	Courtland, Lawrence Co.	Murder
Aug. 2...BENTLEY, CHARLES	Leeds, Jefferson Co.	Murder
Aug. 7...PENNINGTON, JOHN	Enterprise, Coffee Co.	Rape
Sept. 3...FOURNAY, WILLIAM	Chestnut, Monroe Co.	Rape
Dec. 6...THREE UNKNOWN NEGROES	Opp. Covington Co.	Race prejudice

1902

Mar. 24...ZIEGLER, WM.	Locality undetermined	Criminal assault
Apr. 6...REYNOLDS, WILLIAM	Tuscumbia, Colbert Co.	Murder
June 25...CAMPBELL, WILLY	Locality undetermined	Attempted murder
Nov. 3...HARRIS, SAMUEL	Salem, Lee Co.	Murder
Dec. 20...BISHOP, SCOTT	Marbury, Autauga Co.	Murder

1903

June 24...DIGGS, ANDREW	Scottsboro, Jackson Co.	Attempted rape
Nov. 15...YOUNG, CHARLES	Locality undetermined	Attempted rape
" 30...DAVIS, PHILLIP	Locality undetermined	Murder
" 30...CARTER, WALTER	Locality undetermined	Murder
" 30...THOMAS, CLINTON	Locality undetermined	Murder

1904

Apr. 16...SIMS, RUBEN	Little River, Baldwin Co.	Murder
May 1...HALL, CAINES	Kingston, Coffee Co.	Rape
June 22...POPE, EPHREIM	Lamison, Wilcox Co.	Rape
July 1...JONES, JON	Altoona, Etowah Co., Ala.	Rape
Aug. 7...BELL, ED.	Near Selma, Dallas Co.	Murder
Sept. 7...MAPLES, HORACE	Huntsville, Madison Co.	Murder

1905

Mar. 14...PLOWLY, EDW.	Pine Apple, Wilcox Co.	Murder
" 14...PLOWLY, WM.	Pine Apple, Wilcox Co.	Murder
Aug. 23...LATT, OLIVER	Tunnel Springs, Monroe Co.	Murder

1906

Feb. 11...RICHARDSON, BUNKIE	Gadsden, Etowah Co.	Rape and murder
" 20...PEDIGRIE, ——	Andalusia, Covington Co.	Rape
Apr. 29...BROWN, WM.	Riensi	Murder
Oct. 6...ROBINSON, RICHARD	Prichard Sta., Mobile Co.	Rape
" 6...PETERS, HENRY	Prichard, Mobile Co.	Rape
" 20...DOVE, DANIEL	Locality undetermined	Attempted rape

1907

Jan. 4...UNKNOWN	Midway, Bullock Co.	Attempted rape
Mar. 24...HARDING, CLEVELAND	Florence, Lauderdale Co.	Attempted rape
" 26...UNKNOWN	Hartford, Geneva Co.	Rape
Apr. 29...CALHOUN, EBEN	Pittsview, Russell Co.	Murderous assault
Aug. 27...LIPSEY, JNO.	Pickensville, Pickens Co.	Rape
Sept. 3...JOHNSON, JERRY	N. Birmingham, Jefferson Co.	Rape
" 22...DOSSETT, MOSES	Prichard Sta., Mobile Co.	Attempted rape
Nov. 2...SUMROLL, ABRAM	Vinegar Bend, Washington Co.	Murder
" 2...LUCAS, HENRY	Vinegar Bend, Washington, Co.	Complicity in murder
" 3...QUIGLETON, FRED	Talledaga, Talledaga Co.	Murder
" 30...SAUNDERS, NEWT	Opp. Covington Co.	Rape

1908

Apr. 6...CLAYTON, WALTER	Bay Minett, Baldwin Co.	Rape
Aug. 6...MILLER, WM.	Brighton, Jefferson Co.	Dynamiting
Oct. 21...STOVER, ——	Halselle, Choctaw Co.	Attempted rape

1909

Jan. 22...ROBERTSON, DOUGLASS	Mobile, Mobile Co.	Murder
" 24...DAVENPORT	Leighton, Collier Co.	Barn burning
Feb. 1...UNNAMED NEGRO	Bolivar, locality undetermined	Attempted rape
Apr 25...THOMAS, ——	Near Birmingham, Jefferson Co.	Rape
Sept. 4...BALAAM, JOSHUA	Jackson, Clarke Co.	Murder
" 4...BALAAM, LEWIS	Jackson, Clarke Co.	Murder
Nov. 24...ROLSTON, RAY	Anniston, Calhoun Co.	Murderous assault
Dec. 20...MONTGOMERY, CLINTON	Magnolia, Marengo Co.	Murder

ALABAMA—Continued

1910

May 26	MATSON, JESSE	Calera, Shelby Co.	Murder
July 3	McKENNY, HENRY	Dothan, Houston Co.	Attempted rape
Aug. 1	WALLACE, WILLIAM	Axis, Mobile Co.	Rape
Oct. 4	WITHERS, BUSH	Sanford, Covington Co.	Rape
Oct. 8	NEGRO	McFall, Calhoun Co.	Rape
" 9	RICHARDSON, GRANT	Centerville, Bibb Co.	Rape
" 9	DELL, JOHN	Montgomery, Montgomery Co.	Murder

1911

Feb. 12	PETERSON, IVER	Eufaula, Barbour Co.	Attempted rape
Apr. 2	UNNAMED NEGRO	Union Springs, Bullock Co.	Rape
Aug. 30	UNNAMED NEGRO	Clayton, Barbour Co.	Murder
Sept. 20	*MOLPASS, CHAS.*	Locality undetermined	Murder

1912

Jan. 28	*CHANDLER, JOHN*	Bessemer, Jefferson Co.	Murder
Feb. 19	UNNAMED	Dothan, Houston Co.	Murder
Aug. 5	VERGE, SAM	Locality undetermined	Murder
" 28	UNNAMED	Near Gadsen, Etowah Co.	Murder
Nov. 2	SMITH, WM.	Bessemer, Jefferson Co.	Murder
" 18	BERNEY, ——	Wetumpka, Elmore Co.	Murder
Dec. 7	CURTIS, Azariah	Butler, Choctaw Co.	Murder
" 20	UNNAMED	Cuba, Sumter Co.	Murder

1913

Jan. 3	CARSON	Selma, Dallas Co.	Unnamed offense
Aug. 28	UNKNOWN NEGRO	Kilgore	Unnamed cause

1914

Mar. 29	YOUNG, CHARLES	Clayton, Barbour Co.	Murder
Dec. 19	JONES, WILLIAM	Fort Deposit, Lowndes Co.	Murder

1915

Jan. 4	SMITH, EDWIN	Wetumpka, Elmore Co.	Murder
" 4	SMITH, WILLIAM	Wetumpka, Elmore Co.	Murder
" 18	DEELEY, HERMAN	Taylorsville, Bartow Co.	Murder
Aug. 10	FOX, JAMES	Locality undetermined	Murder
" 17	JACKSON, "KID"	Hope Hull, Montgomery Co.	Poisoning mules
" 17	RUSSELL, HENRY	Hope Hull, Montgomery Co.	Poisoning mules
" 17	UNNAMED NEGRO	Hope Hull, Montgomery Co.	Poisoning mules

1916

Jan. 28	BURTON, RICHARD	Boyds, Sumter Co.	Burglary
July 1	WEEKS, LEMUEL	Pickensville, Pickens Co.	Murder

1917

Jan. 10	UNNAMED NEGRO	Greeley, Tuscaloosa Co.	Rape
July 16	UNIDENTIFIED NEGRO	Reform, Pickens Co.	Burglary
" 23	HIBBLER, POE	Pickens Co.	Attempted rape
" 23	POWELL, WILLIAM	Letohatchee, Lowndes Co.	Threat to kill
" 23	POWELL, JESSE	Letohatchee, Lowndes Co.	Threat to kill

ALASKA

1897

Aug. 21	*UNKNOWN MAN*	Skaguay	Larceny
Sept. 11	*MARTIN, WILLIAM G.*	Lake Bennett	Larceny
" 18	*UNKNOWN MAN*	Skaguay	Larceny

1898

Feb. 2	*TANNER, M. F.*		Murder

ARIZONA

1892

June 22	*TWO HORSE THIEVES*	Calabasas, locality undetermined	
Oct. 18	*AN INDIAN*	Ash Fork, Yavapai Co.	Rape

ARIZONA—Continued

1897

Oct. 28....*MADERA, JUAN*....................Morenci, Greenlee Co.........................Murder

1901

July 27....*RIVERA, IGNACIO*...................Hent's Ranch....................................Horse thief

1915

April 20....*LEON, JUAN*.........................Lonely Gulch..............Alleged bandit
"   20....*LEON, JOSE M.*......................Lonely Gulch..............Alleged bandit

1917

May 6....*DALEY, STAR*........................Florence, Pinal County.........................Murder

ARKANSAS

1889

Jan. 15...**REYNOLDS, DEAN**....................Locality undetermined...............Jilting a girl
Mar. 8...**ROBINSON, J. E.**...................Texarkana, Miller Co................................Rape
May 19...**NEELY, A. M.**.......................Forest City, St. Francis Co......Political troubles
June 13...**JOHNSON, ARMSTEAD**............Pine Bluff, Jefferson Co............................Theft
Dec. 16...*FOUR OUTLAWS*.................Maumelle, Pulaski Co..................................

1890

Jan. 1...**UNKNOWN**............................Turner P. O., Phillips Co.....Accessory to
                                                                                    murder
Feb. 14...**LARKIN, WILLIAM**..................Camden, Ouachita Co...........................Murder
May 30....**WEAVER, ROBERT**................Locality undetermined._____......Race prejudice

1891

June 25....**JONES, HENRY**....................Hamburg, Ashley Co..............................Murder
July 7...**BAILEY, JAMES**....................Beebe, White Co.....................................Rape
"   17...*ROSSIMUS, FRANK*............Arkansas City, Desha Co.......Attempted murder
"   18...*RICE, FRANK*......................Arkansas City, Desha Co.......Attempted murder
"   19...*DARMER, JOHN*...................Arkansas City, Desha Co......................Murder
Aug. 30...**MULLIGAN, CHARLES**...........Conway, Faulkner Co............................Murder
Oct. 1...**PATTERSON, BEN**................Hackette, Sebastine...............Strike rioting
"   1...**PEYTON, EDWARD**.............Near Marianna, Lee Co..............Strike rioting
Nov. 8...**RICE, WILLIAM**.................Locality undetermined............Unknown cause
"   20...**HADLEY, NAT**.....................Gurdon, Clark Co.................................Murder
Dec. 14...**UNKNOWN MAN**.................Newton Co.........................Cause unknown
"   21...*SMITH, J. A.*......................Dewitt, Arkansas Co.............................Murder
"   21...*GREGORY, FLOYD*.................Dewitt, Arkansas Co.............................Murder
"   21...**HENDERSON, MOSES**.............Dewitt, Arkansas Co...............................Rape

1892

Jan. 18...*JOHNSON*................................Northern Arkansas...............Suspected murder
"   18...*BAKER, MRS.*........................Northern Arkansas...............Suspected murder
Feb. 9...**BEAVERS, HENRY**................Wilmar, Ashley Co..........Assaulting a woman
"   10...**BRISCO & SON, HAMP**.........Locality undetermined...............Race prejudice
"   10...**BRISCO, MRS.**...................Locality undetermined...............Race prejudice
"   14...**KELLY, JOHN**....................Pine Bluff, Jefferson Co......................Murder
"   14...**HARRIS, GULBERT**..............Pine Bluff, Jefferson Co........Accessory to
                                                                                    murder
"   20...**COY, ED.**...........................Texarkana, Miller Co..............................Rape
"   23...**HARRIS, GEORGE**.................Varner, Lincoln Co.................................Murder
April 1...*STUART, CHAS.*.................Locality undetermined............Attempted rape
May 13...**HENRY, JAMES**....................Little Rock, Pulaski Co...........................Rape
"   21...**STEWART, CHARLES**............Morrillton, Conway Co.........................Murder
"   31...*THREE MEN NAMED MC-
                ARTHUR*......................Perryville, Perry Co....................Advising murder
June 22...*CARSON, HENRY*...................Moark, Clay Co....................................Murder
July 2...**A NEGRO**...........................Wynne, Cross Co.....................................Rape
"   2...**DONNELLY, ROBERT**...........Union Township, Fulton Co.....................Rape
"   14...**MOSELEY, JULIAN**..............Arkansas City, Desha Co._____...........Rape
"   30...**BAKER, EUGENE**...................Monticello, Drew Co............Self-defense
Aug. 4...**CARTER, ALLEN**.................Wynne, Cross Co.....................................Rape
"   10...**JORDON, ROBERT**...............Camden, Ouachita Co............Insulting a woman
"   23...**BOWLES**.................................Gurdon, Clark Co...................................Rape
Sept. 20...**HARRISON**............................Champagnolle, Union Co..........Race prejudice
Dec. 7...**LIGHTFOOT**.........................Near Newport, Jackson Co........................Fraud

ARKANSAS—Continued

1893

Jan. 6	SCROGGS, PAUL	Brinkley, Monroe Co.	Murder
" 6	ALLEN, HENRY	Brinkley, Monroe Co.	Murder
April 19	THORNTON, FLANNEGAN	Morrillton, Conway Co.	Murder
May 9	*CRAM, A. B.*	Bearden, Ouachita Co.	Murder
" 9	"DOC" HENDERSON	Bearden, Ouachita Co.	Murder
" 9	STEWART, JOHN	Bearden, Ouachita Co.	Murder
" 31	WALLACE, JOHN	Jefferson Springs	Rape
Nov. 14	NELSON	Varner, Lincoln Co.	Murder
Dec. 7	GREENWOOD, ROBERT	Cross Co.	Race prejudice
Nov. 20	JONES, NEWTON	Boxley, Newton Co.	Murder

1894

Jan. 5	DAVIS, ALFRED	Lonoke Co.	Stealing
Feb. 9	BRUCE, HENRY	Gulch Co.	Murder
" 9	*PLUNKETT, CHAS. & ROBT.*	Gulch Co.	Murder
Mar. 6	UNKNOWN WOMAN	Near Marche, Pulaski Co.	Unknown offense
May 23	BROOKS, WILLIAM	Palestine, Saint Francis Co.	Asking white woman in marriage
June 22	CAPUS, HENRY	Magnolia, Columbia Co.	Rape
Sept. 22	WASHINGTON, LUKE	McGehee, Desha Co.	Murder
" 22	WASHINGTON	McGehee, Desha Co.	Murder
" 22	CROBYSON, HENRY	McGehee, Desha Co.	Murder

1895

June 20	KING, FRANK	Little Rock, Pulaski Co.	Murder
July 14	TWO NEGROES	Hampton, Calhoun Co.	Alleged murder
Aug. 22	JONES, JAMES	Locality undetermined	Murder
Sept. 5	*FREEMAN, AARON*	Near Hot Springs, Garland Co.	Rape
" 11	CALDWELL, WILLIAM	Near Osceola, Mississippi Co.	Murder
" 11	THOMAS, JOHN	Near Osceola, Mississippi Co.	Murder
" 19	UNKNOWN NEGRO	Locality undetermined	Rape
Nov. 4	ENGLAND, ALBERT	Wynne, Cross Co.	Burglary

1896

July 31	GOULD, GIDFREY	Clarendon, Monroe Co.	Rape
Dec. 9	CRAZY JIM	Milton, Garland Co.	Murder
" 17	UNKNOWN NEGRO	Near Pine Bluff, Jefferson Co.	Murder

1897

May 20	OATES, PRESLEY	Locality undetermined	Theft
Aug. 24	WYATT, WILLIAM	Rison, Cleveland Co.	Murder
" 26	WILLIAMS, EDWARD	Baxter, near Drew Co.	Rape
Sept. 5	UNKNOWN NEGRO	Robroy, Jefferson Co.	Unknown offense
" 16	WATSON, D. L.	Hamilton, locality undetermined	Race prejudice
Oct. 15	PARKER, THOMAS	Kendall, locality undetermined	Killing a white cap
" 17	*COLE*	Wilmot, Ashley Co.	Murder
Nov. 15	PHILKIPS, HENRY	Osceola, Mississippi Co.	Murder
Dec. 8	*MURRAY*	Jenny Lind, Sebastian Co.	Arresting a miner

1898

Jan. 1	UNKNOWN NEGRO	Sherrill, Jefferson Co.	Theft
" 8	DAVAL	Near Reader, Ouachita Co.	Murder
" 8	HUNTLEY	Near Reader, Ouachita Co.	Murder
" 8	TWO NEGROES	Near Reader, Ouachita Co.	Murder
Mar. 15	UNKNOWN	Marcella, Stone Co.	Robbery
April 3	*MERCER, WM.*	Locality undetermined	Murder
June 3	HAYDEN, LEVI	Texarkana, Miller Co.	Assault
July 1	GRAY, GOODE	Rison, Cleveland Co.	Murder
" 14	RIED, JAMES	Monticello, Drew Co.	Murder
" 14	JOHNSON, ALEXANDER	Monticello, Drew Co.	Murder
Aug. 9	MANSE, CASTLE	Clarendon, Monroe Co.	Murder
" 9	RICORD, DENNIS	Clarendon, Monroe Co.	Murder
" 9	SAUNDERS, WILLIAM	Clarendon, Monroe Co.	Murder
" 9	WEAVER, RILLA	Clarendon, Monroe Co.	Murder
Dec. 6	GAINES, NEWTON	Locality undetermined	Rape

ARKANSAS—Continued

1899

Mar. 23...DUCKETT, GENERAL	Little River Co.	Murder
" 23...JONES, BENJAMIN	Little River Co.	Murder
" 23...JONES, JOSEPH	Little River Co.	Murder
" 23...JONES, MOSES	Little River Co.	Murder
" 23...GOODWIN, EDWARD	Little River Co.	Murder
" 23...KING, JOSEPH	Little River Co.	Murder
" 23...UNKNOWN NEGRO	Little River Co.	Murder
April 18...*HARKIN, W. H.*	Clinton, Van Buren Co.	Murder
May 1...DEES, WILLIE	Osceola, Mississippi Co.	Arson
July 24...DAVIS, CHICH	Wilmot, Ashley Co.	Rape

1900

May 26...UNKNOWN NEGRO	West Point, White County	Robbery
June 12...BRODIE, JOHN	Lee County	Attempted murder
June 17...MULLENS, NAT	Earle, Crittenden County	Murder
June 19...*WOODWARD, WILLIAM*	Searcy Co.	Murder
Dec. 21...UNKNOWN NEGRO	Arkadelphia, Clark County	Rape

1901

Feb. 20...BERRYMAN, PETER	Mena, Polk Co.	Assaulting a white person
Mar. 23...*STUNLY, GEORGE*	Pocohantos, Randolph County	Murder
April 6...*HEARN, MAY*	Osceola, Mississippi County	Murder
May 13...KEY, LEE	Knoxville, Johnson Co.	Race prejudice
Aug. 1...*SEIGLER*	Rosston, Nevada Co.	Murder

1902

Mar. 10...McCOY, HORACE	Foreman, Little River Co.	Criminal assault
Aug. 1...NEWTON, LEE	Locality undetermined	Attempted rape
Sept. 3...WILSON, HOG	Stephens, Ouachita Co.	Rape
Oct. 20...YOUNG, CHARLES	Forrest City, Saint Francis	Rape and murder
Nov. 20...WELLS, ELIJAH	Wynne, Cross Co.	Murderous assault

1903

Mar. 20...ROBERTSON, FRANK	Bradley, Lafayette Co.	Arson
April 6...TURNER, JOHN	Warren, Bradley Co.	Attempted rape
" 23...THOMPSON, ALEXANDER	Gurdon, Clark Co.	Murderous assault
July 22...GILBERT, JOHN	Locality undetermined	Murder
" 22...UNKNOWN	Locality undetermined	Murder
Sept. HELLEM	Luxora, Mississippi Co.	Assaulted colored girls
Oct. 6...McCOLLUM, EDWARD	Sheridan, Grant Co.	Murderous assault
Nov. 3...JOHNSON, HENRY	Lake Village, Chicot Co.	Murder
" 8...*CADLE, Z. C.*	Brinkley, Monroe Co.	Murder

1904

Feb. 19...DAYS, GLENCO	Crossett, Ashley Co.	Murder
Mar. 26...SMITH, JAS.	St. Charles, Arkansas Co.	Race prejudice
" 26...SMITH, CHARLES	St. Charles, Arkansas Co.	Race prejudice
" 26...BALDWIN, MACK	St. Charles, Arkansas Co.	Race prejudice
" 26...BAILEY, ABE	St. Charles, Arkansas Co.	Race prejudice
" 26...FLOOD, GARRETT	St. Charles, Arkansas Co.	Race prejudice
" 26...JOHNSTON, KILLIS	St. Charles, Arkansas Co.	Race prejudice
" 26...CARTER, PERRY	St. Charles, Arkansas Co.	Race prejudice
" 26...GRIFFIN, HENRY	St. Charles, Arkansas Co.	Race prejudice
" 26...GRIFFIN, WALTER	St. Charles, Arkansas Co.	Race prejudice
" 26...FLOOD, RANDALL	St. Charles, Arkansas Co.	Race prejudice
" 26...BALDWIN, WM.	St. Charles, Arkansas Co.	Race prejudice
" 26...MADISON, WM.	St. Charles, Arkansas Co.	Race prejudice
" 26...HINTON, AARON	St. Charles, Arkansas Co.	Race prejudice
Aug. 31...TWO UNKNOWN	Stephens, Ouachita Co.	Insulting white women
Sept. 5...UNKNOWN	Crossett, Ashley Co.	Assaulting whites

1905

Jan. 1...*ALLWHITE, LOUIS*	Newport, Jackson Co.	Murder
" 4...JETTON, WHITE	Spring Hill	Murder
April 20...BARRETT, JOHN	Askew, Lee Co.	Murder
July 6...WOODMAN, JAS.	Locality undetermined	Eloping with white girl
Sept. 22...BROWN, FRANK	Conway, Faulkner Co.	Mistaken identity

ARKANSAS—Continued

1906

Feb. 7....CALTON, JAMES...................Elmarth, locality undeter-
        mined.........................Murderous assault
July 8....ANDERSON, WM...................Pillar, locality undetermined...................Rape
" 12....UNKNOWN.......................Near Junction City, Union Co......Attempted rape
Oct. 7....BLACKBURN, H..................Argenta, Pulaski...................Murderous assault
" 8....DAVIS, ANTHONY...............Texarkana, Miller Co...............Attempted rape
Nov. 20....UNKNOWN NEGRO.............Hot Springs, Garland Co.........Attempted rape

1907

Mar. 20....TWO COLORED WOMEN........Stamps, Lafayette Co.............Murderous assault
Dec. 5....MUSSAY, WASHINGTON..........Augusta, Woodruff Co...................Murder

1908

June 20....WILLIAMS, ERNEST.................Parkdale, Ashley Co.............Using offensive
        language

1909

Jan. 18....HILLIARD..........................Hope, Hempstead Co...........Insulting white girl
May 24....AIKENS, ALBERT................Pine Bluff, Jefferson Co...................Rape
" 30....BLAKELY, JOS..................Portland, Ashley Co...................Murder
Dec. 20....BAILY, GEO....................Devill's Bluff, Prairie Co...................Murder

1910

Mar. 19....AUSTIN, ROBERT...............Marion, Crittendon Co...................Murder
" 19....RICHARDS, CHARLES............Marion, Crittendon Co...................Murder
" 25....JONES "JUDGE".................Pine Bluff, Jefferson Co...........Insulting women
April 5....PRIDE, FRANK..................Locality undetermined...................Murder
" 5....MITCHELL, LAURA..............Locality undetermined...................Murder
May 14....McLANE, "DOCK"..............Ashdown, Little River Co.......Murderous assault
June 14....HUNTER, WILLIAM.............Star City, Lincoln Co...........Insulting white
        women
July 6....POWELL, SAM..................Huttig, Union Co..............Robbery and arson
Nov. 26....*CHITWOOD, OSCAR*............Hot Springs...................Murder

1911

Sept. 9....DEAN, ARTHUR................Augusta, Woodruff Co...................Rape
Oct. 16....LUCEY, NATHAN..............Forrest City, Saint Francis Co...................Rape
" 20....LEWIS, CHARLES..............Hope, Hempstead Co...............Insulting women

1912

Mar. 23....LEWIS, SANFORD.............Locality, undetermined...................Murder
July. 5....WILLIAMS, JNO..............Plummerville, Conway Co...................Murder
Aug. 20....FRANKLIN, MONROE..........Russellville, Pope Co...................Rape

1913

June 19....NORMAN, WILLIAM............Near Hot Springs Garland Co...................Rape
Sept. 5....SIMMS, LEE..................Little Rock, Pulaski Co...................Rape

1914

Oct. 28....DAVIS, HOWARD..............Newport, Jackson Co...................Murder

1915

June 15....HALEY, LOY..................Hope, Hempstead Co...................Murder
Sept. 12....BOWERS, JACOB.............Carlisle, Lonoko Co...................Murder
Dec. 3....PATRICK, WILLIAM............Forrest, St. Francis Co...................Murder

ARKANSAS—Continued

1916

Jan. 22.... *U N N A M E D   H I G H W A Y -*
         M A N....Vandervoort, Polk D............ ....
May 27....GILMAN, FELIX.......................Prescott, Nevada Co.......................... ....Murder
Aug. 9....UNNAMED NEGRO.................Stuttgart, Arkansas Co...............................Rape
Oct. 9....DODD, FRANK..............................Dewitt, Arkansas Co...................Attempted rape

1917

Feb. 8...SMITH, JAMES.........................Proctor, Crittenden Co...........................Murder
July 31...AVERY, ANDREW...................Garland City, Miller Co.........................Robbery
Aug. 9...JIMERSON, AARON....................Ashdown, Little River Co....Murderous
                                                                                              assault
Sept. 13...GATES, SAMUEL....................England, Lonoke Co.................Insulting girls
Oct. 8...UNNAMED NEGRO..Robbery

CALIFORNIA

1889

Mar. 18....*SPRAGUE, B. S.*...................Garvanza, Los Angeles Co...................Murder

1891

Feb. 22....*REILLY, OLIVER.*................Salado Independence Co..........................Murder
June 15...AH ANONG TI (CHINESE).....Bridgeport, Mono Co.............................Murder
Aug. 25...LEE OMAN, (CHINESE).........Locality undetermined.............................Rape

1892

July 24....*R UGGLES, JO H N.*...............Redding, Frankiln Co..............Murder and
                                                                                                        robbery
  * 24...*R UGGLES, C HARLES.*...............Redding, Franklin Co............Murder and
                                                                                                        robbery
Sept. 30...*SMIT H, J. W.*......................Locality undetermined...........................Murder
Nov. 11...PLANZ, HENRY.........................San Jose, Santa Clara Co.........Unknown offense

1893

Apr. 7....FULZEN, JESUS (MEXICAN)..San Bernardino, San Bern-
                                                           ardino Co...Murder

1895

July 27....*ADAMS, VICTOR.*...................O'Neals Madera Co.............................Murder
Aug. 26...*JO H NSO N, LAWRE NCE.*........Yreka, Siskiyou Co.............................Murder
  " 26...*N ULL, WILLI AM.*................Yreka, Siskiyou Co.............................Murder
  " 26...*MORE NO, LO UIS.*.................Yreka, Siskiyou Co.............................Murder
  " 26...*SEEMLER, HARLA ND.*...........Yreka, Siskiyou Co.............................Murder
Sept. 27...ARCHOR, WM. (INDIAN).......Bakersfield, Kern Co...........................Murder
Oct. 1...*LITTLEFIELD, JO H N.*.............Round Valley, Inyo Co.......................Murder

1901

May 31...*HALE, FRA N K.*......................Lookout, Modoc Co...................................Theft
  " 31...*HALE, JAMES.*...................Lookout, Modoc Co...................................Theft
  " 31...*HALE, MARTI N.*..................Lookout, Modoc Co...................................Theft
  " 31...*HALE, CALVI N.*...................Lookout, Modoc Co...................................Theft
  " 31...*TANTIS, B. D.*......................Lookout, Modoc Co...................................Theft
July 10...FOOK, TUNG (CHINESE)...........

1904

Mar. 12...UNKNOWN....................................Majane, locality undetermined..Unknown offense
Apr. 16....*PETRIE.*...Dunsmuir, Siskiyou Co.............................Rape

1908

Apr. 23....*SIMPSO N, JOS.*.........................Sikdoo, locality undetermined....................Murder

COLORADO

1893

July 26....*ARATA, NICOLAI.*...............Denver, Denver Co..............................Murder

COLORADO—Continued

1894

June 2....*McCURDY, ALEX*....................Golden, Jefferson Co...Murder

1895

Jan. 9....*WITHERELL, GEORGE*............Canon City, Fremont Co...................Desperado
Mar. 12....*APOLETTI, ANTONIO*............Walsenburg, Huerfano Co............Alleged murder
"   12....*GIACONINO, PIETRO*............Walsenburg, Huerfano Co.........Alleged murder
"   12....*LORENZO, ANTINIO*............Walsenburg, Huerfano Co............Alleged murder
"   12....*ROCHETTI, FRANCISCO*......Walsenburg, Huerfano Co............Alleged murder
"   12....*VETTARI, STANISLAUS*......Walsenburg, Huerfano Co............Alleged murder
"   12....*WELSBY, JOSEPH*................Walsenburg, Huerfano Co............Alleged murder

1896

Apr. 15....*COVINGTON, SAM*................Central City, Gilpin Co.............................Murder
Oct. 14....*HARRIS, GEORGE*................Meeker, Rio Blanco Co...................Bank robbery
"   14....*SMITH, WILLIAM*................Meeker, Rio Blanco Co...................Bank robbery
"   14....*JONES, CHARLES*................Meeker, Rio Blanco Co...................Bank robbery

1900

Jan. 26....*REYNOLDS, THOMAS*.............Canon City, Fremont Co...........................Murder
May 22....**KUNBLERN, CALVIN**.............Pueblo, Pueblo Co...Murder
Nov. 16....*PORTER, PRESTON*...............Locality undetermined.................................Murder

1902

Mar. 25....**WALLACE, WASHINGTON H.**.....La Junta, Otero Co.....................................Assault

1906

Dec. 27....*LEBORG, LAURENCE*............. Las Animas, Bent Co.................................Murder

DELAWARE

1903

June 12....**WHITE, GEORGE**.....................Near Wilmington, New Castle
                                                Co..Rape and murder

FLORIDA

1890

Mar. 29....**SIMPSON, SIMMONS**.................Marianna, Jackson Co.............................Murder
July 18....**JACKSON, GREEN**.................Ft. White, Columbia Co.....................Murder
Dec. 11....**WILLIAMS, DANIEL**...Incendiarism

1891

Feb. 18....**CHAMPION,** ——................Gainesville, Alachua Co.......................Outlaw
"   18....*KELLY, MICHAEL*................Gainesville, Alachua Co.......................Outlaw
June 17....**UNKNOWN NEGRO**.................Fort White, Columbia Co........Unknown offense
"   22....**GRIFFEN, CHARLES**.................Locality undetermined.......................Murder
Aug. 25....**FORD, ANDY**.........................Gainesville, Alachua Co..... ....Bad reputation
Sept. 29....**BARLEY, LEE**.........................De Land, Volusia Co.............................Rape
Dec. 15....**UNKNOWN NEGRO**............Locality undetermined...............................Robbery
"   15....**TWO NEGROES**...................Live Oak, Suwanee Co...............................Murder

1892

Jan. 12....**HENSON, HENRY**........................Micanopy, Alachua Co.............................Murder
Feb. 18....**AUSTIN, WALTER**.................Arcadia, De Soto Co.............................Murder
Mar. 30....**COBB, DENNISS**.................Arcadia, De Soto Co...........Unknown cause
May 25....**WILLIAMS, JAMES**.................Locality undetermined.............................Murder
"   25....**A NEGRO**.........................Locality undetermined.............................Murder

FLORIDA—Continued

June 7	KANEKER, WILLIAM	Apalachicola, Franklin Co.	Rape
July 8	McDUFFIE, HENRY	Orlando, Orange Co.	Stealing
Sept. 7	A NEGRO	Waldo, Alachua Co.	Incendiary

1893

Jan. 26	WILLS, PATROCK	Quincy, Gadsden Co.	Incendiarism
July 12	LARKINS, ROBERT	Ocala, Marion Co.	Rape
Nov. 9	BOGGS, HENRY	Fort White, Columbia Co.	Murder
" 14	THREE NEGROES	Lake City Junction, Columbia Co.	Murder

1894

Jan. 9	SMITH, SAMUEL	Greenville, Madison Co.	Murder
" 14	WILLIS, CHARLES	Ocala, Marion Co.	Desperado
May 13	ROSE, GEORGE	Locality undetermined	Rape
" 15	YOUNG, NIM	Ocala, Marion Co.	Rape
" 29	BURGIS, J. T.	Palatka, Putnam Co.	Conspiracy
Sept. 14	SMITH, JAMES	Starke, Bradford Co.	Attempted rape
Dec. 4	JACKSON, WILLIAM	Ocala, Marion Co.	Rape
" 17	A NEGRO	Marion Co.	Rape

1895

Apr. 2	RAWLES, WILLIAM	Locality undetermined	Murder
May 19	ECHOLS, SAMUEL	Ellaville, Madison Co.	Rape
" 19	CROWLEY, SIMEON	Near Ellaville, Madison Co.	Rape
" 19	BROOKS, JOHN	Near Ellaville, Madison Co.	Rape
" 30	THREE NEGROES	Bartow, Polk Co.	Suspicion of rape
June 9	COLLINS, WILLIAM	Mayo, Lafayette Co.	Attempted rape
" 11	TWO UNKNOWN NEGROES	Mayo, Lafayette Co.	Concealing criminal
July 4	BENNET, ROBERT	Near Lake City, Columbia Co.	Attempted rape
Aug. 18	LEWIS, SAMUEL	Locality undetermined	Murder

1896

Jan. 13	JORDON, HARRY	Alachua, Alachua Co.	Murder
Apr. 20	VAN BRUNT, JOHN	De Land, Volusia Co.	Disorderly conduct
May 7	JONES, CHARLES	Macclenny, Baker Co.	Without cause
" 11	WILSON, HARRY	Madison Co.	Unknown offense
" 11	MURRAY. ———	Madison Co.	Unknown offense
July 6	WILLIAMS, JACOB	Madison Co.	Rape
Sept. 23	HARRIS, CHARLES	Near De Land, Volusia Co.	Rape
" " 23	JOHNSON, ANTHONY	De Land, Volusia Co.	Rape
Nov. 28	DANIELS, ALFRED	Gainesville, Alachua Co.	Arson

1897

Jan. 24	TAYLOR, PIERCE	Tallahasse, Leon Co.	Attempted rape
Mar. 5	SMITH, OTEA	Juliette, Marion Co.	Murder
" 5	GREEN, JACK	Juliette, Marion Co.	Murder
" 5	EDWARDS, HENRY	Juliette, Marion Co.	Murder
" 5	JONES, SAM	Juliette, Marion Co.	Murerr
" 5	MELTON, WASH	Juliette, Marion Co.	Murder
" 15	GILMORE, JAMES	Juliette, Marion Co.	Murder
" 15	MILEY, JAMES	Juliette, Marion Co.	Murder
" 15	MILLER, OTIS	Juliette, Marion Co.	Murder
June 5	BARRETT, ISAAC	Orange Dale, Saint Johns Co.	Murder
Aug. 20	UNKNOWN NEGRO	Apalachicola, Franklin Co.	Attempted rape
Nov. 25	PRICE, HICKS	Starke, Bradford Co.	Rape

1898

Nov. 6	WILLIAMS, ARTHUR	Wellborne, Suwanee Co.	Murder

1899

Feb. 1	MARTIN, CHARLES	Madison, Madison Co.	Unknown offense
June 13	A NEGRO	Dunellon, Madison Co.	Murder
" 13	TWO NEGROES	Dunellon, Madison Co.	Race prejudice
Aug. 9	UNKNOWN NEGRO	Jasper, Hamilton Co.	Rape
Nov. 22	LAWRENCE, WEST	Near Pensacola, Escambia Co.	Rape

FLORIDA—Continued

1900

Mar. 11	UNKNOWN NEGRO	Jennings, Hamilton Co.	Murder
May 14	TWO NEGROES	Brooksville, Hernando Co.	Suspected murder
June 10	UNKNOWN NEGRO	Sneads, Jackson Co.	Murder
June 10	SANDERS, JOHN	Sneads, Jackson Co.	Complicity in murder
" 27	DAVIS, ROBERT	Mulberry, Polk Co.	Murder
" 27	THOMAS, JACK	Live Oak, Suwanee Co.	Attempted rape
" 29	BARCO, JAMES	Panasoffkee, Sumter Co.	Unknown offense
Nov. 27	*WILLIAMS, SPENCER*	Lake City, Columbia Co.	Murderous assault

1901

Jan. 7	DENSON, JAMES	Madison, Madison Co.	Murder
" 7	DENSON'S STEPSON	Madison, Madison Co.	Murder
" 16	McKINNEY, NORMAN	Dunnellon, Marion Co.	Trainwrecking
Feb. 8	WRIGHT, WILLIAM	Dade City, Pasco Co.	Complicity in murder
Feb. 8	WILLIAMS, SAM	Dade City, Pasco Co.	Complicity in murder
May 30	ROCHELLE, FRED	Bartow, Polk Co.	Murder
Sept. 7	UNKNOWN	Chipley, Washington Co.	Rape

1902

July 28	UNKNOWN NEGRO	Bluff springs, Escambia Co.	Unknown offense
Aug. 1	WILLIAMS, ALONZO	San Antonio, Pasco Co.	Rape
Sept. 1	PRICE, MANNY	Newberry, Alachua Co.	Murder
" 1	SCRUGGS, ROBERT	Newberry, Alachua Co.	Murder

1903

Mar. 9	THOMAS, HENRY	Parish, Manatee Co.	Rape
May 3	KENNEDY, DAN	Mulberry, Polk Co.	Murder
" 19	*JARVIS, WASHINGTON*	Madison, Madison Co.	Murder
" 20	RANDALL, AMOS	Mulberry, Polk Co.	Murder
" 20	GORDON, HENRY	Mulberry Polk Co.	Murder
July 18	ADAMS, ——	Lake Butler, Bradford Co.	Rape
" 21	GREEN, CRANE	Pine Barren	Rape
Oct. 9	*WILLIAMS, SAMUEL*	Lawby, Bradford Co.	Refusing information
Dec. 5	LEWIS JACKSON	Near Tampa, Hillsborough Co.	Attempted rape

1904

Jan. 15	CLARK, JUMBO	High Springs, Alachua Co.	Rape
May 20	UNKNOWN	Mulberry, Polk Co.	Unknown offence
Sept. 6	BRADLEY, WASH.	Bronson, Levy Co.	Murder
Oct. 4	*RIVERS, ——*	Perry, Taylor Co.	Attempted rape

1905

July 1	PETERS, DOC	Cottondale, Jackson Co.	Murder

1906

May 17	JORDAN, FRANK	Inverness, Citrus Co.	Murder
June 8	DAVIS, JAMES	Inverness, Citrus Co.	Murder
July 27	BLACK, JOHN	Locality undetermined	Murder
" 27	REAGIN, WM.	Locality undetermined	Murder
Aug. 21	BAPES, JOHN	Mulberry, Polk Co.	Murderous assault
Nov. 9	UNKNOWN NEGRO	Madison, Madison Co.	Rape

1908

Feb. 2	PITMAN, CHAS.	Greenville, Madison Co.	Suspected murder
Mar. 5	*LONG, JOHN*	Newberry, Alachua Co.	Murder
July 29	SHAW, LEANDER	Pensacola, Escambia Co.	Attempted rape
Oct. 5	PRICE, BENJAMIN	Locality undetermined	Rape

1909

Feb. 13	NADER, JACOB	Lakeland, Polk Co.	Rape
Apr. 5	ALEXANDER, DAVID	Pensacola, Escambia Co.	Murder
" 10	SMITH, JNO.	Arcadia, De Soto Co.	Rape
May 9	UNNAMED NEGRO	Duval Co.	Rape
June 6	MORRIS, MAIK	Tallahassee, Leon Co.	Murder
" 15	UNNAMED NEGRO	Arcadia, De Soto Co.	Attempted rape
Sept. 26	ANDERSON, CHAS.	Perry, Taylor Co.	Murder

FLORIDA—Continued

1910

Mar. 7...ELLIS, WADE..........................Tampa, Hillsborough Co.....................Murder
  "   7...ELLIS, SAM.............................Tampa, Hillsborough Co.....................Murder
  "   8...——, NEGRO...........................Tampa, Hillsborough Co.....................Murder
June 11...MATTHEWS, ROBERT..............Locality undetermined.........................Rape
July 9...McINTOSH, SAM...................Kathleen, Polk Co...............Attempted murder
July 30...TWO NEGROES.....................Bonifay, Holmes Co.........................Murder
Aug. 2...FOUR NEGROES...................Bonifay, Holmes Co.............Complicity in mur-
                                                                                            der
Sept. 2...CHRISTIAN, EDWARD...........Graceville, Jackson Co.....................Murder
  "   2...BOWMAN, HATTIE.................Graceville, Jackson Co...Complicity in mur-
                                                                                            der
  " 20...*TICORETEA, CASTENEGO*....Tampa, Hillsborough Co.........Attempted murder
  " 20...*ALBANO, ANGELO*..............Tampa, Hillsborough Co.....Attempted murder
Nov. 26...LOWE, RICHARD..................Mayo, Lafayette Co......Attempted rape
  " 26...MATTHEWS, ROBERT.............Gull Point, Escambia Co.........................Rape

1911

Mar. 5...BAKER, GALVIN...................Marianna, Jackson Co.............Threats to kill
May 21...SIX UNKNOWN NEGROES......Lake City, Columbia Co.....................Murder

1912

Apr. 15...ARLINE, SAM.......................Near Tampa, Hillsborough Co................Murder
July 4...ENGLISH, WM......................Bradentown, Manatee Co......Insulting   white
                                                                                            woman
Sept. 14...MURPHY, H.........................Atlon, Lafayette Co.........................Rape
Nov. 14...NELLIS, PREECH..................Ocala, Marion Co.............................Murder
  " 19...ARCHER, JNO.......................Ocala, Marion Co.............................Murder

1913

July 6...SMITH, ROSCOE....................Yellow River...................................Murder
  "   7...UNNAMED NEGRO.................Bonifay, Holmes Co..........................Rape
  " 10...TEMPERS, KID......................Blountstown, Calhoun Co...................Murder

1914

Nov. 14...EVANS, JOHN.......................St. Petersburg, Pinellas Co..................Murder

1915

Feb. 17...RICHARDS, JOHN..................Sparr, Marion Co................Insulting women
Feb. 28...REED, WILLIAM....................Kissimmee, Osceola Co........................Rape
July 23...OWENS, H. M.......................Trenton, Alachua Co............Popular prejudice,
Aug. 6...LEACH, WILLIAM..................Dade City, Pasco Co.........................Rape
  " 12...*CRUM, AUDRY*....................Osceola, Orange Co............................Murder

1916

Jan. 28...ANDERSON, RICHARDSON......Ocala, Marion Co..............................Murder
Apr. 16...*DUKE, JOHN*......................Bonifay, Holmes Co...........................Murder
  " 17...*DYKES, JOHN*.....................Vernon, Washington Co......................Murder
Aug. 19...YOUNG, STELLA....................Newberry, Alachua Co............Alleged accessory
                                                                                            to murder
  " 19...DENNIS, MARY......................Newberry, Alachua Co........Alleged   accessory
                                                                                            to murder
  " 19...DENNIS, BERT.......................Newberry, Alachua Co...........Alleged   accessory
                                                                                            to murder
  " 19...McHENRY, ANDREW................Newberry, Alachua Co.........Alleged   accessory
                                                                                            to murder
  " 19...HASKINS, JOHN.....................Newberry, Alachua Co........Alleged   accessory
                                                                                            to murder
  " 19...DENNIS, JAMES.....................Newberry, Alachua Co.........Alleged   accessory
                                                                                            to murder

1917

Mar. 29...GARNER, S. G. ....Kissimmee, Osceola Co. ....Refusal to give up
                                                                                            farm
June 25...TRENT, SHEPHERD...............Punta Gorda, De Soto Co...........Attempted rape

GEORGIA

1889

July 1...UNKNOWN NEGRO.................Irwinville, Irwin Co.........................Rape
  " 11...LOVE, MARTIN ....Tunnell Hill, Witfield Co............... ......Rape
Sept. 4...POWERS, WARREN................East Point, Fulton Co........................Rape

GEORGIA—Continued

Oct.	1.. DUNCAN, JOHN	Spring Place, Murry Co.	Living with a white woman
"	12.. MOORE, WILLIAM	Jesup, Wayne Co.	Throwing stones
Nov.	10...THOMAS, JOHN	Midvile, Burke Co.	Rape
"	16..ANTHONY, JOHN	Lincolnton, Lincoln Co.	Attempted rape
Dec.	26... JACKSON, PETER	Jesup, Wayne Co.	Race hatred
"	26...HOPPS, WILLIAM	Jesup, Wayne Co.	Race hatred

1890

Feb.	28.. BROWN, WASHINGTON	Athens, Clark Co.	Rape
Mar.	24.. MARTIN, SAMUEL	Wrightsville, Johnson Co.	Murder
June	10... PRINCE, GEORGE	Elbert Co.	Alleged rape
"	10... POKE, JESSE	Eastman, Dodge Co.	Murder
"	10...PERRY, RICH	Marion Co.	Unpopularity
"	13 ..PENNER, GEORGE	Elberton, Elbert Co.	Rape
"	28.. ROBERTS, ANDREW	Waycross, Ware Co.	Rape
July	11... HARMON, JAMES	Social Circle, Walton Co.	Rape
Oct.	12...WOSTEN, FRANK	Homer, Banks Co.	Incendiarism
"	24...WILLIAMS, JOHN	Waynesboro, Burke Co.	Murder
"	31... TWO NEGROES	Barton Co.	Rape
"	31...POLASCO, ———	Valdosta, Lowndes Co.	Rape
Nov.	1...JONES, OWEN	Pulaski, Candler Co.	Rape
"	19...SIMMONS, JOHN	Cairo, Grady Co.	Rape
Dec.	3....UNKNOWN NEGRO	Rome, Floyd Co.	Unknown cause

1891

Feb.	21 .KING, WESLEY	Locality undetermined	Murder
"	26. .WEST, ALLEN	Abbeville, Wilcox Co.	Rape
July	1...BUCK, DANIEL	Bluffton, Clay Co.	Rape
Aug.	29...OWENS, WILLIAM	Jesup, Wayne Co.	Rape
Sept.	26...MACK, CHAS.	Swainsboro, Emanuel Co.	Rape
Nov.	2...*NIX, LARKIN*	Decatur Co.	Murder
Dec.	16...GOLDEN, WELCOME	Waycross, Ware Co.	Rioting
"	14...KINGUT, ROBERT	Waycross, Ware Co.	Rioting
"	15...UNKNOWN NEGRO	Camak, Warren Co.	Burglary

1892

Jan.	9.... *NUX*, ———	Mitchell Co.	Murder
Mar.	1...*JONES*, ———	Ware Co.	Murder
Apr.	5...FIVE NEGROES (5)	Near Lithonia, Dekalb Co.	Rape
"	14...WEST, WILLIAM	Locality undetermined	Murder
May	17...THREE NEGROES (3)	Clarksville, Habershaw Co.	Suspected robbery
"	21...SMITH, SERBORN	Covington, Newton Co.	Rape
June	11...MORELAND, ANDERSON	Forsythe, Monroe Co.	Rape
July	21...UNKNOWN NEGRO	Jesup, Wayne Co.	Supposed offense
Aug.	25...HOWARD, BENJ.	Josselin, Liberty Co.	Murder
Sept.	8...WILLIAMS, JESSE	Eastman, Dodge Co.	Attempted rape
Oct.	26...WILSON, JAMES	Dalton, Whitfield Co.	Race prejudice
Nov.	26...*SCOTT, GESTER*	Calhoun, Gordon Co.	Murder
Aug.	30...JESSY, JOHN	Near Forsyth, Monroe Co.	Rape

1893

Mar.	1...HILL, THOMAS	Spring Place, Murray Co.	Rape
May	23...MUCHLEA, EPHRIM	Hazelhurst, Jeff Davis Co.	Murder
"	23...UNKNOWN NEGRO	Hazelhurst, Jeff Davis Co.	Murder
July	17...DEAN, WARREN	Locality undetermined	Rape
Oct.	22...JENKINS, EDWARD	Clayton Co.	Murder
Dec.	2...HOLT, LUCIUS	Concord, Pike Co.	Murder
"	19...FERGUSON, WILLIAM	Adel, Berrien Co.	Turning State's evidence
"	25...THOMAS, CALVIN	Locality undetermined	Unknown offense

1894

Feb.	10....COLLINS, ———	Athens, Clarke Co.	Enticing servant away
"	15...COLLINS, ROBERT	Oglethorpe, Macon Co.	Race prejudice
Mar.	5...RHODES, SYLVESTER	Collins, Jasper Co.	Murder
Apr.	6...AHREN, DANIEL	Greensboro, Greene Co.	Rape
"	10...*CASH, EDWARD*	Greensboro, Greene Co.	Rape
"	20...*WORLEY, HENRY*	Murry Co.	Unknown offense, by white caps
"	26...EVARTS, ROBERT	Locality undetermined	Rape
May	22...A NEGRO	Miller Co.	Rape
June	13...A NEGRO	Blackshear, Pierce Co.	Rape
"	18...OPIETRESS, OWEN	Forsythe, Monroe Co.	Rape

GEORGIA—Continued

June 28...FRANKLIN, FAYETTE ....Mitchell Co............................Rape
Sept. 19...GOOSENBY, DAVID.................Atlanta, Fulton Co.....................Rape
Nov. 8...LAWRENCE, LEE....................Jasper Co..............................Rape
Dec. 23...TAYLOR, SAMUEL...................Brooks Co.............................Murder
  "   23...FRAZIER, CHARLES................Brooks Co.............................Murder
  "   23...PIKE, SAMUEL....................Brooks Co.............................Murder
  "   23...SHERARD, HARRY..................Brooks Co.............................Murder
  "   23...THREE UNKNOWN NEGROES
         (3).................................Brooks Co.............................Murder

1895

Jan. 9...COLDHAND, GEORGE................Colquitt Co...........................Murder
Mar. 2...ROBERTSON, CHARLES.............Allendaletown, Wilkinson Co...........Murder
  "   14...GIBSON, ARMOR...................Forsyth, Monroe Co......................Rape
May   2...BROWNLEE, THOMAS...............Butts Co............................Informing
  "   22...*CONNELL, WILLIAM*.............Montgomery Co.........................Murder
June 18...HARRIS, GEORGE.................Near Dublin, Laurens Co..........Attempted rape
July 2...CHANDLER, SAMUEL..............Monroe, Walton Co............Unknown offense
Aug. 12...HARRIS, WILLIAM................Colquitt Co...............Attempted assault
Oct. 4...SMITH, NEAL.....................Locality undetermined...................Rape
Nov. 4...JEFFERSON, LEWIS..............Homersville, Clinch Co..................Rape
  "   23...*PERDUE, L. W.*................Locality undetermined...................Rape
  "   25...HANCOCK, BALAM.................Gibson, Glasscock Co.........Attempted rape
Dec. 1...*SUTTON, LONG.*................Unadilla, Dooly Co..................Desperado
  "   1...*SUTTON, HENRY.*..............Unadilla, Dooly Co..................Desperado
  "   8...*SMITH, JAMES.*...............Monticello, Jasper Co...............Informer

1896

Feb. 9...*BLAKE, HY.*...................Locality undetermined.........Illicit distilling
May 12...HARDEE, WILLIAM...............Nicols, Coffee Co.....................Assault
June 1...SLAYTON, JESSE................Columbus, Muscogee Co..................Rape
  "   1...MILES, WILLIAM...............Columbus, Muscogee Co..................Rape
Sept. 16...WARREN, LEM..................Terrell Co.............................Rape
  "   27...BOONE, HARRISON..............Sparta, Hancock Co.........Shooting at officer
Oct. 7...WILLIAMS, CHARLES............Locality undetermined...............Murder
  "   15...MILNER, HENRY................Griffin, Spalding Co...................Rape

1897

Jan. 5...GUST, SIDNEY..................Locality undetermined.........Race prejudice
  "   9...HENDERSON, ANTHONY..........Unadilla, Dooly Co..................Murder
  "   22...WHITE, WILLIAM..............Jeffersonville, Twiggs Co...........Murder
  "   22...FORSYTHE, CHARLES...........Jeffersonville, Twiggs Co...........Murder
  "   27...BRANNAN, GEORGE.............Locality undetermined..............Assault
May 18...CAPT. LEWIS..................Lumpkin, Stewart Co...........Alleged arson
July 19...*RYDER, W. L.*...............Waverly, Harris Co..................Murder
  "   23...WILLIAMS, OSCAR.............Griffin, Spalding Co.........Attempted rape
Aug. 23...GREEN, ANDREW...............Lovett, Laurens Co..................Murder
Sept. 2...SCOTT, BEN..................Echols Co................Stealing cattle
  "   12...GIBSON, CHARLES.............Mason, Bibb Co.....................Murder
Oct. 2...JOHNSON, FRANK..............Locality undetermined................Rape
Nov. 18...RUFF, JOSHUA................Gibson, Glasscock Co...................Rape
  "   19...*CONNELL, WILLIAM*.........Dublin, Laurens Co..................Murder

1898

Feb. 1...BELIN, JOHN.................Locality undetermined...............Murder
  "   13...*DILLARD, WHIT*............Blue Ridge, Fannin Co..............Murder
Mar. 24...ALLEN, JOSEPH..............Moultrie, Colquitt Co........Attempted rape
May 27...OLLIVER, RICHARD...........Donaldsonville, Decatur Co..........Murder
Aug. 8...MEADOWS, JOHN..............Carmel, Meriwether Co........Attempted rape
  "   20...UNKNOWN NEGRO.............Americus, Sumter Co................Murder
Sept. 7...WILLIAMS, JOHN.............Fowlstown, Decatur Co................Rape
  "   11...BURTON, GEORGE............Digby, Spalding Co..................Rape
Nov. 23...MERRIWEATHER, EDWARD....Monticello, Jasper Co..........Alleged rape
Dec. 6...GLOVER, JACOB.............Monticello, Jasper Co...............Murder
  "   6...ANDERSON, JAMES..........Locality undetermined..............Murder
  "   26...*BOLTON, JEFF.*..........Harmony Grove, Jackson Co............Arson

1899

Feb. 11...BIVINS, GEO. L............Leesburg, Lee Co...........Alleged rape
  "   11...HOLT, WILLIAM............Leesburg, Lee Co...........Alleged rape
  "   11...FOOT, GEORGE............Leesburg, Lee Co...........Alleged rape
Mar. 16...CATLEN, BUD.............Palmetto, Campbell Co.................Arson
  "   16...BINGHAM, HENRY.........Palmetto, Campbell Co.................Arson
  "   16...HUTSON, TIP............Palmetto, Campbell Co.................Arson
  "   16...BROWN, EDWARD.........Palmetto, Campbell Co.................Arson

GEORGIA—Continued

Mar. 16...BIGLEY, JOHN............................Palmetto, Campbell Co...Arson
Apr. 25...HOSE, SAMUEL.................................Newman, Cowetta Co................Murder and rape
"   25...STRICKLAND, ELIJAH..............Palmetto, Campbell Co..........Alleged complicity
                                                  in murder
"   27...DANIEL, MITCHELL. ....Leesburg, Lee Co.....................Inflammatory lan-
                                                  guage
May 22...LINTON, THOMAS.....................Locality undetermined.................Race prejudice
June 16...WILLIAMS, ———.........................Near Odum, Wayne Co................Attempted rape
"   16...CLARK, DAVID.............................Near Odum, Wayne Co.............Resisting arrest
July 23...SAMMIN, LOUIS........................Safford, Early Co.........................Robbery and
                                                  murder
"   23...TWO UNKNOWN NEGROES (2).Safford, Early Co.....................Robbery and
                                                  murder
"   23...FISH-HEAD GUS..........................Safford, Early Co.......................Robbery and
                                                  murder
"   23...JOHNSON, WASHINGTON........Safford, Early Co......................Robbery and
                                                  murder
"   25...MACK, CHARLES.........................Safford, Early Co...................Complicity in
                                                  murder
"   25...UNKNOWN NEGRO....................Near Leesburg, Lee Co.........Alleged complicity
                                                  in murder
Aug.   1...JONES, SOLOMON........................Forrest, Columbia Co................Attempted rape
"   3...HENDERSON, LOUIS..................Blakely, Early Co...................................Rape
"   11...McCLUE, WILLIAM.....................Clem, Carroll Co.......................Attempted rape
Sept. 14...UNKNOWN NEGRO....................Ty Ty, Tift Co..Rape
Oct. 24...GOOSBY, JOHN...........................Locality undetermined............Attempted murder
Nov. 23...UNKNOWN NEGRO....................Jackson, Butts Co.....................Attempted rape

1900

Mar. 18...**BARLEY, JOHN**..........................Marietta, Cobb Co...................Attempted rape
Apr.   3...**BROOKS, ALLEN**......................Berryville..Rape
May   4...**JONES, MARSHALL**.................Douglas, Coffee Co...............................Murder
"   13...**WHITNEY, ALEX.**.....................Harlem, Columbia Co..........................Murder
"   14...**WILLIS, WILLIAM**....................Grovetown, Columbia Co.....................Murder
June   9...**ADAMS, SIMON**.........................Near Columbus, Muscogee Co....Attempted rape
"   11...**JEFFERSON, LENNY**...............Metcalf, Thomas Co.............Attempted rape
"   27...**HINES, JORDAN**......................Molena, Pike Co......................Unknown offense
Sept.   8...**WELLY, GRANT**.......................Thomasville, Thomas Co.. ....Assaulting a white
                                                  man
Oct. 19...**HARDEMAN, FRANK**..............Willaston..Rape
"   24...**GUER, JAMES**...........................Liberty Hill, Pike Co.............Race prejudice
"   24...**CALEAWAY, JAMES**................Liberty Hill, Pike Co............Race prejudice
Dec.   8...*RUFUS, BUD.*...............................Near Rome, Floyd Co.. ....Murder
"   28...**FULLER, GEORGE**...................Marion Co...Arson

1901

Jan.   3...**READ, GEORGE**.........................Rome, Floyd Co........................Suspected rape
"   3...**THOMPSON, STERLING**.......Campbell Co.............................Race prejudice
"   5...**UNKNOWN NEGRO**................Near Quitman, Brooks Co..........................Rape
Mar.   2...**MOODY, JOHN.**.......................Bryan Co..................................Cause unknown, by
                                                  white caps
"   13...**HARRIS, SHERMAN**................Shellman, Randolph Co.......................Murder
"   18...**UNKNOWN NEGRO**................Randolph Co..Murder
Apr. 15...**GORDON, KENNEDY**.............Portal, Bulloch Co....................Attempted rape
"   29...**GROUSLSBY, WILLIAM**........Elberton, Elbert Co................Murderous assault
May 10...**JOHNSON, HENRY**.................Valdosta, Lowndes Co.........Murderous assault
June 29...**UNKNOWN NEGRO**................Georgetown, Quitman Co........Attempted rape
July 25...**ERLE, FRANK**...........................Vidalia, Montgomery Co.....................Robbery
Aug. 10...**UNKNOWN NEGRO**................Ways Station, Bryan Co...........................Rape
Nov.   1...**UNKNOWN NEGRO**................Allentown, Wilkinson Co........Attempted rape

1902

Mar. 29...**YOUNG, RICHARD**..................Near Savannah, Chatham Co... ....Murder
Apr.   1...**ALLEN, WALTER**....................Rome, Floyd Co......................Attempted
                                                  criminal assault
"   22...**YOUNG, HARRY**.......................Locality undetermined.............Unknown offense
July 28...**McCAULEY, ARTHUR**...........Locality undetermined..........................Murder
"   28...**WISE, JOHN**..............................Pembroke, Bryan Co...............................Rape
Aug. 31...**BROSIN, JOHN**.........................Monticello, Jasper Co..............Attempted rape
Oct. 23...**BROWN, BENJ.**........................Tallapoosa, Haralson Co........................Rape

1903

Feb.   7...**HILL, LEE**.................................Wrightsville, Johnson Co.....................Murder
"   24...**FAMBRO, WILLIAM**...............Griffin, Spalding Co................Insulted white
                                                  woman
Apr. 23...**RAINEY, ANDREW**..................Bainbridge, Decatur Co................................Arson

GEORGIA—Continued

May 22	HOPKINS, WILLIAM	New Bainbridge, Decatur Co.	Rape
June 1	GORMAN, BENJ.	Locality undetermined	Murder
" 8	PEAVEY, BANJO	Fort Valley, Houston Co.	Murder
" 24	McCOY, GARFIELD	Newton, Baker Co.	Murder
" 24	McKINNEY, GEORGE	Newton, Baker Co.	Murder
" 24	ANNETT, WILEY	Newton, Baker Co.	Murder
July 14	CLAUS, EDWARD	Eastman, Dodge Co.	Mistaken identity
Sept. —	UNKNOWN NEGRO	Whigham, Grady Co.	Rape
Oct. 16	UNKNOWN NEGRO	Cordele, Crisp Co.	Unknown offense

1904

May 15	CUMMINGS, JNO.	Appling, Columbia Co.	Rape
June 1	THOMPSON, ARTHUR	Arlington, Calhoun Co.	Murder
Aug. 16	REED, PAUL	Statesboro, Bulloch Co.	Murder
" 16	CATO, WM.	Statesboro, Bulloch Co.	Murder
" 17	ROGERS, ALBERT	Statesboro, Bulloch Co.	Race prejudice
" 17	SON OF ROGERS	Statesboro, Bulloch Co.	Race prejudice
" 17	LESUERE, RUFUS	Thomaston, Upson Co.	Assault
" 22	GLOVER, JAS.	Locality undetermined	Rape
" 28	SCOTT, ——	Rebecca, Turner Co.	Murder
" 30	McBRIDE, SEBASTIAN	Portal, Bulloch Co.	Race prejudice
Sept. 18	WARE, JNO.	Royston, Franklin Co.	Murder
" 21	TROY, JACK	Talbotton, Talbot Co.	Murder
" 21	*MARSHALL, EDW*	Talbotton, Talbot Co.	Murder
Oct. 12	WEAVER, MOSES	Tifton, Tift Co.	Murder
Nov. 29	SIMMONS, HURBERT	Neal, Pike Co.	Murder

1905

June 29	AYCOCK, LON J.	Watkinsville, Oconee Co.	Murder
" 29	ROBINSON, RICH.	Watkinsville, Oconee Co.	Murder
" 29	ROBINSON, LEWIS	Watkinsville, Oconee Co.	Murder
" 29	ELDER, CLAUDE	Watkinsville, Oconee Co.	Murder
" 29	ALLEN, RICH.	Watkinsville, Oconee Co.	Murder
" 29	YERLY, GENE	Watkinsville, Oconee Co.	Murder
" 29	HARRIS, ROBT.	Watkinsville, Oconee Co.	Murder
" 29	PRICE, SANDY	Watkinsville, Oconee Co.	Attempted rape
Oct. 8	SEABRIGHT, THOS.	Bainbridge, Decatur Co.	Rape
" 29	GOODMAN, AUGUSTUS	Bainbridge, Decatur Co.	Murder

1906

May 14	WOMACK, WM.	Eastman, Dodge Co.	Rape
" 23	*IRWIN, JOHN*	Chipley, Harris Co.	Murder
July 11	PEARSON, ED.	Swainsboro, Emanuel Co.	Murderous assault
" 31	CARMICHAEL, FLOYD	Lakewood	Rape
Sept. 10	MILLER, CHAS.	Culloden, Monroe Co.	Attempted rape

1907

May 7	HARRIS, CHAS.	Dearing, McDuffie Co.	Murder
" 21	FIVE NEGROES (5)	Reidsville, Tattnall Co.	Race riot
July 1	*POSEY "DOCK"*	Dalton, Witfield Co.	Rape
" 2	HERBERT, GEO.	Cowen, ——	Murderous assault
Oct. 27	WILKS, JNO.	Byron, Houston Co.	Robbery

1908

Jan. 9	COLEY, THOS.	Goldsboro, ——	Murderous assault
" 9	WEBB, ISAAC	Goldsboro, ——	Murderous assault
Feb. 17	UNKNOWN NEGRO	Stateboro, Bulloch Co.	Rape
" 24	THOMPSON GILBERT	Stateboro, Bulloch Co.	Rape
	(Alleged rape, proved innocent afterwards.)		
" 26	UNKNOWN NEGRO	Valdosta, Lowndes Co.	Conspiracy to do violence
Mar. 6	CURRY, ROBERTSON	Hawkinsville, Pulaski Co.	Murder
" 6	HENRY, JOHN	Hawkinsville, Pulaski Co.	Murder
June 27	WILKINS, WALTER	Waycross, Ware Co.	Rape
" 27	BAKER, ALBERT	Waycross, Ware Co.	Rape
" 27	UNNAMED NEGRO	Hickox, Wayne Co.	Complicity in rape
July 29	WILLIAMS, ALONZO	Ohoopee, Tombs Co.	Attempted rape
Aug. 7	LOKIE, CHAS.	Tifton, Tift Co.	Insulting remarks to white woman
" 25	WILLIAMS, VANCE	Louisville, Jefferson Co.	Murder
Sept. 5	TOWNE, JOHN	Damascus, Early Co.	Rape
" 22	THOMAS, GEO.	Ft. Gaines, Clay Co.	Murderous assault
Oct. 11	WHITE, HENRY	Younker, Dodge Co.	Murderous assault

1909

Feb. 19	WYATT, ROLLEY	Locality undetermined	Murder

GEORGIA—Continued

Feb. 22	*THREE WHITE MEN* (3)	Mineral bluff, Fannin Co.	Rape
Mar. 2	FOWLER, JOS.	Blakely, Early Co.	Murder
May 24	AIKENS, ALBERT	Lincolnton, Lincoln Co.	Murderous assault
June 22	CORNAKER, WM.	Talbotton, Talbot Co.	Unnamed offense
" 22	HARDY, JOS.	Talbotton, Talbot Co.	Instigation of murder
" 25	REESE, ALBERT	Cuthbert, Randolph Co.	Murderous assault
July 1	UNNAMED NEGRO	Barnett, Warren Co.	Burglary
" 20	GREEN, KING	Gum Branch, Liberty Co.	Insulting women
" 31	ANDERSON, SIMON	Wellston, Houston Co.	Window peeping
Aug. 27	CLARK, BENJ.	Tarrytown, Montgomery Co.	Murder
" 27	SWEENEY, JOHN	Tarrytown, Montgomery Co.	Complicity
" 27	CLARK, B.	Sopertown, Montgomery Co.	Murder
Dec. 1	HARVARD, JNO.	Cochran, Bleckley Co.	Murder

1910

Feb. 20	LUMPKIN, DAN.	Columbus Co.	Alleged complicity in murder
Mar. 2	—— —— NEGRO	Vidalia, Toombs Co.	Attempted rape and murder
Apr. 15	ROYAL, ALBERT	Amboy, Turner Co.	Rape
" 15	JACKSON, CHAS.	Amboy, Turner Co.	Rape
May 27	WILSON, CHAS.	Albany, Dougherty Co.	Rape
July 27	RALENT, EVAN	Locality undetermined	Attempted rape
" 31	—— NEGRO	Near Cairo, Grady Co.	Rape
Apr. 11	TABOR, JAMES	Alamo, Wheeler Co.	Rape
Sept. 6	TWO NEGROES (2)	Clark Co.	Attempted burglary and murder
Nov. 8	WALKER, JOHN	Montezuma, Macon Co.	Murder
" 8	BARNES, WILLIAM	Montezuma, Macon Co.	Murder

1911

Jan. 22	JOHNSON, WM.	Locality undetermined	Murder
Feb. 25	JONES, ROBERT	Augusta, Richmond, Ga.	Murder
" 25	VEASE, JOHN	Augusta, Richmond, Ga.	Murder
Apr. 7	HALE, CHARLES	Lawrenceville, Gwinnett Co.	Rape
Apr. 8	JORDAN, DAWSON	Ellaville, Schley Co.	Murder
" 8	PICKETT, CHARLES	Ellaville, Schley Co.	Murder
" 8	BURTON, MURRAY	Ellaville, Schley Co.	Murder
May 18	McLEOD, JOHN	Swainsboro, Emanuel Co.	Murder
" 21	SMITH, BENJAMIN	Swainsboro, Emanuel Co.	Murder
" 22	MOORE, JOSEPH	Crawfordsville, Taliferro Co.	Murder
June 30	ALLEN, THOMAS	Monroe, Walton Co.	Rape
" 31	WATTS, FOSER	Monroe, Walton Co.	Suspicioned rape
July 11	McGROFF, WM.	Baconton, Mitchell Co.	Murder
Aug. 29	DAVIS, PETER	Ft. Gaines, Clay Co.	Murder
Oct. 5	UNNAMED NEGRO	Dublin, Laurens Co.	Attempted rape
" 11	CHAPWAN, ANDREW	Locality undetermined	Attempted rape
" 19	LOVELACE, TERRY	Manchester, Meriwether Co.	Murderous assault
" 28	WALKER, DANIEL	Washington, Wilkes Co.	Murder
Dec. 21	WARREN, JOHN	Donald, Liberty Co.	Murder

1912

Jan. 22	HEMMING, EUGENE	Hamilton, Harris Co.	Murder
" 22	MOORE, JNO.	Hamilton, Harris Co.	Murder
" 22	CRUTCHFIELD, JNO.	Hamilton, Hamilton Co.	Murder
" 22	HATHAWAY, BELLE	Hamilton, Hamilton Co.	Murder
" 30	HAMILTON, ALBERT	Cordele, Crisp Co.	Rape
Feb. 4	POWELL, CHAS.	Macon, Bibb Co.	Assault and Robbery
Mar. 21	BURK, HOMER	Cochran, Bleckley Co.	Murder
Apr. 26	ETHERIDGE, HENRY	Near Jackson, Butts Co.	Race prejudice,
June 25	BOSTWICK, ANN	Locality undetermined	Murder
Aug. 13	COTTON, T. Z.	Columbus, Muscogee Co.	Murder
Sept. 10	EDWARDS, ROBT.	Cummings, Forsyth Co.	Complicity in murder
Oct. 5	YARBOROUGH, ——	Americus, Sumter Co.	Rape
Nov. 30	WILLIAMS, CHESBLEY	Cordele, Crisp Co.	Murder

1913

Mar. 4	TWO UNNAMED NEGROES (2)	Cornelia, Habersham Co.	Murder
May 5	OWENSBY, SAMUEL	Hogansville, Troup Co.	Murder
June 21	UNNAMED NEGRO	Americus, Sumter Co.	Murder

GEORGIA—Continued

July 28	SHAKE, JOHN	Locality undetermined............Murderous assault
Aug. 15	LOVETT, ROBERT	Morgan, Calhoun Co.........................Murder
Aug. 25	SWANSON, VIRGIE (F)	Greenville, Meriwether Co.....Alleged murder, proved innocent

1914

Sept. 20	BROWN, NATHAN	Rochelle, Ogle Co...................................Murder

1915

Jan. 15	BARKER, SAMUEL	Monticello, Jasper Co............Resisting arrest for murderous assault
" 15	BARKER, JESSE	Monticello, Jasper Co............Resisting arrest for murderous assault
" 15	CHARLES, EULA (F)	Monticello, Jasper Co............Resisting arrest for murderous assault
" 23	MORRIS, PETER	Arlington, Calhoun Co.........................Murder
Feb. 4	CULBERSON, A. B.	Evens, Columbia Co...............................Rape
Apr. 16	SHEFFIELD, CAESAR	Valdosta, Lowndes Co.............................Theft
June 14	HEVENS, SAMUEL	Toccoa, Habersham Co............................Rape
July 5	*GREEN, WILLIAM & SON* (2)	Macon, Bibb Co.......................Alleged murder
" 21	FLAMBE, PETER	Cochran, Pulaski Co............Accessory to murder
" 21	JACKSON, ——	Cochran, Pulaski Co............Accessory to murder
Aug. 17	*FRANK, LEO M.*	Near Milledgeville.............Alleged rape and murder
Aug. 17	RIGGINS, JOHN	Bainbridge, Decatur Co............................Rape
Oct. 21	GREEN, ALONZO & SON (2)	Wayside, Jones Co............................Murder
Dec. 20	BLAND, SAMUEL	Eastman, Dodge Co..................Unnamed cause
" 20	STEWART, WILLIAM	Eastman, Dodge Co..................Unnamed cause

1916

Jan. 21	LAKE, FELIX	Sylvester, Worth Co.............................Murder
" 21	LAKE, FRANK	Sylvester, Worth Co.............................Murder
" 21	LAKE, DEWEY	Sylvester, Worth Co.............................Murder
" 21	LAKE, MAJOR	Sylvester, Worth Co.............................Murder
" 21	LEAMON, RODIUM	Sylvester, Worth Co.............................Murder
Feb. 12	HARRIS, HARVIN	Near Macon, Bibb Co..........................Murder
" 25	McCORTELE, JESS	Cartersville, Bartow Co.............Attempted rape
Aug. 21	LEWIS, ——	Valdosta, Lowndes Co..............Alleged burglary
Sept. 21	WHITE, HENRY	Durand, Meriwether Co............................Rape
" 26	HUDSON, PETER	Cuthbert, Randolph Co..........................Murder
" 26	STURGIS, ELIJAH	Cuthbert, Randolph Co..........................Murder
" 29	SHULER, MOXIE	Bainbridge, Decatur Co.............Attempted rape
" 29	TWO UNNAMED NEGROES (2)	Gordon, Wilkinson Co............Accessory to murder
Oct. 4	CONNELL, MARY	Leary's, Calhoun Co............Accessory to murder
" 7	SMITH, CHARLES	Near Sandersville, Washington Co...................................Murder

1917

Mar. 1	CLINTON, LINTON	Meigs, Thomas Co...............................Rape
Mar. 28	NOWLING, JOE	Pelham.........................Reason unknown
Sept. 18	MONCRIEF, RUFUS	Whitehall, Clarke Co............................Rape
Nov. 16	STATEN, JESSE	Quitman, Brooks Co............Insulting white woman
Nov. 17	JOHNSON, COLLINS	Sale City...............Disputing white man's word
" 17	JOHNSON, D. C.	Sale City...............Disputing white man's word
Dec. 15	DEKLE, CLAXTON	Metter................Killing in quarrel

IDAHO

1892

Oct. 17	*EIGHT HORSE THIEVES*	Deer Flat, —— ....

1893

Jan. 5	*ROBERTS, ALBERT*	Locality undetermined...................Murder

IDAHO—Continued

1904
June 3....*MYERS, T. M.*........................Grangeville, Idaho Co.........................Murder

1011
Sept. 9.... *HALLICK, PETER*...............Grangeville, Idaho Co............ ....Wife beating

ILLINOIS

1891
June 29...*FRISBY, ROYAL*...................Sparland, Marshall Co....................By white caps

1892
Feb. 3....*MILLER, AMOS*..........................Cairo, Alexander Co....................................Murder

1893
June 3....**BUSH, SAM**................................Decatur, Macon Co..............................Rape
July 14...**BUTLER, ALLEN**.........................Lawrenceville, Lawrence Co......Criminal abortion

1894
June 26....*PINKERTON, WILLIAM*......Spring valley, Bureau Co...............................Rape

1805
May 25.... *HALLS, JOHN*........................Danville, Vermillion Co................................Rape
"   25....*ROYCE, WILLIAM*..................Dnaville, Vermillion Co................................Rape

1896
Feb. 12....*GRANT*.......................................Sullivan, Moultrie Co.................................Murder

1897
Aug. 19.... *UNKNOWN TRAMP*................Manheim, Cook Co.................Murderous assault

1898
Nov. 7....**STEWART, F. W.**......................Lacon, Marshall Co....................................Rape
Dec. 21...*SIMMS, WM.*...........................Near Decatur, Macon Co...........................Murder

1902
Feb. 26....**HUGHES, WOODFORD**...............Locality undetermined...........Disreputable   character
Sept. 4.......**BROWN, EDWARD**...................Locality undetermined.................Attempted rape

1903
Apr. 26...**UNKNOWN NEGRO**....................Thebes, Alexander Co.................Attempted rape
June 6....**WYATT, DAVID**.........................Bellville, Saint Clair Co.....................Murder
July 23...**MAYFIELD, I. D.**........................Danville, Vermillion Co.........................Murder

1908
Aug. 15...**BURTON, SCOTT**..........................Springfield, Sangamon Co......................Race riot
"   16....**DONIGAN, GEO.**.........................Springfield, Sangamon Co......................Race riot

1909
Nov. 3....**JONES, WM.**............................Cairo, Alexander Co...............................Murder

1913
Sept. 12...**TWO UNNAMED NEGROES**.......Tamms, Alexander Co............Murderous assault

1914
Oct. 12...*CLAZA, ALBERT*...................Willisville, Perry Co.................................Murder

1915
June 10...**STRANDS, JOSEPH**.................Johnston City, Williamson Co..................Murder

INDIANA

1889
June 12...*DEVINE, JAMES*...................Corydon, Harrison Co...............................Murder
"   12...*TENNYSON, CHAS.*.............Corydon, Harrison Co...............................Murder
July 20...**WILLIS, PETER**............................Warsaw, Kosciusko Co..............................Rape

INDIANA—Continued

1890

Feb. 8....LADD, ELI..Blountsville, Henry Co..............Crime unknown, desperado
Nov. 18...SMITH, HENRY.....................Locality undetermined.........................Rape

1891

May 22...JENNINGS, JAMES..................Locality undetermined.........................Rape
Aug. 22...*HAWKINS, CHARLES*.........Shelbyville, Shelby Co..........................Murder

1894

Jan. 11...*WAGONER, SHERMAN*.........Mitchell, Lawrence Co...........................Murder

1897

Sept. 15...*LEVI, LYLE*........................Valparaiso, Porter Co..........................Burglary
"   15....*ANDREWS, ROBERT*....Valparaiso, Porter Co..........................Burglary
"   15....*GORDON, CLIFFORD*.....Valparaiso, Porter Co..........................Burglary
"   15....*JENKINS, WILLIAM*.....Valparaiso, Porter Co..........................Burglary
"   15....*SHUBLE, HEINE*.............Valparaiso, Porter Co..........................Burglary

1898

Dec. 24...*TYLER, MARION*...............Scottsburg, Scott Co...............Murderous assault

1900

Dec. 16...ROWLAND, BUD.................Rockport, Spencer Co............................Murder
"   16...HENDERSON, THOMAS...........Rockport, Spence rCo............................Murder
"   17...ROLLO, JOHN......................Booneville, Warwick Co...............Complicity in murder

1901

Feb. 26....WARD, GEORGE.................Terre Haute, Vigo Co............................Murder

1902

Nov. 20...DILLARD, JAS.................Sullivan, Sullivan Co............................Rape

IOWA

1889

July 1...AN INDIAN......................Gravity, Taylor Co............................Rape

1890

Jan. 15...SMITH, GEORGE................Locality undetermined...............Unknown cause

1893

Mar. —...*FRAZIER, WILLIAM*............Albia, Monroe Co............................Murder

1894

Apr. 30....*NILSON, REDDY*...............Missouri Valley, Harrison Co....................Murder
June 25...*STACEY, WILLIAM*............Iowa Falls, Hardins Co........................Swindling

1896

Jan. 18...UNKNOWN NEGRO.................Mitchelville, Polk Co............................Assault

1901

Aug. 5...HEFFEN, WILLIAM..............Moscow, Muscatine Co............................Murder

1907

Jan. 9...*CULLEN, JAMES*.................Charles City, Floyd Co............................Murder

KANSAS

1889

June 4...*OLIPHANT, NATHANIEL*...Topeka, Shawnee Co............................Murder
"   4...*CLEARY, PATRICK*.................Lincoln, Lincoln Co............................Murder
Sept. 9...FISHER, RICHARD.................Hiawatha, Brown Co...............Horse stealing

1892

Jan. 16....*HEHMAN, AUGUSTUS*.........Rosalia, Butler Co............................Murder
Sept. 14...THOMPSON, JAMES.................Larned, Pawnee Co............................Rape
Nov. 29...TRUE, COMMODORE.............Hiawatha, Brown Co............................Murder

KANSAS—Continued

1893

Apr. 20... ADAMS, DAN. ....Salina........................ ....Murderous assault
Aug. 21...WILSON, JOHN...................Leavenworth, Leavenworth Co. ....Rape

1894

Apr. 24 LUGGLE, JEFF. ....Cherokee, Crawford Co......................... ....Murder
May 9 *McKINDLEY, W.* .... Sharon Springs, Wallace Co. .... Murder
"   9...*McKINDLEY, LEWIS*..........Sharon Springs, Wallace Co. ....Murder

1895

Apr. 3 *WALTERS, NEWTON*...............Locality undetermined......... ... ...Murder

1898

June 13...*BECKER, JOHN*......................Great Bend, Barton Co.........................Murder

1899

Mar. 28...*SANDERSON, HENRY*.......Locality undetermined............. ... .Murder
Apr. 25...WILLIAMS, CHARLES...........Galena, Cherokee Co.................... ......Murder
Oct. 30...MILLS, GEORGE.....................Weir, Cherokee Co................ ....Murder

1900

Jan. 20 *SMITH, GEORGE*......................Fort Scott, Bourbon Co........... ....Murder
"   20...*SMITH, EDWARD*..................Fort Scott, Bourbon Co.... ... .Murder

1901

Jan. 15 ALEXANDER, FRED..................Leavenworth, Leavenworth Co..Murder and rape
May 13 HERMAN, DR........................Topeka, Shawnee Co...................Race prejudice

1902

Dec. 25 GODLEY, MONTGOMERY.........Pittsburg, Crawford Co....................Murder

1916

Sept. 21 *DUDLEY, BERT*,.......................Olathe, Johnson Co. ....Murder

KENTUCKY

1889

May 20. THORNTON, JOS.......................Wickliffe, Ballard Co........... ....Rape
June 24...*CRAVASSO, TONY AND BRO.*Cumberland Gap, Whitley Co......Murder
"   26...*ARDELL, CHARLES*...............Shepherdsville, Bullitt Co....... ....Murder
July 23...MALONE, DANIEL.....................Covington, Kenton Co............... .. ....Rape
"   23...KELLY, JAMES......................Paris, Bourbon Co........................Rape
Nov. 24...*SMITH, JOSEPH A.*...............Trenton, Todd Co.......................Murder
Dec. 9 ...*TURNER, JOHN*.....................Greensburg, Green Co......................Murder
"   19...JONES, DOC.............................Owensboro, Daviess Co...................Murder

1890

Apr. 18...MOODY, SAMUEL.....................Auburn, Logan Co.........................Murder
Aug. 17...HENDERSON, JOHN.................Midway, Woodford Co............... ...Murder
Oct. 2...HUMPHREYS, ERNEST.............Princeton, Caldwell Co...................Murder

1891

Apr. 16...SKAPP, WILLIAM.....................Old Union...........................Murder
May 22...*WILCOX, JOHN*......................Sandy Hook, Elliot Co...................Rape
"   22...*WILCOX, H Y.*........................Sandy Hook, Elliot Co...................Rape
July 20...BROWN, MARK.........................Shelbyville, Shelby Co...................Rape
"   25...GRANGE, JOHN.........................Franklin, Simpson Co....................Threats
Aug. 28...DUDLEY, JAMES......................Georgetown, Scott Co....................Murder
Sept. 15...*GILLILAND, JAMES H.*.........Somerset, Pulaski Co................ .....Murder
"   15...*GILLILAND, JOSIAH*.............Somerset, Pulaski Co..... ... . Murder

1892

Jan. 28...GIBSON, LEE.............................Owenton, Owen Co............. ... . Murder
June 1...WILLIS, NICK...........................Lebanon, Marion Co........... ... ...Rape
"   8...PORTER, AUSTIN.......................Grayson, Carter Co..................Wife-murder
"   10...HILL, CHARLES.......................Paducah, McCracken Co............... ......Rape
July 12...*REDFERIN, J. R.*.....................Franklin, Simpson Co....................Murder
"   29...McDANIELS, LEE......................Oaks Crossing...................Attempted rape
Aug. 16...MURPHY, LOGAN.....................Mt. Sterling, Montgomery Co..............Murder
Sept. 2...WILCOXSON, JOHN..................Edmonton, Metcalf Co.... . ... Murder
Dec. 19...BOND, JAMES.... ....Guthrie, Todd Co........ .... Attempted rape
"   28...A NEGRO.................................Bowling Green, Warren Co.............. ... .Rape

KENTUCKY—Continued

1893

Jan.	12	MOORMAN, EDWARD	Guston, Meade Co.	Murder
"	12	MOORMAN, RICHARD	Guston, Meade Co.	Murder
May	3	*COLLINS, JAMES*	Sherman, Grant Co.	Stealing horse
July	7	MILLER, CHARLES	Bardwell, Carlisle Co.	Alleged rape
Aug.	3	*POOLE, FELIX*	Owensboro, Daviess Co.	Rape
"	18	WALTON, CHARLES	Morganfield, Union Co.	Murder
"	19	NEGRO TRAMP	Paducah, McCracken Co.	Rape
"	28	TAYLOR, LEONARD	Newcastle, Henry Co.	Murder
Sept.	1	McNEAL, JUDGE	Cadiz, Trigg Co.	Attempted rape
"	2	ARKINSON, WILLIAM	McKinney, Lincoln Co.	Rape
Dec.	16	GIVENS, HENRY	Nebo, Hopkins Co.	Alleged poisoning stock

1894

Jan.	7	*MITCHELL, JOSHUA*	Leesburg	Unknown offense by white caps
"	21	GUMBLE, M. G.	Jellico Mines, Whitley Co.	Rape
Mar.	2	TYE, LEN	Hariem	Kidnapping
June	20	HAINES, ARCHIE	Mason Co.	Horse stealing
"	21	HAINES, BURT	Mason Co.	Horse stealing
"	20	HAINES, WILLIAM	Mason Co.	Horse stealing
"	24	GODLY, CALEB	Bowling Green, Warren Co.	Rape
July	10	HOWARD, MARION	Scottsville, Allen Co.	Rape
"	26	TYLER, WILLIAM	Carlisle, Nicholas Co.	Attempted rape
Aug.	14	BOSTON, MARSHALL	Frankfort, Franklin Co.	Rape
Oct.	1	*RICH, BERRY*	Marion Co.	Suspected robbery
"	8	*RICHARDSON, AL.*	Irvine, Estill Co.	Rape and murder
"	14	*MORTON, OSCAR.*	Stanton, Powell Co.	Murder
"	15	GRIFFEY, WILLIS	Princeton, Caldwell Co.	Attempted rape
Nov.	8	NALLS, GABE	Blackford, Webster Co.	Incendiarism
"	8	NALLS, ULYSSESS	Blackford, Webster Co.	Incendiarism

1895

Jan.	1	*BLAU, THOMAS*	Mt. Sterling, Montgomery Co.	Murder
Apr.	26	RAY, GEORGE	Gensonton,	Being disreputable
May	16	*HOWESTON, JOHN*	Marion, Crittenden Co.	Rape
"	23	THOMPSON, CLAUDE	De Koven, Union Co.	Attempted rape
July	1	*COLSTON, ABITHAL*	Trigg Co.	Murder
"	1	SMITH, MOLLIE	Trigg Co.	Murder
"	9	*HOWLETT HOWTON & SON*	Lewiston	Unknown offense
"	15	HUGGARD, ROBERT	Winchester, Clark Co.	Alleged rape
Aug.	26	LEWIS, HARRISON	Springfield, Washington Co.	Murder
Sept.	2	BUTCHER, WILLIAM	Hickman, Fulton Co.	Murder
Nov.	21	TWO NEGROES	Henderson, Henderson Co.	Rape
"	25	UNKNOWN NEGRO	Calvert, Marshall Co.	Train-wrecking
Dec.	29	*DEVER, WILLIAM*	Lebanon, Marion Co.	Murder
"	29	*WEST, MRS. T. J.*	Lebanon, Marion Co.	Mob indignation

1896

Feb.	17	MARTIN, FOMIT	Monticello, Wayne Co.	Barn-burning
May	11	UNKNOWN NEGRO	Fulton, Fulton Co.	Murder
Sept.	14	WHITE, THOMAS	Aurora, Fulton Co.	Unknown cause
Dec.	18	*PROCTOR, PINK*	near Russellville, Logan Co.	Murder
"	18	*PROCTOR, ARCH*	near Russellville, Logan Co.	Murder
"	21	STONE, JAMES	Mayfield, Graves Co.	Rape
"	22	FINLEY, GEORGE	Mayfield, Graves Co.	Theft
"	26	HOLT, ALFRED	Owensboro, Daviess Co.	Murder

1897

Feb.	4	MORTON, ROBERT	Rockford, Rockcastle Co.	Writing insulting letters
Mar.	8	UNKNOWN NEGRO	Rock Springs	Stealing
Apr.	14	*BRAYDEE, WILLIAM*	near Middleboro, Bell Co.	Murder
July	22	BRINKLEY, EPHRIAM	Madison	Bad reputation
Aug.	15	WILSON, GEORGE	Meyers	Unknown cause
"	22	*SULLIVAN, ELEANY*	Williamsburg, Whitley Co.	Rape
Sept.	26	BRUSHROD, RAYMOND	Hainesville	Rape

1898

Feb.	23	ALLEN, RICHARD	Mayfield, Graves Co.	Robbery
"	23	HOLMES, THOMAS	Mayfield, Graves Co.	Murder
June	16	CALLS, GAMS	Glasgow, Barren Co.	Rape
"	26	SCOTT, GEORGE	Russellville, Logan Co.	Rape

KENTUCKY—Continued

Oct. 2...**BAUER, ARCH**............Tompkinsville, Monroe Co... Murderous assault
Dec. 16 *GOIN, PLEAS* ....near Middletown, Jefferson Co............Murder

1899

May 11...*HOLLAND, WALTER*............Meyers...............Rape
June 27...*STEVENS, HENRY* ....Fulton, Fulton Co. Highway robbery
Dec. 6...**COLEMAN, RICHARD**............Maysville, Mason Co............Murder

1900

Oct. 18...**WARFIELD, FRATEN**............Elliston, Grant Co............Attempted rape

1901

Sept. 12...**HOWARD, FRANK**............Wickliff, Ballard Co............Murder
" 12...**REED, SAM**............Wickliff, Ballard Co............Murder
" 12...**HARRIS, ERNEST**............Wickliff, Ballard Co............Murder
Oct. 2...**FIELDS, JUMBO**............Shelbyville, Shelby Co............Murder
" 2...**GARNETT, CLARENCE**............Shelbyville, Shelby Co............Murder
Oct. 31...*ESTERS, SILAS*............Hodgenville, Larue Co............Forcing white boy
to commit crime

1902

Jan. 11...**MAYS, JAS.**............Spyfield............Criminal assault
Feb. 6...**BROWN, THOMAS**............Nicholasville, Jessamine Co... Criminal assault
" 15...**DULY, BELL**............Fulton, Fulton Co............Suspected murder
Mar. 20...**DRAKE, ELIJAH**............Madrid Bend, Breckenridge
Co............Larceny
" 20...**STEWART, JAS.**............Madrid Bend, Breckenridge
Co............Implicated in lar-
ceny
Apr. 10...**BLAMBARD, THOMAS**............Fulton, Fulton Co............Murder
" 30...**DEWLEY, ERNEST**............Brandenburg, Meade Co......Murderous assault
Nov. 16...*BUCKLES, HARLAN*............Elizabethtown, Hardin Co............Murder

1903

July 14...*THACKSON, WILLIAM*............Maysville, Mason Co............Murder
Oct. 9...**HALL, THOMAS**............Kevil, Ballard Co............Murder

1904

Jan. 24...**RADFORD, LEWIS**............Guthrie, Todd Co............Murder
June 14...**THOMPSON, MARIE**............Lebanon Junction, Bullitt Co............Murder
July 17...**UNKNOWN**............Locality undetermined............Murder
Aug. 30...**BUMPASS, JOE**............Near Hickman, Fulton Co............Rape

1905

May 22...**SHAW, ROBERT**............Waitman, Hancock Co............Murder
July 7...**BEARD, LEON**............Normandy, Spencer Co............Rape
Oct. 12...**LEAVELL, FRANK**............Elkton, Todd Co............Attempted rape

1906

Jan. 22...**BAKER, ERNEST**............Cadiz, Trigg Co............Murder

1907

Aug. 16...**CLIFFORD, WM.**............Maple Grove............Rape and murder

1908

May 31...**McDOWELL, JACOB**............Providence, Webster Co............Murder
Aug. 1...**JONES, VIRGIL**............Russellville, Logan Co............Expressing sympa-
thy with murder
of white man
" 1...**JONES, ROBT.**............Russellville, Logan Co............Expressing sympa-
thy with murder
of white man
" 1...**JONES, THOS.**............Russellville, Logan Co............Expressing sympa-
thy with murder
of white man
" 1...**RILEY, JOSEPH**............Russellville, Logan Co............Expressing sympa-
thy with murder
of white man
Oct. 4...*DAVID WALLACE, WIFE
AND TWO CHILDREN*............Hickory Grove, Simpson Co.... Making threats
Dec. 17...*HILL, ELMER*............Monticello, Wayne Co............Cause not given

KENTUCKY—Continued

1909

Apr. 9	BRAME, BENJ	Hopkinsville, Christian Co	Attempted rape
June 3	MAXEY, JNO.	Frankfort, Franklin Co	Murder
Aug. 10	MILLER, WALLACE	Cadiz, Trigg Co	Attempted rape

1910

Apr. 1	*CARROLL*	Goff	By night riders

1911

Jan. 15	PATTERSON, WADE	Shelbyville, Shelby Co	Insulting women
" 15	WEST, JAMES	Shelbyville, Shelby Co	Insulting women
" 15	MARSHALL, GENE	Shelbyville, Shelby Co.	Murder
Apr. 21	POTTER, WILLIAM	Livermore, McLean Co	Murder
25	*FOUR UNKNOWN WHITES*.	Campton, Wolfe Co	Unknown cause

1913

Sept. 26	RICHARDSON, JOSEPH	Leitchfield, Grayson Co	Rape

1914

Nov. 13	TEN NEGROES	Rochester, Bulter Co	By night riders
" 13	ALLEY, HENRY	Hillside, Muhlenberg Co	By night riders

1915

Jan. 15	*MOLINNDRO, P.*	Lovelaceville, Ballard Co	Night riders
Feb. 13	*UNDERWOOD, HOUSTON*	Irvine, Estil Co.	Unknown
" 14	*TINKER, THOMAS*	Mayfield, Graves Co.	Murder
June 4	BELL, ARTHUR	Princeton, Caldwell Co.	Rape
Sept. 10	*JOHNSON, CLAUDE*	Hickman, Fulton Co.	Murder
Nov. 26	BUCKNER, ELLIS	Henderson, Henderson Co.	Rape

1916

Oct. 16	HENLEY, BROCK	Paducah, McCracken Co	Rape
" 16	THORNHILL, JAMES	Paducah, McCracken Co	Expressing sympathy with Henley

1917

Mar. 12	SANDERS, WILLIAM	Mayville, Macon Co.	Robbery
May 20	*DEMPSEY, LAURENCE*	Fulton, Fulton Co	Murderous assault

LOUISIANA*

1889

Jan. 25	WAKEFIELD, SAMUEL	New Iberia, Iberia Co	Murder
Feb. 1	ROSEMOND, ——	New Iberia, Iberia Co	Alleged cattle stealing
" 10	HANDY, HAYWARD	Houghton	Self-defense
Apr. 18	HECTOR, Jr.	New Iberia, Ineria Co.	Murder
" 19	UNKNOWN NEGRO	Bayou Desard	Rape
May 18	UNKNOWN NEGRO	Columbia, Caldwell Co.	Burglary
June 5	CONLEY, DICK	Tangipahoa, Tangipahoa Co.	Unknown cause
" 5	HUEY, ——	Tangipahoa, Tangipahoa Co.	Unknown cause
July 12	KEYES. FELIX	Lafayette, Lafayette Co.	Murder
Nov. 18	UNKNOWN NEGRO	Vidalia, Concordia Co.	Incendiarism

1890

Jan. 3	HOLMES, HENRY	Bossier Parish	Cause not given
" 8	WARD, HENRY	Bayou Sara, West Feliciana Co	Murder
Mar. 15	WILLIAM, PHILIP	Napoleonville, Assumption Co.	Rape
June 16	SWAYEY, GEORGE	East Feliciana.	Political causes
" 29	COLEMAN, JOHN	Shreveport, Caddo Co.	Murder
Aug. 22	ALEXANDER, WILLIAM	Baton Rouge, East Baton Rouge Co.	Attempted rape

1891

Nov. 21	UNKNOWN NEGRO	Near Baton Rouge, East Baton Rouge Co.	Race prejudice
Mar. 14	*SCAFFEDI, ANTONIO*	New Orleans, Orleans Co.	Alleged conspiracy to murder
" 14	*MACLECHA, JOSEPH*	New Orleans, Orleans Co.	Alleged conspiracy to murder
" 14	*MONASTERO, PIETRO*	New Orleans, Orleans Co.	Alleged conspiracy to murder
" 14	*COMSO, JAMES*	New Orleans, Orleans Co.	Alleged conspiracy to murder
" 14	*GUACCI, TOCCO*	New Orleans, Orleans Co.	Alleged conspiracy to murder

*"Co." should read "Parish" wherever found.

LOUISIANA—Continued

Mar. 14	*ROMERO, FRANK*	New Orleans, Orleans Co.	Alleged conspiracy to murder
" 14	*MARCHESI, ANTONIO*	New Orleans, Orleans Co.	Alleged conspiracy to murder
" 14	*TRAHINA, CHARLES*	New Orleans, Orleans Co.	Alleged conspiracy to murder
" 14	*CONRITEZ, LORETTO*	New Orleans, Orleans Co.	Alleged conspiracy to murder
" 14	*BAJNETTI, ANTONIO*	New Orleans, Orleans Co.	Alleged conspiracy to murder
" 14	*PALITZ, MANUEL*	New Orleans, Orleans Co.	Alleged conspiracy to murder
May 23	*ANDERSON, WILLIAM*	Louisiana State Line	Rape
" 23	*ANDERSON, JOHN*	Louisiana State Line	Rape
" 30	**HAMPTON, TURNIP**	Claiborne	Larceny
June 2	**HUMMEL, SAMUEL**	Point Cenpee Parish	Murder
" 2	**CAMPBELL, ALEX.**	Point Cenpee Parish	Accessory to murder
" 2	**UNKNOWN NEGRO**	Point Cenpee Parish	Accessory to murder
Oct. 20	*RUSS, JOHN*	Columbia, Caldwell Co.	Murder
" 30	**SNOWDEN, ——**	Monroe, Ouachita Co.	Incendiarism
" 30	**PARKE, JACK**	Abitz Springs, Saint Tammany Co.	Murder
" 31	**UNKNOWN NEGRO**	Poole's Landing	Cause unknown
Nov. 4	*SMITH, J. T.*	Morehouse Parish	Murder
" 4	*FELTON, W. S.*	Morehouse Parish	Murder
" 10	**HAGLE, JOHN**	Homer, Claiborne Co.	Unknown cause
" 27	**MIXY**	Many, Sabine Co.	Rape
Dec. 17	**ELY, JOHN R.**	Holloway, Rapides Co.	Murder
" 30	**UNKNOWN MAN**	Blackwater, Concordia Co.	Murder

1892

Jan. 7	**DESCHARNER, L. N.**	Rayville, Richland Co.	Murder
" 7	**FOSTER, CALVIN**	Rayville, Richland Co.	Murder
" 9	**ANDREWS, NATHAN**	Caddo Parish	Murder
Mar. 13	**ELLA ——**	Rayville, Richland Co.	Attempted murder
" 28	**TILLMAN, JACK**	Gretna Parish	Race prejudice
Apr. 6	**FOUR NEGROES**	Fishville	Murder
" 23	*FREEMAN, ——*	Smithland	Murder
" 27	*TRAMP*	Point Conpee	Robbery and murder
May 22	**A NEGRO**	Near Monroe, Ouachita Co.	Murder
" 23	**A NEGRO**	Near Bastrop, Morehouse Co.	Murder
June 1	**WALKER, ——**	Sparta, Bienville Co.	Alleged rape
Sept. 6	**LAURENT, ED.**	Bunkie, Avoyelles Co.	Threats
" 6	**MAGLOIRE, GABRIEL**	Bunkie, Avoyelles Co.	Threats
" 8	**DIXON, SAM**	Kenner, Jefferson Co.	Attempted murder
" 15	**PATTON, JAMES**	Bonita, Morehouse Co.	Murder
Oct. 6	**WALKER, BENJAMIN**	Concordia	Attempted rape
" 25	*COURTNEY, JAMES*	Plaquemine, Iberville Co.	Attempted rape
Nov. 2	**SON AND DAUGHTER OF JOHN HASTINGS**	Calahoula	No offense
" 5	**HASTINGS, JOHN**	Calahoula	Murder
" 30	*MAGEE, RICHARD*	Benton, Bossier Co.	Murder
" 30	*CARMICHAEL, ——*	Benton, Bossier Co.	Murder
Dec. 29	**FOX, LEWIS**	Luling, Saint Charles Co.	Murder
" 29	**GRIPSON, ADAM**	Luling, Saint Charles Co.	Murder

1893

Jan. 6	*LAFARGUES, BEN*	Avangeles Parish	Murder
" 21	**LANDRY, ROBERT**	St. James Parish	Alleged murder
" 21	**"CHICKEN" GEORGE**	St. James Parish	Alleged murder
" 21	**DAVIS, RICHARD**	St. James Parish	Alleged murder
" 25	**FISHER, WILLIAM**	Algiers, New Orleans Co.	Murder
May 12	**HALOWAY, ISRAEL**	Napoleonville, Assumption Co.	Rape
July 6	**UNKNOWN NEGROES**	Poplar Head	Rape
Aug. 14	**SMITH, MONROE**	Springfield, Livingston Co.	Rape
Oct. 24	**TWO NEGROES**	Knoxpoint	Stealing
Dec. 28	**GREEN, TILLMAN**	Columbia, Caldwell Co.	Attempted assault

1894

Jan. 18	**UNKNOWN NEGRO**	Bayou Sara, West Feliciana Co.	Suspected incendiarism
Apr. 23	**STANGATE, SAMUEL**	Tallulah, Madison Co.	Murder
" 23	**CLAXTON, THOMAS**	Tallulah, Madison Co.	Murder
" 23	**HAWKINS, DAVID**	Tallulah, Madison Co.	Murder

LOUISIANA—Continued

Apr.	27	CLAXTON, THELL	Tallulah, Madison Co.	Murder
"	27	HARVEY, SCOTT	Tallulah, Madison Co.	Murder
"	27	McCLY, JERRY	Tallulah, Madison Co.	Murder
"	27	CLAXTON, CAMP	Tallulah, Madison Co.	Murder
May	15	WILLIAMS, COAT	Pine Grove, Saint Helena Co.	Murder
June	4	UNDERWOOD, THOMAS	Monroe, Ouachita Co.	Murder
"	10	JACOBS, MARK	Bienville, Bienville Co.	Race prejudice
"	14	DAY, J. H.	Monroe, Ouachita Co.	Suspected arson
"	28	WHITE, EDWARD	Hudson	Attempted rape
July	26	McCLURE, VANCE	New Iberia, Iberia Co.	Attempted rape
Sept.	9	WAGGONER, LINK	Minden, Webster Co.	Murder
"	14	WILLIAMS, ROBERT	Concordia Parish	Murder
Dec.	23	KING, GEORGE	New Orleans, Orleans Co.	Assault
"	28	SHERMAN, SCOTT	Morehouse Parish	No offense

1895

June	24	*FRY, JOHN*	Gretna, Jefferson Co.	Arson
July	24	BELZAIRE, OVIDE	Youngsville, Lafayette Co.	Race prejudice
Sept.	22	SMITH, WILLIAM	Hammond, Tangipahoa Co.	Murder
"	26	FRANCIS, FELICIAN	Near New Orleans, Orleans Co.	Unknown offense

1896

Jan.	10	SMART, A. L.	Near Monroe, Ouachita Co.	Murder
"	12	*MORRIS, MR. AND MRS.*	Near New Orleans, Orleans Co.	Miscegenation
"	12	*MORRIS, PATRICK*	Near New Orleans, Orleans Co.	Miscegenation
Feb.	29	FRANCIS, GILBERT	St. Joseph, Tensas Co.	Robbery and murder
"	29	*FRANCIS, PAUL*	St. James, St. James Co.	Robbery and assault
"	29	*FRANCIS, GILBERT*	St. James, St. James Co.	Robbery and assault
Mar.	16	LOVE, BIRD	Raybille, Richland Co.	Robbery
"	23	PIZER, ISAAC	Near Shreveport, Caddo Co.	Attempted rape
"	24	SENEGAL, LOUIS	Carencro, Lafayette Co.	Rape
May	19	DAZZELE, JOSEPH	St. Bernard Parish	Attempted rape
"	21	UNKNOWN NEGRO	Bossier Parish	Unknown offense
June	12	STARKES, WALTER	Baldwin, St. Mary Co.	Rape
July	13	PORTER, JAMES	Minden, Webster Co.	Murder
"	13	DUNLEY, MOND	Minden, Webster Co.	Murder
"	13	RENDRICK, COURTNEY	Monroe, Ouachita Co.	Murderous assault
"	15	JAMES, FRANK	Bayou Sara, West Feliciana	Murder
"	27	McGEE, ISAAC	Homer, Claiborne Co.	Rape
Aug.	3	*MULLEN, LOUIS*	Bunkie, Avoyelles Co.	Attempted rape
"	5	WEIGHTMAN, HIRAM	Franklin, Saint Mary Co.	Attempted murder
"	9	*SALADINO, L.*	Halumlee,	Murder
"	9	*LOCENO, DECIMO*	Halumlee,	Murder
"	9	*MARCUSO, ANGELO*	Halumlee,	Murder
Sept.	16	McCAULEY, JAMES	Monroe, Ouachita Co.	Rape
"	24	HAWKINS, ALEXANDER	Gretna, Jefferson Co.	Slapping a child
Oct.	9	HAMILTON, LOUIS	Bossier Point	Arson
Dec.	22	BURKE, JERRY	Clio, Livingston Co.	Attempted murder

1897

Jan.	17	UNKNOWN NEGRO	White Castle, Iberville Co.	Highway robbery
"	19	WILLIAMS, GUS	Amite City	Murder
"	19	JOINER, ARCHIE	Amite City	Murder
"	19	JOHNSON, GUS	Amite City	Murder
May	15	JACKSON, CHARLES	Redwood	Train-wrecking
July	13	THOMPSON, ATTICUS	Forest, West Carroll Co.	Insulting white woman
"	24	DAVIS, JACK	Baldwin, Saint Mary Co.	Rape
Aug.	10	GORDON, JOHN		Murder
Oct.	1	OLIVER, WM.	Jefferson	For disobeying ferry regulations
"	2	FURRAN, WASH.	Monroe, Ouachita Co.	Rape
"	15	BOLTE, DOUGLAS	Quarantine, Plaquemines Co.	Running
Dec.	13	ALEXANDER, JAMES	Near Plaquemine, Iberville Co.	Murder
"	13	ALEXANDER, CHARLES	Near Plaquemine, Iberville Co.	Murder
"	13	THOMAS, JOSEPH	Near Plaquemine, Iberville Co.	Murder

1898

Mar.	9	HARRIS, WILLIAM	Near New Orleans, Orleans Co.	Robbery
"	9	PIGGE, ANDREW	Near New Orleans, Orleans Co.	Robbery
Apr.	2	BELL, WILLIAM	Amite, Tangipahoa Co.	Murder
"	26	LEWIS, COLUMBUS	Lincoln Parish	Resisting arrest

LOUISIANA—Continued

May   6....BURREL, DENNIS........................New Orleans, Orleans Co..............................Murder
June   3....STREET, WILLIAM......................Doyline, Webster Co.................Attempted murder
  "   15....NEGRO...Oak Ridge, Morehouse Co......Assault on officer
Nov. 17....MORRELL, CHARLES.................Edgard, St. John the Baptist Co........Burglary
Dec.   6....HEARN, ———...........................Benton, Bossier Co.....................................Murder
  "   6....RICHARDSON, ———...................Benton, Bossier Co.....................................Murder

1899

June 14....GRAY, EDWARD.........................St. Peter.......................................Race prejudice
July 16....JONES, GEORGE.......................St. Charles Parish.............................No offense
  "   16.... *SMITH, SI.*...............................Gainsville..Murder
  "   21.... *CERENO, JO.*..........................Talullah, Madison Co...................Accomplice in
                                                                                                                    murder
  "   21.... *DEFALTA, CHARLES*...............Talullah, Madison Co...................Accomplice in
                                                                                                                    murder
  "" 21.... *DEFALTA, FRANK*....................Talullah, Madison Co...................Accomplice in
                                                                                                                    murder
  "   21.... *DEFALTA, JO.*........................Talullah, Madison Co...................Accomplice in
                                                                                                                    murder
  "   21.... *DEFERROCH, SY.*...................Talullah, Madison Co...................Accomplice in
                                                                                                                    murder
  "   27....UNKNOWN NEGRO....................Lindsay, East Feliciana Co...Mistaken identity
Aug.   9....BROWN, ECHO...........................Amite City.................................Various crimes
  "   11....SINGLETON, MAN......................Grant Point..........................Attempted rape
Oct. 10.... *LAPLACE, BASIL*....................St. James Parish..........................Unknown offense
  "   15.... *SMITH JAMES L.*...................Wilson, East Felicina Co....................Desperado
Dec. 13....UNKNOWN NEGRO....................Jones, Morehouse Co..Rape

1900

Apr. 22....HUGERLY, JOHN........................Allentown........................Plot to kill whites
  "   22....AMES, EDWARD.........................Allentown........................Plot to kill whites
May 15....HARRIS, HENRY........................Lena, Rapides Co.................... ......Attempted rape
June 12....COBB, SETH...............................Devall Bluff..........................Making threats
  "   23.... *GILMORE, FRANK*....................Livingston Parish. ....Rape
Sept. 1....AMOS, THOMAS J......................Cheneyville, Rapides Parish.....................Murder
  "   21....BICKHAM, GEORGE...................Ponchatonla, Tangipahoa Parish...........Burglary
  "   21....BOWMAN, NATHANIEL.............Ponchatonla, Tangipahoa Parish...........Burglary
  "   21....ELLIOTT, CHARLES....................Ponchatonla, Tangipahoa...................Burglary
  "   21....ROLLINS, ISAIAH.......................Ponchatonla, Tangipahoa Parish...........Burglary
Oct. 19....JOHNSON, NUBRY:.....................Near Baton Rouge, East
                                                                       Baton Rouge Parish...............................Murder

1901

Jan. 24....UNKNOWN NEGRO....................Doylands..Rape
Feb. 17....JACKSON, THOMAS...................St. Peter, St. Landry Parish......................Murder
  "   21....VITAL, THOMAS.........................Fenton, Jefferson Davis Co..........................Rape
Mar. 5....DAVIS, WILLIAM........................Blanchard, Caddo Co...................................Rape
May 4....BRIGMAN, FELTON....................Rodessa, Caddo Co.......................................Rape
  "   4....JOHNSON, GRANT......................Alden Bridge, Bossier Co......For keeping a gamb-
                                                                                                                    ling house
June 5....DICKSON, "DIC"..........................Minden, Webster Co.................................Murder
  "   20....SMITH, PROPHET.......................Bossier, Bossier Co..................................Murder
  "   20....MOLAND, F. C.............................Bossier, Bossier Co..................................Murder
July 15....THOMAS, LOUIS.........................Girard, Richland Co..Theft
  "   19....UNKNOWN NEGRO....................Crowley, Acadia Parish..............Resisting arrest
Sept. 1....WEST, SAM.................................E. La. Parish.........................Attempted rape
Oct. 12....MORRIS, WILLIAM.....................Balltown...Rape
Nov. 24....THOMPSON, FRANK...................Shreveport, Caddo Co..............................Murder
Dec. 7....POYDRASS, SAM.........................Lake Charles, Calcasieu Co......Murderous assault

1902

Jan. 26....TWO NEGROES...........................West Carrol Parish.................................Murder
Feb. 20....BIBB, OLIVER..............................Winona...Accessory to
                                                                                                                    murder
Mar. 19....WOODWARD, JOHN...................Vidalia, Concordia Co.............................Murder
Apr. 1....FRANKLIN, GEO.........................Homer, Claiborne Co.............Attempted murder
  "   10....UNKNOWN NEGRO....................Victoria, Natchitoches Co.....................Murder
May 4.... *SIMS, JOHN*..............................Oak Ridge, Morehouse Co...Sheltering murderer
  "   13....DUBLANO, NICHOLAS...............Loreauville, Iberia Co...........Attempted criminal
                                                                                                                    assault
Sept. 8....MOBLEY, WM..............................Winona.................................Attempted rape
Oct. 17....UNKNOWN NEGRO....................Calcasieur Parish.................................Murder
Nov. 26....LAMB, JOSEPH...........................Francisville....................................Attempted rape

LOUISIANA—Continued

1903

Jan. 19	*UNKNOWN WHITE MAN*	Locality undetermined	Unknown offense
" 20	MOMAS, JOSEPH	Luling, Saint Charles Co.	Murder
Feb. 7	LEE, CORNELIUS	Plaquemine, Iberville Co.	Murderous assault
June 12	DUPREE, FRANK	Forest Hill, Rapides Co.	Murder
" 24	HARRIS, JACK	Concordia Parish	Assault on white man
" 24	WHITTLE, LAMB	Concordia Parish	Assault on white man
July 26	STURS, JENNIS	Near Shreveport, Caddo Co.	Murder
Oct. 16	KENNY, GEORGE	Taylor Town, Bossier Co.	Threats to kill
Nov. 2	CRADDVELS, JOSEPH	Taylor Town, Bossier Co.	Murder
Dec. 27	CARR, JAMES	Millview	Murder

1904

May 8	PIPER, FRANK	Alexandria, Rapides Co.	Making threats
Sept. 18	*ALLISON, JOHN*	McGhees Station	Murder

1905

June 1	WILSON, THOS.	Batchelor, Pointe Coupee Co.	Murder
Apr. 26	*CRAIGHEAD, R.*	Homer, Claiborne Co.	Murder
Aug. 12	UNKNOWN NEGRO	Eros, Jackson Co.	Murder
Nov. 26	WILLIAMS, MONSIE	Tangipahoa, Tangipahoa Co.	Attempted rape

1906

Feb. 24	PAGE, WILTZIE	Bienville, Bienville Co.	Suspected rape
Mar. 18	CARR, WM.	Plaquemine, Iberville Co.	Theft
" 28	"COTTON"	Carrolle, Red River Co.	Attempted rape
May 8	WHITNEY, GEO.	Ethel, East Feliciana Co.	Insulting lady
" 23	JACKSON, THOS.	Blanchard, Caddo Co.	Robbery
" 29	ROGERS, R. T.	Tallulah, Madison Co.	Murder
Aug. 26	SHAUFILET, ALFRED	Calhoun, Ouachita Co.	Attempted rape
Nov. 29	DOMINGO, ANTON	Lafayette, Lafayette Co.	Disorderly conduct

1907

Mar. 15	WILLIAMS, FLINT	Monroe, Ouachita Co.	Murder
" 15	GARDNER, HENRY	Monroe, Ouachita Co.	Murder
Apr. 16	STRAUSS, CHAS.	Bunkie, Avoyelles Co.	Attempted rape
" 17	KILBOURNE, FRED.	Clinton, East Feliciana Co.	Attempted rape
May 3	EALY, SILAS	Bossiers' City, Bossier Co.	Rape
June 1	JOHNSON, HENRY	Echo, Rapides Co.	Attempted rape
" 10	WILSON, JAS.	Gibsland, Bienville Co.	Attempted rape
" 28	JACKSON, MATHIAS	Near Alexandria, Rapides Co.	Rape
" 28	DORANS, RALPH	Ruby, Rapides Co.	Rape
Dec. 13	UNKNOWN NEGRO	Mer Rouge, Morehouse Co.	Murderous assault

1908

Feb. 5	MITCHELL, ROBERT	Oak Grove, West Carroll Co.	Murder
June 4	*COOPER, BIRD*	Homer, Claiborne Co.	Murder
July 18	THREE UNNAMED NEGROES	Jonesville, Catahoula Co.	Suspected arson
Aug. 3	HARRIS, ANDREW	Bethany, Caddo Co.	Attempted rape
Sept. 19	MILES, JOHN	Locality undetermined	Robbery and assault
Oct. 12	HECTOR, NICHOLAS	New Iberia, Iberia Co.	Desperado

1909

July 30	ANTOINE, EMILE	Grand Prairie	Murder
" 30	THOMAS, ONEXZIME	Grand Prairie	Murder
Aug. 15	UNNAMED NEGRO	Morehouse Parish	Bringing suit against white man
" 24	WAY, WM.	Monroe, Ouachita Co.	Murderous assault
Sept. 8	HILL, HENRY	Mangham, Richland Co.	Rape
Oct. 1	ARD, APS.	Near Greensburg, Saint Helena Co.	Murder
" 12	*RODRIGUEZ, MICHAEL*	Slabtown	Robbery
" 27	GIFFORD, JOSEPH	Floyd, West Carroll Co.	Murder
" 27	HILL, ALEX.	Floyd, West Carroll Co.	Murder
Nov. 20	ESTES, JAMES	Delhi, Richland Co.	Murder
" 27	RACHEL, HENRY	Shreveport, Caddo Co.	Rape

1910

Mar. 14	DENTON, ELY	Rayville, Richland Co.	Murder
July 10	*FREEMAN, J. D.*	Rayville, Richland Co.	Not given

LOUISIANA—Continued

Aug. 25 . PORTER, LAURA..................................Monroe, Ouachita Co.................Keeping disreputable house
Sept. 14... GLOVER, ISAAC............................Springfield, Livingston Co...................Murder

1911

Jan. 20 . POULSON, OVAL........................Opelousas, Saint Landry Co......................Murder
July 24 ..TAYLOR, MILES.........................Claibourne Parish...Murder
Sept. 15...BYRD, WALTER...........................Winnsboro, Franklin Co......Murderous assault
Nov. 8...NIXON, WILLIAM ....Delhi, Richland Co...................................Murder

1912

Apr. 9....MILES, THOMAS ....Shreveport, Caddo Co..............Insulting white women
"   25...UNNAMED ....Delhi, Richland Co...................Unnamed offense
May 3 .ALLUMS, ERNEST.....................Locality undetermined...........Insulting white women
Sept. 25... JOHNSON, SAM..........................Grand Cane, De Soto Co...........................Murder
Nov. 28...BURKE, WOOD............................Benton, Bossier Co..................Murderous assault
"   28...HEARD, JAS. ....Benton, Bossier Co..................Murderous assault
"   28...JIMMERSON, SILAS...................Benton, Bossier Co. ....Murderous assault
Dec. 28...CADORE "NORM"......................Baton Rouge, East Baton.........................Murder
Rouge Co.

1913

Aug. 27...COMEAUX, JAMES.....................Jennings, Jefferson Davis Co...Murderous assault
Oct. 22...EATON, WARREN ....Monroe, Ouachita Parish ....Insulting white woman
Dec. 16...WILLIAMS, ERNEST....................Blanchard, Caddo Co...............................Murder
"   16...WILLIAMS, FRANK.......................Blanchard, Caddo Co...............................Murder

1914

May 7...UNKNOWN NEGRO........................St. James, St. James Co.............................Murder
"   12...HAMILTON, EDWARD................Shreveport, Caddo Parish...............................Rape
Aug. 7...GRIFFIN, PRESTO......................Munroe, Ouachita Parish..........................Murder
"   7 . GRIFFIN, CHARLES.................Munroe, Ouachita Parish..........................Murder
"   7...HOLMES, HENRY.......................Munroe, Ouchaita Parish..........................Murder
"   9...UNKNOWN NEGRO..................Munroe, Ouachita Parish......Suspicion of murder
"   12...ROMEO, ————.........................Slidell, St. Tammany Co.............................Murder
Dec. 2...LEWIS, TOBE..............................Sylvester Station....................................Murder
"   2...DURDEN, MUNROE.................Sylvester Station....................................Murder
"   3...McKNIGHT, KANE...................Sylvester Station....................................Murder
"   11...WASHINGTON, CHARLES.....Mooringsport, Caddo Parish.....................Murder
"   11...HENDERSON, BREAD.............Mooringsport, Caddo Parish.....................Murder
"   12...LEWIS, WATKINS....................Shreveport, Caddo Parish.........................Murder

1915

July 16....COLLINS, THOMAS.....................Bunkie, Aroyelles Co..............Murderous assault
Aug. 21...UNNAMED NEGRO....................Grand Bayou, Red River Co......Attempted rape
"   26...UNNAMED NEGRO....................Conshama.................................Attempted rape

1916

May 25...TALLY, U. G.................................McNary, Rapides Co...................Attempted rape
Aug. 29...HAMMETT, JESS......................Vivian, Caddo Co........................Attempted rape

1917

Mar. 1...HOOPER, EMMA ....Hammond, Tangipahoa Parish.................Murder
May 11...BROOKS, HENRY......................Shreveport, Caddo Parish....Intimacy with white woman
July 10...RUFFIN, MARVEL ....Edgard, Baptist Parish...........................Vagrancy
"   29...ROUT, DANIEL....................Amite, Tangipahoa Co............................Murder
"   29...ROUT, JERRY ....Amite, Tangipahoa Co............................Murder
Oct. 12...JOHNSON, FRED ....New Orleans, Orleans Parish..................Robbery

MAINE
1907

Aug. —....HIGGINS, LOUIS......................Bancroft, Aroostook Co.............................Rape

MARYLAND
1889

Dec. 3....VERMILLION, JOSEPH........Marlboro..Arson

1891

May 12....GREEN, ASBURY.......................Centerville, Queen Annes Co......................Rape

MARYLAND—Continued

1892
May 18....TAYLOR, JAMES..................Chestertown, Kent Co..................Rape

1894
Oct. 20....WILLIAMS, ———..................Upper Marlboro, Prince
Georges Co..................Attempted rape

1895
May 27....HENSON, JACOB..................Elliot City..................Murder
July   2....*PRICE, MARSHAL C.*..................Denton, Caroline Co...................Murder
Nov. 17....BOWENS, JAMES..................Frederick, Frederick Co.........................Rape

1897
June   9....ANDERSON, WILLIAM..................Princess Anne, Somerset Co..................Rape

1898
May 26....KING, GARFIELD..................Salisbury, Wicomico Co. ....Murder
Oct.   2....SMITH, WRIGHT..................Annapolis, Anne Arundel Co....Attempted rape

1900
Mar. 26....HARRIS, LEWIS..................Belair, Harford Co..................Rape

1906
June 14....WATSON, ED...................Pocomoke City, Worcester
Co...................Murderous assault
Dec. 21....DAVIS, HENRY..................Annapolis, Anne Arundel Co..................Rape

1907
July 28....REED, JAS...................Crisfield, Somerset Co..................Murder
Oct.   5....BURNS, WM...................Cumberland, Alleghany Co..................Murder

1909
Mar.   8....RAMSAY, WM...................Rosedale..................Unnamed cause

1911
Dec. 25....DAVIS, KING..................Brooklyn, Anne Arundel Co..................Murder

MICHIGAN

1889
May 27....MARTIN, ALBERT..................Port Huron, Saint Clair Co..................Rape

1891
Sept.   2....TWO UNKNOWN TRAMPS..................Maybee Station, Monroe Co..................Murder

1902
Aug. 29....*LABARGE, JOHN*..................Locality undetermined..................Prospective   elope-
ment

MINNESOTA

1893
May   6....*DEMEAN, JOHN*..................Near Duluth, Saint Louis Co..................Rape
 "   28....AN INDIAN..................Cass Lake, Cass Co..................Murder

1896
Sept. 10....*TWO TRAMPS*..................Glencoe, McLeod Co..................Murder

MISSISSIPPI

1889
Feb.   7....UNKNOWN NEGRO..................Amite Co..................Rape
 "   22....SMITH, D. H...................Artesia, Loundes Co..................Colonizing Negroes
 "   23....WESLEY, THOMAS..................Port Gibson, Claiborne Co..................Attempted rape
 "   28....PERKINS, ———..................Port Gibson, Claiborne Co....Unknown offense
May 21....MITCHELL, JAMES..................Kosciusko, Attala Co..................Rape
 "   31....UNKNOWN NEGRO..................Thomastown, Leake..................Rape
June   1....HERRON, ROBERT..................Eureka..................Race hatred

MISSISSIPPI—Continued

July	12	LUSTER, PRINCE	Iuka, Tishomingo Co.	Rape
"	16	BURRES, SWAN	Iuka, Tishomingo Co.	Murder
"	20	THREE NEGROES (3)	Clinton, Hinds Co.	Murder
"	31	TALBOT, THOS.	Kemper Co.	Rape
Aug.	14	BOWEN, KEITH	Aberdeen, Monroe Co.	Rape
"	23	LEWIS, SHERMAN	Luccalena	Rape
"	30	*HARRIS, THOMAS*	Amory, Monroe Co.	Suspected burglar
Sept.	9	ALLEN, GEORGE	Le Flore Co.	Incendiarism
"	12	MORTIMER, LEWIS	Shell Mound, Lefiroy Co.	Murder
Oct.	12	ROBERT, BIGGS	Hernando, De Soto Co.	Rape
"	21	UNKNOWN NEGRO	Lake Comorant, De Soto Co.	Rape
"	26	HARROLD, JOSEPH	Near Columbus, Loundes Co.	Rape
Nov.	15	STANFORD BROTHERS (2)	Hazelhurst, Copiali Co.	Murder
"	16	WASHINGTON, GEORGE	Magnolia, Pike Co.	Attempted rape
"	16	UNKNOWN NEGRO	Hazelhurst, Copiali Co.	Murder

1890

Mar.	2	MARTIN, BURKE	Greenville, Washington Co.	Murder
May	22	ANDERSON, GRANT	Columbus, Loundes Co.	Alleged rape
June	3	STEVENSON, GEORGE	Hattiesburg, Forrest Co.	Alleged rape
Sept.	4	ROGERS, JOHN	Water Valley, Yalobusha Co.	Attempted rape
"	11	CRUMP, STEPHEN	Amory, Monroe Co.	Rape
"	11	BOLTER, GEORGE	Amory, Monroe Co.	Rape
Nov.	14	McGREGORY, ——	Water Valley, Yalobusha Co.	Rape
"	18	WALLACE, SANDY	Longstown	Rape
Dec.	7	MARTIN, DENNIS	Roebuck Landing	Murder
"	9	LEMON, MOSES	Roebuck Landing	Threats

1891

Jan.	2	SHARP, ——	Neshoba Co.	Robbery
"	3	*UNKNOWN WHITE MAN*	Neshoba Co.	
"	10	UNKNOWN INDIAN	Neshoba Co.	Murder
Feb.	6	JACKSON, GREEN	Greenville, Washington Co.	Alleged murder
"	16	BROWN, WILLIAM	Roxie, Franklin Co.	Rape
"	19	BULL, JOHN (Indian)	Battlefield	Murder
Mar.	7	HODGE, LOUIS	Louisville, Winston Co.	Attempted rape
Apr.	21	CURTIS, CHAS.	Liberty, Amite Co.	Rape
May	2	WALTERS, MONROE	Hudson	Alleged murder
"	11	BARRENTINE, JOHN	Loundes Co.	Murder
"	11	LEE, WESLEY	Loundes Co.	Murder
"	11	WALKER, MONROE	Loundes Co.	Murder
June	15	UNKNOWN NEGRO	Brookhaven, Lincoln Co.	Rape
July	1	GATES, WILLIAM	West Point, Clay Co.	Rape
"	6	CENTRY, HENRY	Near Vicksburg, Warren Co.	Murder
"	7	DOUGLAS, WALLACE	Whitaker Station, Wilkinson Co.	Robbery
"	14	GILLESPIE, SAM	De Soto, Loundes Co.	Race prejudice
Aug.	24	ANDREWS, LUCIUS	Magnolia, Pike Co.	Bad reputation
Sept.	1	*MURRELL, ANDREW*	Conden	Bank robbery
"	5	UNKNOWN NEGRO	Oxford, Lafayette Co.	Rape
"	28	STEVENSON, LOUISE	Hollandale, Washington Co.	Accessory to murder
Nov.	22	GLADNEY, DANIEL	Atlanta Co.	Race prejudice
"	30	RAINSEY, ARTHUR	Meridian, Lauderdale Co.	Race prejudice
Dec.	20	NEGRO	Meridian, Lauderdale Co.	Rape

1892

Feb.	28	ROBINSON, JOHN	Shaw Station, Bolivar Co.	Robbery
Mar.	8	RICE, JOHN	Boyle Station, Bolivar Co.	Incendiarism
"	8	CENTER, RICHARD	Boyle Station, Bolivar Co.	Incendiarism
May	2	A NEGRO	Greenville, Washington Co.	Rape
June	19	JOHNSON, JOHN	McComb City, Pike Co.	Murder
July	5	TOOLEY, SMITH	Vicksburg, Warren Co.	Murder
"	19	DAVIS, DOC.	Near Jackson, Hinds Co.	Rape
Aug.	14	MAGEE, PORT	Westville	Suspicion of rape
Oct.	5	FOUR DESPERADOES (4)	Near Beandon, Rankin Co.	
"	6	TWO DESPERADOES (2)	Copiah Co.	
Nov.	8	*TALBERT, JAMES*	Fort Stephens	Murder
Dec.	15	NEGRO CONVICT	Greenwood, Leflore Co.	Murder

1893

Jan.	30	CARR, THOMAS	Kosciuscko, Attala Co.	Race prejudice
Feb.	9	HARREL, FRANK	Dickey,	Incendiarism
"	9	FELDER, ——	Dickey,	Incendiarism
"	10	FORMAN, RICHARD	Near Grenada, Grenada Co.	Burglary
July	12	FLEMMING, HENRY	Columbus, Loundes Co.	Murder
Aug.	22	HART, CHARLES	Lyons, Station, Coahoma Co.	Race prejudice

MISSISSIPPI—Continued

Sept. 8	JACKSON BENJAMIN	Quincy, Monroe Co.	Murder
" 11	SMITH, FRANK	Newton, Newton Co.	Attempted rape
" 15	JACKSON, BENJAMIN	Jackson, Hinds Co.	Alleged well poisoning
" 15	JACKSON, MAHALA	Jackson, Hinds Co.	Alleged well poisoning
" 15	CARTER, LOUISA (F)	Jackson, Hinds Co.	Alleged well poisoning
" 15	HEALEY, W. A.	Jackson, Hinds Co.	Alleged well poisoning
" 15	BEAGLEY, RUFUS	Jackson, Hinds Co.	Alleged well poisoning
Dec. 23	ALLEN SLOAN	West, Holmes Co.	Suspected murder
" 23	UNKNOWN NEGRO	Fannin, Rankin Co.	Suspected robbery

1894

Mar. 30	SAYBRICK	Fishers Ferry	Murder
May 7	*HICKS, A.*	Rocky Springs, Claiborne Co.	Suspected arson
" 29	SMITH, HENRY	Clinton, Hinds Co.	Burglary
June 4	MURDOCK, READY	Yazoo City, Yazoo Co.	Alleged rape
" 9	WILLIAMS, LEWIS	Hewitt Springs	Alleged rape
" 15	THOMAS, LUKE	Biloxi, Harrison Co.	Murder
" 28	LINTON, GEORGE	Brookhaven, Lincoln Co.	Attempted rape
July 6	POND, GEORGE	Fulton, Itawamba Co.	Attempted rape
" 6	HOOD, ——	Amite Co.	Murder
" 6	BARKHEAD, LEWIS	Amite Co.	Rape
" 7	POND, AUGUSTUS	Tupelo, Lee Co.	Attempted rape
" 14	UNKNOWN NEGRO	Biloxi, Harrison Co.	Attempted rape
" 20	MYERS, ALLEN	Rankin Co.	Conjuring
" 24	UNKNOWN WOMAN (F)	Simpson Co.	Race prejudice
Dec. 26	CARTER, WILLIAM	Winston Co.	Murder

1895

Jan. 7	COSTELLO, SPENCER	Flora, Madison Co.	Murder and Robbery
Mar. 29	BETAT, ROBERT	Bluff Creek	Arson
May 23	UNKNOWN NEGRO	Rodney, Jefferson Co.	Rape
June 17	*DAWSON, R. W.*	Natchez, Adams Co.	Murder
" 19	CHANDLER, WILLIAM	Abbeyville, Lafayette Co.	Attempted rape
" 29	BOWEN, THOMAS	Brook Haven, Lincoln Co.	Rape
July 6	PICKET, THEODORE	Jackson, Hinds Co.	Larceny
" 18	THOMAS, ANDREW	Scranton	Rape
" 25	JOHNSON, THOMAS	Hattiesburg, Forrest Co.	Murder
" 28	BURWELL, CHARLES	Meridian, Lauderdale Co.	Assault
Sept. 2	UNKNOWN NEGRO	Simpson Co.	Miscegenation
Nov. 29	*YARBOROUGH,* ——	Crystal Springs, Copiak Co.	Murder

1896

Apr. 3	MAYBERRY, HARVEY	Teysels,	Rape
June 27	YOUNG, PERRY	Winona, Montgomery Co.	Rape
Oct. 21	A NEGRO	Sunnyside	Murder
Nov. 18	COLLIER, MIMMS	Steenston	Attempted rape

1897

Jan. 10	TWO NEGROES (2)	Vardaman, Calhoun Co.	Murder and robbery
" 20	HENDERSON, PETER	Ittabena, Leflore Co.	Murder and assault
Mar. 28	HOLLINSHEAD, T. W.	Waynesboro, Wayne Co.	Informer
Apr. 3	HAINES, ——	Belen, Quitman Co.	Murder
" 10	UNKNOWN NEGRO	Near Vicksburg, Warren Co.	Unknown offense
" 16	EVANS, JESSE	Edwards, Hinds Co.	Rape
May 27	COOPER, JAMES	Hemlock	Attempted murder
June 25	MOSES, JOHN M.	Crystal Springs, Copiah Co.	Murder
" 28	GILIAM, PARY	Aberdeen, Monroe Co.	Robbery and assault
July 28	SELLERS, JAMES	Pittsboro, Calhoun Co.	Murder
Oct. 6	CROWER, HENRY	Hernando, De Soto Co.	Rape
" 16	WILLIAMS, WILLIAM	Hamburg, Franklin Co.	Rape
Dec. 10	JONES, CHAS.	Weason, Copiah Co.	Murder
" 16	WALLER, THOMAS	Near Brookhaven, Lincoln Co.	Murder
" 27	HOPKINS, JAMES	Glendora, Tallahatchie Co.	Murder

1898

Jan. 1	JONES, JAMES	Macon, Noxubee Co.	Arson
" 7	WATTS, JAMES	Pea Ridge	Insults

MISSISSIPPI—Continued

Jan.	7	COLE, SAM	Pea Ridge	Insults
"	26	*PEARSON, MARY*	Near Natchez, Adams Co.	Murder
Mar.	2	*MOORE, FREDERICK*	Senatobia, Tate Co.	Murder
"	6	JONES, WILLIAM	Lake Cormorant	Rape
"	20	ANDERSON, ALEX	Grenada, Grenada Co.	Attempted rape
July	12	GOULD, WESLEY	Leland, Washington Co.	Mistaken identity
"	19	PATTERSON, WM.	Westville	Murder
Aug.	11	WALKER, MULLOCH	Corinth, Alcorn Co.	Highway robbery
Nov.	27	THREE NEGROES (3)	Near Meridian, Lauderdale Co.	Assaulting white man
Dec.	6	WHITE, ——	Tallahatchie Co.	Murder

1899

Mar.	11	ALLEN, THOMAS	McGee	Unknown offense
"	23	BOYD, WILLIS	Silver City, Yazoo Co.	Race prejudice
"	23	REED, C. C.	Silver City, Yazoo Co.	Race prejudice
"	23	WILSON, MINOR	Silver City, Yazoo Co.	Race prejudice
Apr.	6	JAMESON, FOREST	Brookfield	Murder
"	6	ANDERSON, MOSES	Brookfield	Murder
June	11	BROOKS, SIMON	Sardis, Panola Co.	Robbery
"	20	PATRICK, DANIEL	Scranton	Rape
July	24	UNKNOWN NEGRO	Pushington,	Rape
"	25	NOARK, HENRY	Hattiesburg, Forrest Co.	Attempted rape
"	26	HAYES, STANLEY	Near Brandon, Rankin Co.	Attempted rape
Aug.	11	WILSON, WILLIAM	Port Gibson, Claiborne Co.	Attempted rape
Sept.	6	STERN, WILLIAM	Rosemeath	Murder
"	20	OTIS, WILLIAM	Rawles Springs, Forrest Co.	Unknown offense
Oct.	21	LUFLORE, JOSEPH	St. Anne	Arson and murder
Dec.	23	MARTIN, JAMES	Bolton, Hinds Co.	Murder
"	23	WEST, FRANK	Bolton, Hinds Co.	Murder

1900

Mar.	4	CROSBY, JAMES	Tutwiler, Tallahatchie Co.	Threats to kill
"	10	CLAYTON, THOMAS	Hernando, De Soto Co.	Rape
"	27	EDWARD, WILLIAM	Deep Creek Bridge, Perry Co.	Murder
Apr.	16	YORK, MOSES	Near Tunica, Tunica Co.	Murder
"	19	McAFEE, HENRY	Brownsville, Hinds Co.	Attempted rape
May	1	RATCLIFF, HENRY	Gloster, Amite Co.	Attacking white man
"	1	GORDON, GEORGE	Albin, Tallahatchie Co.	Attacking white man
"	7	UNKNOWN NEGRO	Amity Co.	No offense
"	16	HINSON, SAMUEL	Cushtusha	Assault
June	3	PETE, DAGO	Tutwiler, Tallahatchie Co.	Rape
"	10	ASKEW, ——	Mississippi, Harrison Co.	Suspected murder
Aug.	13	BETTS, JACK	Corinth, Alcorn Co.	Rape
Sept.	12	FLOYD, ZED	Tunica, Tunica Co.	Murder
"	14	BROWN, FRANK	Tunica, Tunica Co.	Murder
"	14	BROWN, WILLIAM	Tunica, Tunica Co.	Murder
"	14	MOORE, DAVID	Tunica, Tunica Co.	Murder
Oct.	23	BARNES, GLOSTER	Near Vicksburg, Warren Co.	Murder
Nov.	8	*NABORS, KIT*	Coahoma, Coahoma Co.	Murder
Dec.	19	TWO UNKNOWN NEGROES (2)	Arcadia, Issaquena Co.	Murder
"	20	LEWIS, ——	Gulfport, Harrison Co.	Murder

1901

Feb.	1	MATTHEWS, WARNER	Ocean Springs, Jackson Co.	Rape
"	18	ISHAM, FRED	Macon, Noxubee Co.	Arson
"	18	ISHAM, HENRY	Macon, Noxubee Co.	Arson
"	26	*KNOX, JOHN*	Scranton, Jackson Co.	Murder
Mar.	20	BELL, TERRY	Terry, Hinds Co.	Race prejudice
May	22	*CALVERT, MILT*	Griffith	Attempted rape
July	11	*THREE SUSPECTED CATTLE THIEVES* (3)	Erwin, Washington Co.	
"	11	*AMEO, JOHN AND VICTOR* (2)	Erwin, Washington Co.	
"	20	*PHILIPS, JESSE P.*	Cleveland, Bolivar Co.	Murder
Aug.	1	McCRAY, BETSY	Carrolton, Carroll Co.	Implicated in murder
"	1	McCRAY, IDA	Carrolton, Carroll Co.	Implicated in murder
"	1	McCRAY, BELFIELD	Carrolton, Carrol Co.	Implicated in murder
"	4	PRICE, WILLIAM	Carrolton, Carrol Co.	Alleged complicity in murder
Sept.	1	HILL, RICHARD	Philadelphia, Neshoba Co.	Murder
Nov.	4	UNKNOWN NEGRO	Perry Co.	Rape

MISSISSIPPI—Continued

1902

May 13	MULLER, HORACE	Cookamie Co.	Attempted murder
July 15	ODY, WILLIAM	Clayton, Tunica Co.	Attempted rape
July 20	TWO NEGROES	Cross Roads	Race prejudice
Aug. 4	McDANIEL, JOHN	Smithdale, Amite Co.	Lawlessness
" 17	JOHNSON, CHAS.	Walnut Grove, Leake Co.	Rape
Sept. 28	CLARK, THOMAS	Corinth, Alcorn Co.	Murder
Oct. 20	UNKNOWN NEGRO	Estabutchie, Jones Co.	Attempted rape
Nov. 1	UNKNOWN NEGRO	Darling, Quitman Co.	Murder
" 20	YOUNGBLOOD, JOHN	Summit, Pike Co.	Complicity in murder
" 20	UNKNOWN NEGRO	Summit, Pike Co.	Complicity in murder

1903

Jan. 10	HOLLINS, JOHN	Drew, Sunflower Co.	Attempted assault
May 3	BRYANT, ROBERT	Vicksburg, Warren Co.	Murder
" 20	HART, MOSE	Corinth, Alcorn Co.	Murderous assault
" 28	UNKNOWN NEGRO	Woodville, Wilkinson Co.	Arson
June 4	DENNIS, ROBERT	Greenville, Washington Co.	Alleged rape
" 8	FOUR NEGROES (4)	Smith Co.	Complicity in murder
" 8	NEGRO WOMAN	Smith Co.	Complicity in murder
" 12	KINCAID, GEORGE	Near Cleveland, Bolivar Co.	Murderous assault
July 7	JARRETT, CATO	Stouts Crossing	Murder
Sept. —	JONES, GEORGE	Mayersville, Issaquena Co.	Arson
" —	WILLIAMS, WILL	Centerville, Wilkinson Co.	Murder
Oct. 27	*McALPIN, WILLIAM*	Smith Co.	Murder
" 29	UNKNOWN NEGRO	Hattiesburg, Forrest Co.	Attempted rape
Nov. 5	ADAMS, SAMUEL	Pass Christian, Harrison Co.	Rape
Dec. 24	HILSON, ELI	Brookhaven, Lincoln Co.	Race prejudice

1904

Jan. 14	RILEY, BUSH	Tallula, Issaquena Co.	Murder
Feb. 7	HOLBERT, LUTHER AND WIFE (2)	Doddsville	Murder
" 7	THREE UNKNOWN MEN (3)	Near Doddsville	Murder

1904

Mar. 17	UNKNOWN NEGRO	Saucier, Harrison Co.	Murder
" 19	SAWYER, FAYETTE	Cleveland, Bolivar Co.	Murder
" 19	HARRIS, BURKE	Cleveland, Bolivar Co.	Murder
May 24	UNKNOWN NEGRO	O'Neil, Amite Co.	Murder
June 3	VAN HORNE, ——	Trail Lake, Ozark Co.	Murder
" 3	CLARK, ——	Trail Lake, Ozark Co.	Murder
" 4	MAYFIELD, ——	Trail Lake, Ozark Co.	Murder
June 26	DUNHAM, STERLING	Europa, Webster Co.	Rape
July 9	UNKNOWN		Attempted rape
" 10	TUCKER, JESSE	Houston, Chickasaw Co.	Attempted rape

1905

Jan. 4	UNKNOWN NEGRO	Benoit, Bolivar Co.	Unknown offense
Mar. 5	UNKNOWN NEGRO	Helm Station, Washington Co.	Murder
June 25	MOBERLY, PIERCE	Near Meridian, Lauderdale Co.	Murder
July 19	HARRIS, HENRY	Near Glendora, Tallahatchie Co.	Murder
" 25	HARRIS, WM.	Near Glendora, Tallahatchie Co.	Murder
Aug. 4	LEWIS, ED.	Hattiesburg, Forrest Co.	Murder
" 4	GEORGE, KID	Hattiesburg, Forrest Co.	Murder
" 16	YOUNG, HENRY	Lake Cormorant, De Soto Co.	Murder
Sept. 1	REES, ALT	Rosetta Wilkinson Co.	Rape
" 14	JAMES, WM.	Tallahatchie Co.	Informing
" 19	McDOWELL, JOHN	Rankin Co.	Unknown offense
Oct. 10	JAMES, JOHN	Woodville, Wilkinson Co.	Attempted rape
Nov. 22	SIMMS, DAVID	Coahoma, Coahoma Co.	Murder
Dec. 11	GREEN, JAMES	Boyle, Bolivar Co.	Rape

1906

Jan. 17	UNKNOWN NEGRO	Penola	Attempted rape
May 8	SIMMS, SAM	Jackson, Hinds Co.	Killing a horse
" 23	YOUNGER, GEO.	Columbus, Lowndes Co.	Murder
June 11	AMBROSE, WOOD	Prentiss, Jefferson Davis Co.	Murder
" 30	UNKNOWN NEGRO	De Kalb, Kemper Co.	Alleged rape
Sept. 7	TWO NEGROES (2)	Laurel, Jones Co.	Attempted rape
Oct. 6	UNKNOWN NEGRO	Basin, George Co.	Rape

MISSISSIPPI—Continued

Oct. 25 CROMPTON, THOS..............Centerville, Wilkinson Co........ ...... Murder
Nov. 8 HINKS, "JET".............................Lee Co.............................Murder
Dec. 5 YOUNG, WES...............Near Valley Park, Issaquena Co. ...Murder

1907

Jan. 23 BELL, HENRY..................Greenwood, Leflore Co. ....Rape
June 8 JOHNSON, ABE ....Near Yazoo City, Yazoo Co.......Race rioter
  " 8 JOHNSON, HARRY ......Near Yazoo City, Yazoo Co.......Race rioter
  " 9 FOX, LEE ....Near Yazoo City, Yazoo Co.......Race rioter
July 20 TRICE, ANDREW..........Olive Branch, De Soto Co.........Murder
  " 29 WASHINGTON, SAM....Near Vicksburg, Warren Co........Murder
Oct. 11 JACKSON, WM..........Tunica, Tunica Co.......Burglary
  " 11 SHOOTS, JAS............Tunica, Tunica Co.......Burglary
  " 11 ROBINSON, GEO........Tunica, Tunica Co.......Burglary
  " 23 SYKES, HENRY...........Van Vleet, Chickasaw Co.....Insulting women
  " 27 MEYER, ——..............Carrollton, Carroll Co............Complicity in murder
  " 29 GERMAN, CHAS............Near Belen, Quitman Co.......Rape
Dec. 16 HUSBAND, PAT..................McHenry, Stone Co.....................Rape

1908

Jan. 2 UNNAMED NEGRO.............Brookhaven, Lincoln Co...........Murder
  " 28 TWO UNNAMED NEGROES (2) ..Commerce (near) Tunica Co............Murder
Feb. 10 PIGATT, ELI...Brookhaven, Lincoln Co........Rape
Mar. 10 POE, DAVID........Van Cleave, Jackson Co.....Incendiarism
  " 10 RANSTON, THOS.......Van Cleave, Jackson Co.....Incendiarism
  " 10 JENKINS BROS. (2)........Van Cleave, Jackson Co.....Incendiarism
Apr. 5 BURR, JOHN............Wesson, Copiah Co.............Murder
Aug. 28 WILLIAMS, JOHN........Ittababa, Leflore Co.............Arson
Sept. 8 PATTON, LAWSON.......Oxford, Lafayette Co............Murder
  " 20 JONES, CHAS........Yazoo City, Yazoo Co.............Murder
Oct. 10 DAWSON, DEE........Hickory, Newton Co.......Alleged complicity in murder
  " 10 FULLER, WM.......Hickory, Newton Co.......Alleged complicity in murder
  " 10 JOHNSON, FRANK.......Hickory, Newton Co.......Alleged complicity in murder
  " 11 DAVIS, JOSEPH........Lula, Coahoma Co.............Murder
  " 11 DAVIS, FRANK........Lula, Coahoma Co.............Murder
  " 15 JACKSON, W. J......Hernando, De Soto Co............Theft
Nov. 2 HODGES, WM......Union, Newton Co............Rape
  " 10 LEIDY, HENRY......Biloxi, Harrison Co............Rape

1909

Jan. 16 WILLIS, "PINK".........Poplarville, Pearl River Co.......Attempted rape
Feb. 9 BUSKIN, ROBBY........Houston, Chickasaw Co.............Murder
Mar. 12 GORDON, JOSEPH.......Greenwood, Leflore Co............Murder
Apr. 11 MONTGOMERY, HORACE.........Greenville, Washington Co.......Murder
Aug. 17 ROBINSON, WM......Greenville, Washington Co.......Unnamed cause
Oct. 28 FOUR, UNNAMED (4). ....Kemper Co.............Murder
Nov. 25 *CHAMBERS, MORGAN*..........Meehan, Lauderdale Co............Robbery

1910

Apr. 19 O'NEIL, THOMAS.............Meridian, Lauderdale Co............Murder
June 12 CURL, ELMER.............Mastadon.............Murder
  " 15 MITCHELL, OTTO............Durant, Holmes Co.......Attempted murder
  " 28 JONES, ——........Braxton, Simpson Co.............Murder
Sept. 1 THOMPSON, NICHOLAS........Armory.....................Rape

1911

June 16 BRADFORD, WILLIAM.....Chunky, Newton Co.............Desperado
Nov. 7 MOSELEY "JUDGE".........Lockhart, Lauderdale Co.......Murderous assault

1912

Jan. 15 GILES, NEELEY.........Sucarnoochee, Kemper Co...........Murder
Feb. 14 HAMILTON, MANN.........Starkesville, Oktibbeha Co............Rape
Apr. 3 COLEMAN, ALEX........Starkesville, Oktibbeha Co.......Attempted rape
May 7 UNNAMED........Greenville, Washington Co.......Attempted rape
  " 7 EDD, G. W........Near Macon, Noxubee Co..........Murder
Dec. 17 UNNAMED........Jackson, Hinds Co...........Murderous assault

1913

Jan. 30 UNNAMED NEGRO......Drew, Sunflower Co. ....Murder
Feb. 7 WILLIAMS, ANDREW.....Houston, Chickasaw Co............Murder
  " 23 WEBB, WILLIE........Drew, Sunflower Co............Murder

MISSISSIPPI—Continued

June 27...ROBINSON, WILLIAM......Lambert, Quitman Co.......................Murder
July 15...TOWNER, SAMUEL........Alligator, Bolivar Co. .... Murder
Sept. 21...CROSBY, HENRY....................Louisville, Winston Co.........Annoying a white woman
"   28...JONES, WALTER.............Harriston, Jefferson Co..............Murder
"   28...JONES, WILLIAM..........Harriston, Jefferson Co............ Murder
Oct. 15...BROWNLEE, WALTER.........Hinchcliff, Quitman Co................Alleged rape, proved innocent

1914

Feb. 16...McQUIRK, JOHNSON........Love Station, De Soto Co......Murder
"   24...PETTY, SAM.............Leland, Washington Co.......................Murder
July 14...BAILEY, JOSEPH...........Comorant....................Murder
Oct. 25...MILLER, MAYSHE........Aberdeen, Monroe Co........ Murderous assault
Nov. 3...BURNS, THOMAS..........Hernando, De Soto Co.....................Murder
"   24...SULLIVAN, FREDERICK......Byhalia, Marshall Co.....................Arson
"   25...SULLIVAN, MRS. FREDERICK.Byhalia, Marshall Co.....................Arson

1915

Jan. 20...JOHNSON, EDWARD ....Vicksburg, Warren Co.........Murder and stealing cattle
Feb. 10...HILL, ALEXANDER ....Brookville, Noxubee Co............Murder
May 15...UNNAMED NEGRO ....Lousiville, Winston Co.................Insulting white woman
June 28...UNNAMED NEGRO..........Cedar Bluffs, Clay Co..........Attempted rape
July 11...UNNAMED NEGRO.........De Kalb, Kemper Co...................Theft
July 16...MITCHELL, WILLIAM......Sardis, Panola Co.........Murderous assault
Oct. 11...TWO UNNAMED NEGROES (2) Clarksdale, Coahoma Co.....................Murder
"   30...*HUYLER, JOSEPH*.........Columbus, Loundes Co.......................Murder
Nov. 12...TAYLOR, JOHN.........Aberdeen, Monroe Co........Murderous assault

1916

Mar. 20...BROWN, JEFF...............West Point, Clay Co.........Attempted rape
Oct. 6...NANCE, ALLEN............Greenwood, Le Flore Co........Murderous assault

1917

June 2...HAYNES, VAN.........Columbia, Marion Co..........Murder
"   2...HEMPTON, PRATT .....Columbia, Marion Co..............Murder

MISSOURI

1889

Jan. 21...THOMAS, HENRY.......Bolar.................... Murder
May 7...*THREE CORBER BROTHERS*.Tiptonville.................Murder
June 21...GRIZZARD, ALFRED...........Tiptonville...............Gambling
Aug. 3...SMITH, BENJAMIN.........La Plata, Macon Co..................Rape
Sept. 12...*DAVIS, JOHN*.........Stafford.....................Murder
"   17...BURKE, GEO............Columbia, Boone Co..................Rape
Nov. 17...*GEBHART, JOSEPH*.......Kennett, Dunklin Co...............Safe-breaking

1890

Sept. 3...SMITH, THOMAS.........Poplar Bluff, Butler Co...............Murder

1891

Jan. 20...TRUXTON, OLLI.......Glasgow, Howard Co.......Rape

1892

Jan. 22...*HEPLER, ROBERT*.........Nevada, Vernon Co.................Murder
Feb. 12...*GORDON, LEWIS*........Carrollton, Carroll Co...............Rape
"   14...*BRIGHT, JOHN F*......Taney Co.................Wife-murder
Apr. 27...SIMS, DAVID...........Clarkton, Dunklin Co..............Unknown reason

1893

Feb. 18...HUGHES, JOHN............Moberly, Randolph Co..........Insulting whites
"   21...*MAYES, RICHARD*......Springfield, Green Co..........Attempted rape
Sept. 16...*BURKE, REDMOND*.......Breckenridge, Caldwell Co.....Wife-beating, by white caps

1894

Jan. 17...BUCKNER, JOHN..........Valley Park, Saint Louis Co...........Rape
"   22...UNKNOWN NEGRO........Verona, Lawrence Co..............Rape
Feb. 27...*CARTER, A*.........West Plains, Howell Co.................Murder
"   27...*MONTGOMERY, B.*.......West Plains, Howell Co.................Murder
June 29...HAYDON, ULYSSESS......Monett, Barry Co....................Murder
July 2...JOHNSON, JOSEPH........Hillers Creek, Barry Co................Rape
Nov. 5...*UNKNOWN MAN*.......Roscoe, Saint Clair Co..........Offense unknown

MISSOURI—Continued

1895

Feb. 17	*TRACY, GEORGE*	Kingston, Caldwell Co.		Murder
Aug. 15	**DIVENS, EMMETT**	Fulton, Callaway Co.		Murder
Oct. 11	**HENDERSON, WILLIAM**	Jackson, Cape Girardeau Co		Rape

1896

June 27....*COCKING, JAMES*................La Plata, Macon Co......................Murder
" 30...*WAYLAND, CECIL*................Near Hannibal, Marion Co................Rape
July 27...*CRAWFORD, M.*................Near Tipton, Moniteau Co....Attempted rape
Sept. 4...*LARKIN, THOMAS*................Vineland, Jefferson Co......................Rape
Dec. 6...*WINNER, JESSIE*................Lexington, Lafayette Co......................Murder
" 6...*NELSON, JAMES*................Lexington, Lafayette Co......................Murder

1897

May 22....*MITCHELL, JOHN*................Mountain Grove, Wright Co......................Larceny
" 22. *COFFMAN, JACK*................Mountain Grove, Wright Co......................Larceny
July 10...**BROWN, ERASTUS**................Villa Ridge, Franklin Co......................Rape
Nov. 18...*FARGO, SILAS P.*................Liberty, Clay Co......................Alleged arson

1898

Feb. 2....**WARD,** ——................Galena, Stone Co......................Murder
June 6....**YOUNG, CURTIN**................Clarkville, Pike Co......................Murder
" 6....**YOUNG, SAM**................Clarkville, Pike Co......................Murder
" 30....**WILLIAMS, HENRY**................Macon, Macon Co......................Rape
Aug. 11...*JONES,, BENJAMIN*................Liberty, Clay Co......................Murder
Nov. 29....**NEGRO**................Near New Madrid, New Madrid Co........Murder

1899

July 23....**EMBREE, FRANK**................Steinmetz, Howard Co......................Rape
Nov. 1....**HAYDEN, THOMAS**................Near Fayette, Howard Co......................Murder
" 16....*HUFF, WILLIAM*................Bloomfield, Stoddard Co......................Murder

1900

Apr. 28....**CHOWAGEE, MUNDEE**................Marshall, Platte Co......................Murder
May 4....**DARLEY, HENRY**................Liberty, Clay Co......................Rape

1901

Jan. 3....**SIMPSON, NELSON**................Neelyville, Butler Co..............Race prejudice, by white caps
Mar. 2....**McNEAL, ARTHUR**................Richmond, Howard Co......................Murder
July 26....*MACK, JOHN*
Aug. 19....**GODLEY, WILLIAM**................Pierce City, Lawrence Co....Suspected murder
" 19....**GODLEY, FRENCH**................Pierce City, Lawrence Co....Suspected murder
" 20....**HAMPTON, PETER**................Pierce City, Lawrence Co....Suspected murder

1902

Feb. 17....**WRIGHT, LOUIS**................New Madrid, New Madrid Co..Assaulting white man
Mar. 26....**WRIGHT, OLIVER**................Higbee, Randolph Co................Unknown offense
May 25...*WITHERUPS, ABRAHAM*....Paris, Monroe Co......................Murder
July 17...*ANDERSON, JOSHUA*................Lexington, Lafayette Co......................Murder
Aug. 12...**GATES, HARRY**................Lexington, Lafayette Co......................Murder

1903

Jan. 21....**CLARK, ANDY**................Leeper, Wayne Co......................Murder
Apr. 15....**GILYARD, THOMAS**................Joplin, Jasper Co......................Murder
May 3....**MALONE, D.**................Caruthersville, Pemiscot Co................Prejudice
" 3....**MOONEYHON, W. J.**................Caruthersville, Pemiscot Co................Prejudice

1905

May 12....**PETTIGREW, ROBT.**................Belmont, Mississippi Co......................Kidnapping

1906

Apr. 4....**DUNCAN, HARRY**................Springfield, Green Co................Alleged rape
" 14....**COPELAND, JAMES**................Springfield, Green Co......................Rape
" 15....**ALLEN, WILLIAM**................Springfield, Green Co......................Murder

1909

Aug. 1....*JOHNSON, GEO.*................Platte City, Platte Co......................Murder

1910

May 30....**NEGRO**................New Madrid, New Madrid Co................Murderous assault

MISSOURI—Continued

July 3....COLEMAN, ROBERT............Charleston, Mississippi Co..............Murder
  "   3....FIELD, SAM................Charleston, Mississippi Co..............Murder

1911

Oct. 11....RICHARDSON, A. B............Caruthersville, Pemiscot Co..............Robbery
  "   11....WOODS, BENJ................Caruthersville, Pemiscot Co..............Rape

1914

Mar. 10....SHIELDS, DALLAS............Fayette, Howard Co..............Murder
June 17....KOLLINS, ISAAC............West Plains, Howell Co..............Unknown cause
  "   17....COLLINS, MRS. PARALEE........West Plains, Howell Co............Unknown

1915

Feb 21....WILLIAMS, W. F............Mt. Pleasant, Bates Co..............Murder
Sept. 1....LANE, RUDD................Louisiana, Pike Co..............Theft

1916

Jan. 3....SYKES, SAMUEL............Hayti, Pemiscot Co..............Attempted murder
Apr. 3....CHANDLER, FAYETTE............Near St. Charles..............Murder

MONTANA

1889

June 5.._TWO HIGHWAY ROBBERS..Marysville, Lewis and Clarke Co..............
  "   28.._HOCK, JOHN................Piegan..............Murder

1891

May 15....JUIDEN, ————..............Dewey,..............Murder
July 26....CLANCY, JOSEPH............Billings, Yellowstone Co..............Murder
Sept. 2....THREE CATTLE THIEVES..Custer Co..............

1892

Jan. 30....FOUR HORSE THIEVES..............

1898

Dec. 10....FISHER, ELI..............Mistaken identity

1901

July 16....LIBEREO, SALVATOR............Judith, Fergus Co..............
Oct. 2....BRADY, JAMES E............Helena, Lewis and Clarke Co..............Rape
Oct. 7....WILSON, MATTHEW............Helena, Lewis and Clarke Co....Attempted rape

1903

June 19....BROWN, JOHN............Bad Lands..............Murder
Aug. 14....UNKNOWN MAN............Dupyer, Teton Co..............Unknown offense,
                                                            by white caps
Oct. 14....JACKSON, WALTER............Hamilton, Ravalli Co..............Murder

1912

Apr. 18....HOFNER, HARRY............Forsyth, Rosebud Co..............Murder

1913

Apr. 5....COLLINS, J. C............Mondak, Sheridan Co..............Murder

1917

Aug. 1....LITTLE, FRANK............Butte, Silver Bow Co............I. W. W. Leader

NEBRASKA

1889

Feb. 5....HAGGERMAN, GEORGE..........Schuyler, Colfax Co..............Horse stealing
Mar. 28....GANNON, ————..............Ainsworth..............Horse stealing
  "   28....BABCOCK, ————..............Ainsworth..............Horse stealing
  "   28....REMUS, ————..............Ainsworth..............Horse stealing
May 22....PEKWEK, FRANK............Weston, Saunders Co..............Wife-beating
  "   31.._NEWELL, JOHN T............Deyapaha Co..............By vigilantes
June 22....FOLEY, NICHOLAS............Elgin, Antelope Co..............Murder
July 15....MANDIN, H. A............Bassett, Rock Co..............Horse stealing

1891

Oct. 9....COE, JOSEPH............Omaha, Douglas Co..............Rape
Dec. 18....UNKNOWN TRAMP............Emmett, Holt Co..............Rape

NEBRASKA—Continued

1894

Feb. 2....**HURST, GEORGE**.................Neely.........................Murder
July 2....*HILLS, RAPPLE AND SON*....Bush Creek..................Arson
  "   2....*UNKNOWN MAN*..............Bush Creek..................Arson

1895

Jan. 1....*SCOTT, BARRET*.................O'Neill, Holt Co................Frauds
Mar. 18....*HOLTON, MRS. W. E*..........Keyapaha Co.................By vigilantes
Apr. 14....*POWELL, DEAN*................Keyapaha Co.................Cattle rustler
  " 14....*CHAMBERLAIN, FRED'K*....Keyapaha Co.................Cattle rustler

1911

June 19....*SELLERS, CHAS*.................Near Cody, Cherry Co................Murder

NEW JERSEY

1900

GAMBOLA, JOHN....................Hackensack, Bergen Co....................Murder

NEW YORK

1892

June 2....**LEWIS, ROBERT**....................Port Jervis, Orange Co....................Rape

1896

Jan. 10....*SMITH, GEORGE H*.................Ransonville, Niagara Co....................Murder

1916

Dec. 14....*BOLETA, PAULO*.....................Greenwich, Washington Co.....Murderous assault

NEW MEXICO

1889

July 22....*TWO HORSE THIEVES*.........Kelly, Socorre Co....................
July 26....*CHACHA, JOSEPH*.................Wallace....................Murder

1893

Apr. 14....*HARDIN, WILLIAM*..............Monticello, Sierra Co....................Murder
May 7....*MARTINEZ, ANTONIO*........Los Lunas, Valencia Co....................Murder
  "   7....*BARCELOZ, ANTONIO J*....Los Lunas, Valencia Co....................Murder
  "   7....*ANJOU, VICTORIANO*........Los Lunas, Valencia Co....................Murder
  " 30....*LUCERO, CELIO*..................Las Vegas, San Miguel Co....................Murder
June 19....*UNKNOWN COW-BOY*.........Dunseath....................Murder

1895

Oct. 17....*YOUNG, DANIEL E*..............Oak Canon....................Unknown offense

1905

Sept. 2....**WOODWARD, ARTHUR**........Silver City, Grant Co............Murderous assault
  "   2....**WOODWARD, TALCUM**........Silver City, Grant Co............Murderous assault

1914

Mar. 31....*PADILLA, ADOLFE*..............Santa Fe, Santa Fe Co....................Murder

NEVADA

1897

June 10....MOUSE (INDIAN)....................Muddy Creek....................Murder
Dec. 7....*UBER, ADAM*........................Genoa, Douglas Co....................Murder

1903

Sept. 17....CHINAMAN........................Tonopah, Nye Co....................Race prejudice

1905

Feb. 22....*UNKNOWN MAN*....................Hazen....................Robbery

NORTH CAROLINA

1889

Sept. 9	SIGMOND, JOHN	Stanley Creek, Gaston Co.	Rape
" 11	BOONE, DAVID	Morganton, Burke Co.	Murder
" 11	*STACK, FRANK*	Morganton, Burke Co.	Murder
Oct. 25	*BERRIER, ROBERT*	Lexington, Davidson Co.	Murder

1890

Dec. 24	FREEMAN, KINCH	Winton, Hertford Co.	Murder

1891

Sept. 8	BESS, MACK	Nearland	Attempted rape
" 25	RANKIN, HEZEKIAH	Asheville, Buncombe Co.	Murder

1892

May 3	PURDEE, LYMAN	Elisabethtown, Bladen Co.	Murder
June 10	*WENTELY, ALEX*	Charlotte, Mecklenburg Co.	Murder
" 12	BURRIS, J. A.	Albermarle, Stanly Co.	Murder
Sept. 13	*ALLISON, THOS. N.*	Mt. Airy, Surry Co.	Murder
Nov. 15	BURNETT, WM.	Oxford, Granville Co.	Rape

1893

Jan. 6	UNKNOWN NEGRO	Pocket Township	Murder
Feb. 24	WHITSON, THOMAS	Asheville, Buncombe Co.	Murder
" 24	WHITSON, WILSON	Asheville, Buncombe Co.	Murder
June 2	LINCOLN, ISAAC	Ft. Madison	Insulting women

1894

Feb. 25	*SLAUGHTER, P.*	Sparta, Alleghany Co.	Murder

1895

Jan. 4	*BEGERON, JOHN F.*	Idalit	Murder

1896

Apr. 22	CHARMERS, ROBERT	Cranberry, Avery Co.	Incendiarism

1897

Nov. 27	WILLIS, NATHAN	Town Creek, Brunswick Co.	Murder
Mar. 2	INDIAN DOCTOR	Morganton, Burke Co.	Name and offense unknown
" 2	*GIRL*	Morganton, Burke Co.	Name and offense unknown
May 29	KISER, JOSEPH	Concord, Cabarrus Co.	Suspected murder
" 29	JOHNSON, THOMAS	Concord, Cabarrus Co.	Suspected murder

1899

Jan. 11	JONES, HENRY	Harps Cross	Murder
May 11	TWO NEGROES	Pitt Co.	Murder

1900

Mar. 4	RATCLIFFE, GEORGE	Clyde, Haywood Co.	Rape
" 22	RITTER, GEORGE	Carthage, Moore Co.	Informer
Sept. 1	UNKNOWN NEGRO	Forest City, Rutherford Co.	Murder

1901

Aug. 21	HOUGH, LUKE	Wadesborough, Anson Co.	Murder

1902

Mar. 25	WALKER, JAMES	Washington, Beaufort Co.	Murder
June 11	GILLESPIE, HARRISON	Salisbury, Rowan Co.	Murder
Aug. 25	JONES, THOMAS	SevenSprings, Wayne Co.	Rape

1904

May 19	UNKNOWN	Seaboard, Northampton Co.	Rape

1905

Aug. 27	MOORE, JOHN	Clark, Craven Co.	Murderous assault

1906

May 28	*JOHNSON, J. V.*	Wadesboro, Anson Co.	Murder
Aug. 6	GILLESPIE, NEASE	Salisbury, Rowan Co.	Murder

NORTH CAROLINA—Continued

Aug. 6	GILLESPIE, JOHN	Salisbury, Rowan Co	Murder
" 6	DILLINGHAM, JACK	Salisbury, Rowan Co	Murder
Nov. 15	HARRIS, WM	Near Asheville, Buncombe Co	Murder

1908

Jan. 12	UNNAMED NEGRO	Pine Level, Johnston Co	For giving poor entertainment, lynched by Negroes

1910

May 26	NEGRO	Charlotte, Mecklenburg Co	Rape
Oct. 8	NEGRO	Pelham, Caswell Co	Robbery

1913

Aug. 26	McNEELY, JOSEPH	Charlotte, Mecklenburg Co	Murder

1914

Jan. 27	WILSON, JAMES	Wendell, Wake Co	Murder

1915

Aug. 29	*THREE NIGHT RIDERS*	Graham Co	

1916

Jan. 12	RICHARDS, JOHN	Goldsboro, Wayne Co	Murder
Apr. 5	BLACK, JOSEPH	Kinston, Lenoir Co	Attempted murder

NORTH DAKOTA

1912

Nov. 7	*BAKER, GEO.*	Steele, Kidder Co	Murder

1913

Dec. 16	*KULBERTSON, CLIVE*	Williston, Williams Co	Murder

OHIO

1891

Apr. 10	*BOLES, WILLIAM*	Kenton, Hardin Co	Murder

1892

Jan. 14	CORBIN, HENRY	Oxford, Butler Co	Murder
Feb. 30	*LYTLE, JAMES*	Findlay, Hancock Co	Wife-murder
Apr. 1	UNKNOWN NEGRO	Millersburg, Holmes Co	Unknown cause

1894

Jan. 12	PARKER, ROSCOE	West Union, Adams Co	Murder
Apr. 15	NEVILLE, SEYMOUR	Rushsylvania, Logan Co	Rape

1895

May 31	*WEATHEROFF, NELSON*	Logan, Hocking Co	Attempted rape
Aug. 21	ANDERSON, NOAH	New Richmond, Clermont Co	Murder

1897

June 4	MITCHELL, CHARLES	Urbana, Champaign Co	Rape

1904

Mar. 7	DIXON, RICHARD	Springfield, Clark Co	Murder

1910

July 8	*ETHERINGTON, CARL*	Newark, Licking Co	Murder

1911

June 27	UNNAMED NEGRO	Cleveland, Cuyahoga Co	Murder

OKLAHOMA

1889

Apr. 23	UNKNOWN MAN		Murder

1891

Mar. 28	HUDSON, ELROD	Russellville, Pittsburg Co	Incendiarism

OKLAHOMA—Continued

1892
Dec. 21....CORA, ———..................................Near Guthrie, Logan Co..................By Indians

1893
Sept. 18.... YOUMANS, A..Cause not given
"   22....FIVE INDIANS..Cause not given
"   24... UNKNOWN MAN.....................Hennessey, Kingfisher Co..........Cause not given
"   29...A BOHEMIAN.....................Alva, Woods Co....................................Murder
Nov. 18....HORSE THIEF.....................Near Ponca, Kay Co...............................

1894
Apr. 19....BISHOP, DOCK..........................Wakongo...........................Horse-stealing
"   19....LATHAM, F..........................Wakongo...........................Horse-stealing
"   20...SEVEN HORSE THIEVES...Hennessey, Kingfisher Co........................
May 26...TWO INDIANS...................Hennessey, Kingfisher Co.......................Rape
Sept. 20...**UNKNOWN HORSE THIEF**....Lincoln..........................

1895
Jan.   1....THREE HORSE THIEVES..Kingfisher, Kingfisher Co.......................
May 15....CALVIN, JOHN.....................Near Ingalls.....................Informing
"   15...DUNN, WILLIAM.................Near Ingalls.....................Informing
July   1...TWO HORSE THIEVES.......Near Guthrie, Logan Co........................
Oct. 22...UMBRA, JAMES (MEXICAN)..Hennessey, Kingfisher Co.............Cattle stealing
"   22....MEXICAN JOHN (MEXICAN).Hennessey, Kingfisher Co————Cattle stealing

1896
Jan. 15...FOLEY, THOMAS..................Ft. Holmes...........................Highwayman
"   15...."WILD HORSE".....................Ft. Holmes...........................Highwayman
"   15...UNKNOWN.....................Ft. Holmes...........................Highwayman
"   15...INDIAN.....................Ft. Holmes...........................Highwayman
Sept. 16...**MORRIS, B. S.**.....................Watonga, Blaine Co.....................Murder
"   19....COAX, ELMER.....................Pawnee, Pawnee Co.....................Murder

1897
Feb.   4...LINTON, HENRY.....................................Outlawry
"   4....ROBINSON, JOSEPH..Outlawry

1898
Oct.   1....**JOHNSON, PETER**................Edmond, Oklahoma Co.....................Larceny

1899
Aug.   2.... KIRK, TAYLOR...................Cloud Chief, Washita Co.....................Murder

1901
May 10....CHANDLER, J. L...Suspected killing
                                                                                                      cattle
May 25....**CAMPBELL, WILLIAM**................Pond Creek, Grant Co.....................Murder

1906
May 23...**UNKNOWN MAN**.....................Choctaw Nation, Oklahoma Co.............Murder
July   2...**UNKNOWN.**.....................Chickasha, Grady Co.....................Rape

1907
Mar. 31...**WILLIAM, JAS,**...........................Colbert, Bryan Co.................Attempted rape
July 16...**BAILEY, FR.**.....................Near Oklahoma City, Oklahoma Co........Murder
Dec. 24...**GARDEN, JAS.**.....................Muskogee, Muskogee Co.....................Murder

1909
Apr. 19...MILLER, J. B.........................Ada, Pontotoc Co.....................Murder
"   19...BURRELL, D. B........................Ada, Pontotoc Co.....................Complicity in
                                                                                                      murder
"   19...WEST, JESSE.........................Ada, Pontotoc Co.....................Complicity in
                                                                                                      murder
"   19...ALLEN, JOS.........................Ada, Pontotoc Co.....................Complicity in
                                                                                                      murder
June 26....**SHENNIEN, SYLVESTER**........Wilburton, Latimer Co.....................Murder

1910
Aug. 15...BUCKLEY, JOS.........................Weleetka, Okfuskee Co.....................Murder
Nov. 15...**NEGRO.**.....................Mannford, Creek Co.....................Murder

OKLAHOMA—Continued

1911

May 25	LAURA NELSON and SON	Okemah, Okfuskee Co.	Murder
Aug. 18	UNNAMED NEGRO	Durant, Bryan Co.	Murder
" 24	CARTER, PETER	Purcell, McClain Co.	Rape
Oct. 22	SUDDETH, EDWARD	Corneta	Murder
Dec. 6	WALKER, BUD	Mannford Creek, Co.	Murder

1912

Jan. 1	TURNER, SAM	Muldrow, Sequoyah Co.	Murder

1913

Jan. 2	UNNAMED NEGRO	Wagoner Co.	Rape
June 13	SIMMONS, DENNIS	Anadarko, Caddo Co.	Murder
Aug. 14	FRANKLIN, SANDERS	Paul's Valley, Garvin Co.	Murder
" 14	RALSTON, HENRY	Paul's Valley, Garvin Co.	Murder
Nov. 4	CUDJO, JOHN	Wewoka, Seminole Co.	Murder

1914

Jan. 27	DICKERSON, BENJAMIN	Noble, Cleveland Co.	Murder
Mar. 31	SCOTT, MARIE	Wagoner Co.	Murder
Aug. 7	WILLIAMS, CROCKETT	Eufaula, McIntosh Co.	Murder

1915

May 9	WARD, DR. E. B.	Norman, Cleveland Co.	Murder
Aug. 6	BERRY, EDWARD	Shawnee, Pottawatomie Co.	Rape
Sept. 4	WASHINGTON, GEORGE	Wagoner, Wagoner Co.	Attempted rape

1916

Apr. 3	MARTIN, OSCAR	Idabel, McCurtain Co.	Rape
" 9	DUDLEY, CARL	Lawton, Comanche Co.	Murder
Sept. 20	FOREMAN, JOHN	Nowata, Nowata Co.	Accessory to murder
" 29	POWELL, ——	Nowata, Nowata Co.	Accessory to murder

1917

June 16	CONLY, HENRY	Holdenville, Hughes Co.	Rape

OKLAHOMA
(INDIAN TERRITORY)

1889

Feb. 13	*STEIN, CHARLES*		Murder
" 20	*PUCKET, JOHN*	Lyon Creek, Adair Co.	Unknown offense
" 20	*PUCKET, MRS. JOHN*	Lyon Creek, Adair Co.	Unknown offense

1891

Mar. 3	UNKNOWN NEGRO	Woodward, Woodward Co.	Rape

1894

Apr. 20	*"DUTCH JOHN"*	Tukon, locality undetermined	Cattle stealing
Sept. 16	IN KI WISH	Locality undetermined	Indian police, by desperadoes

1895

Mar. 12	*TWO HORSE THIEVES*	Enterprise, Haskell Co.	

1896

July 14	*THREE UNKNOWN MEN*	Reagan, Johnston Co.	Stealing horses

1898

Jan. 8	McGEESEY, JOHN (INDIAN)	Maud P. O., Pottawatomie Co.	Murder and outrage
" 8	SIMPSON, PALMER (INDIAN)	Maud P. O., Pottawatomie Co.	Murder and outrage
Aug. 9	*NAIL, WILLIAM*	Braggs, Muskogee Co.	Murder

1901

Feb. 28	MILLER, JOHNSON (INDIAN)	Holdenville, Hughes Co.	Murder

OREGON

1891
Apr. 24...*HUNT, A. J.* ....Locality undetermined......................... ....Murder

1894
Aug. 2...*THOMPSON, W. S.*....................Lake View, Lake Co................. ....Murder

1902
Sept. 15...FISHER, ALONZO........ ....Mansfield............... ....Rape

1914
July 17... *UNKNOWN*...................... ....Whitney, Baker Co................. ....Rape

PENNSYLVANIA

1891
May 23....*HAMPTON, DENNIS*..............Barnsley, Chester Co...................... ... ...Murder

1894
Mar. 15...PURYEA, RICHARD....................Locality undetermined............... .. ..Murder

1899
Dec. 13...PIERCE, DAVID..........................Dunbar, Fayette Co................................Murder

1911
Aug. 13....WALKER, ZACHARIAH.............Coatesville, Chester Co............................Murder

SOUTH CAROLINA

1889
Jan. 26...BREWINGTON, WM. ....Wadis Station..Murder
May 17...DANFORD, TUT............................Mt. Carmel, McCormick Co...For turning State's
                                                                                                        evidence
June 22...CALDWELL, ANDY ....Ridgewater_____ ....Rape
"   28...McNIGHT, A._____Union Co..Quarreling
Dec. 28...JOHNSON, RIPLEY....................Barnwell, Barnwell Co..............................Murder
"   28...ADAMS, MICHAEL....................Barnwell, Barnwell Co..............................Murder
"   28...BELL, PETER............................Barnwell, Barnwell Co..............................Murder
"   28...MONOLL, RAFE........................Barnwell, Barnwell Co................_____......Murder
"   28...FURZ, HUGH............................Barnwell, Barnwell Co..............................Murder
"   28...JOHNSON, HUDSON.................Barnwell, Barnwell Co..............................Murder
"   28...PHOENIX, ROBERT J.................Barnwell, Barnwell Co..............................Murder
"   28...JONES, JUDGE.........................Barnwell, Barnwell Co..............................Murder

1890
Jan. 11...BLACK, WILLIAM......................Barnwell, Barnwell Co............................Burglary
May 5...LEAPHART, WILLIE...................Lexington, Lexington Co.............Alleged rape
                                                                                          (proved innocent)
Dec. 3....JOHNSON, HENRY.....................Central, Pickens Co.................................Rape

1891
Dec. 10...LUNDY, RICHARD........................Edgefield Co._____............Murder

1892
May 9...A NEGRO...................................Berkley Co..Murder
"   16...A NEGRO...................................Berkley Co..Murder
"   31...SHAW, DAVID............................Gray Court, Laurens Co............................Larceny
Nov. 18...McFATTON, DUNCAN.................Cheraw, Chesterfield Co._____ ...Murder
"   28...WHITE, NATHAN.......................Quaker Creek..Incendiarism

1893
Apr. 24...*PETERSON, JOHN*...................Denmark, Bamberg Co..............................Rape
May 6...GAILLARD, SAM...Rape
"   10...BANKS, HAYWARD........... ....Columbia, Richland Co. ....Rape
July 18...MEETZE, DUB............................Lexington Co.............................Stealing horse
Aug. 23...DAVIS, JACOB............................Greenwood, Greenwood Co.........................Rape
Nov. 8...KENNEDY, ROBERT.....................Spartanburg, Spartanburg Co.....Attempted rape

SOUTH CAROLINA—Continued

1894

June 2....CRAWFORD, JEFF.................................Bethune, Kershaw Co...............................Murder
 "   3....GILL, HARRY..Lancaster, Lancaster Co.............Unknown cause
 "   3....A NEGRO..Lancaster, Lancaster Co.........Highway robbery
July 14....MASON, JAMES.......................................Abbeville Co.......................Giving information
Nov. 29....UNKNOWN NEGRO...........................Landrum, Spartanburg Co........Cause unknown

1895

June 26....STOKES, WILLIAM.................................Colleton Co.................................Attempted rape
July 15....JACKSON, IRA..Piedmont, Greenville Co...............Alleged rape
Oct. 17....*BLAKE, WILLIAM*................................Hampton, Hampton Co...............................Murder
Nov. 24....RICHARDS, JOHN...................................Abbeville, Abbeville Co...........................Murder
 "   24....WATTS, THOMAS....................................Abbeville, Abbeville Co...........................Murder
Dec. 5....KEARSE, ISOM..Colleton Co.....................................Larceny
 "   5....KEARSE, HANNAH.................................Colleton Co...............................Knowledge of
                                                                                                                larceny
 "   7....BLAKE, WILLIAM...................................Hampton, Hampton Co...............Alleged murder

1896

Feb. 29....KENNEDY, MELVILLE.........................Windsor, Aiken Co...........................Alleged rape
Apr. 23....PRICE, THOMAS....................................Westville, Kershaw Co..........................Assault
July 6....UNKNOWN NEGRO...............................Lincoln Co..Rape
 "   18....DICKS, DANIEL......................................Ellenton, Aiken Co...............................Rape

1897

Jan. 6....BROWN, LAWRENCE..............................Stilton................................Suspected arson
 "   8....UNKNOWN NEGRO...............................Orangeburg, Orangeburg...........................Arson
 "   8....COOPER, SIMON....................................Sumter, Sumter Co.............................Murder
Feb. 13....UNKNOWN NEGRO...............................Saluda, Saluda Co.................................Rape
July 23....GRAY, JAMES..Golboro..Rape
Dec. 29....TURNER, SAM..Kingstree, Williamsburg Co...................Murder

1898

Jan. 4....HUNTER, DAVID....................................Clinton, Laurens Co.....................Violation of
                                                                                                                 contract
Feb. 22....BAKER, F. B..Lake City, Florence Co.............Race prejudice
 "   22....BAKER, DORA..Lake City, Florence Co.............Race prejudice
Oct. 23....MACKIE, JOSEPH..................................Edgefield Court House, Edge-
                                                                        field Co.............................Suspected murder
 "   23....SULLIVAN, LUTHER.............................Edgefield Court House, Edge-
                                                                        field Co.............................Suspected murder
Nov. 9....McKENNY, HAMPTON..........................Phoenix...............................Alleged murder
 "   9....JACKSON, COLUMBUS...........................Phoenix...............................Alleged murder
 "   9....WILLIAMS, JESSE..................................Phoenix...............................Alleged murder
 "   9....WILLIAMS, DRAYTON..........................Phoenix...............................Alleged murder
 "   9....ETHERIDGE, ROSE................................Phoenix...............................Alleged murder
 "   9....DARLING, JEFF......................................Phoenix...............................Alleged murder
 "   10....COLLINS, BENJAMIN.............................Phoenix...............................Alleged murder
 "   10....HARRISON, ESSX..................................Phoenix...............................Alleged murder
 "   18....GOODE, ELIZA..Greenwood, Greenwood Co...........Race prejudice

1899

June 18....PATRICK, LOUIS...................................Bayne...Murder

1900

Jan. 11....SALTER, RUFUS....................................West Springs........................Suspected of arson
Feb. 17....BURTS, WILLIAM.................................Basket Mills............................Threats to kill

1901

Jan. 16....ROBINSON, CHARLES...........................Elko, Barnwell Co.................................Rape
July 14....HAINES, ————.................................Thickety, Union Co............................Murder
 "   21....CORNISH, WILLIAM.............................Port Royal, Beaufort Co......................Murder
Oct. 21....UNKNOWN NEGRO...............................Hampton, Hampton Co......................Burglary
Nov. 24....LADISON, JOHN....................................Anderson Co.....................................Murder

1902

June 5....BLACK, JAS..Ravenals, Charleston Co......................Murder
Dec. 27....WIDEMAN, OLIVER.............................Troy, Greenwood Co...........................Murder
 "   27....WIDEMAN, MRS.....................................Troy, Greenwood Co...........................Murder

SOUTH CAROLINA—Continued

1903

July 1...EVANS, CHARLES......................Norway, Orangeburg Co..............Suspicioned of murder
"   1...TWO UNKNOWN NEGROES....Norway, Orangeburg Co................Suspicioned of murder
"   1...ELROD, REUB........................Piedmont, Greenville Co..............Race prejudice
"   20...HEAD, DENNIS.......................Aiken Co.............................Mistaken identity
"   20...BUTLER, JESSE.......................Aiken Co.............................Mistaken identity
Nov. 24...NELSON, CHARLES..................Jefferson, Chesterfield Co....................Rape
"   28...FAGLER, JOHN........................Ross Station...............................Attempted rape

1904

Jan. 15...LEE "GEN."..........................Dorchester Co.............................Attempted rape
June 30...WILLIAMS, CAIRO..................Scranton, Florence Co.................... Murder
July 5...TAYLOR, JOHN.....................Chesterfield Co..........................Attempted rape
Sept. 24...UNKNOWN..........................Waterloo, Laurens Co......................Rape
Oct. 1...MORRISON, JOHN..................Kershaw, Kershaw Co......................Murder

1905

Sept. 20...PENDLETON, ALLEN..............Abbeville, Abbeville Co...........................Murder
Dec. 20...DA LOACH, FRANK................Barnwell, Barnwell Co...........................Murder
Dec. 20...DA LOACH, JOHN................Barnwell, Barnwell Co...........................Murder

1906

June 14...HUGHES, MOSES..................Union, Union Co..............................Alleged arson
Aug. 20...DAVIS, ROBT.......................Greenwood, Greenwood Co...................... Rape
"   20...ETHRIDGE, ROBT....................Mont Willing...........................Attempted rape
"   22...SPAIN, WM............................St. George, Dorchester Co...........Attempted rape
Nov. 15...DAVIS, MARK.......................Near Newberry, Newberry Co..........................Murderous assault

1907

May 7...UNKNOWN............................Marion Co................................Rape
June 2...HUDSON, GEO......................Trenton, Edgefield Co................Attempted rape and murder

1909

Jan. 6...UNNAMED NEGRO................Lexington, Lexington Co..........................Rape
"   6...DAVIS, ARTHUR....................Florence, Florence Co..........Dispute with white man
June 11...SIMMONS, TUILLIE...............Branchville, Orangeburg Co..................Murder
"   11...SAMUELS, FRANK..................Branchville, Orangeburg Co..................Murder

1910

Nov. 26...CLARK, FLUTE......................Little Mountain, Newberry Co..............Murder

1911

Oct. 10...JACKSON, WILLIS.................Near Greenville, Greenville Co..............Rape

1912

Mar. 13...DUBLIN, ALFRED................Olar, Bamberg Co...........................Arson
"   13...DUBLIN, RICHARD................Olar, Bamberg Co...........................Arson
"   13...RIVERS, PETER......................Olar, Bamberg Co...........................Arson
"   29...WHISONANT, FRED................Blacksburg, Cherokee Co.......Murder and assault
"   29...BRONSON, JOS......................Blacksburg, Cherokee Co......Murder and assault
Nov. 23...THOMAS, WM.......................Newberry, Newberry Co..........Murder
Dec. 21...FITTS, HENRY.......................Norway, Orangeburg Co.......Refusal to pay a note

1913

Aug. 12...PUCKETT, RICHARD..............Laurens, Laurens Co.......................Rape

1914

July 13...CARSON, ROSE......................Elloree, Orangeburg Co.........................Murder
Nov. 24...WILSON, DILLARD................Shiloh, Sumter Co............................Murder
Dec. 4...GRIER, WILLIAM...................Coward, Florence Co...........Frightening women
Dec. 16...SEYMOUR, ALLEN..............Hampton, Hampton Co......................Rape

1915

June 14...SMITH, JULES........................Winnsboro, Fairfield Co...........................Rape

SOUTH CAROLINA—Continued

1916
Oct. 21....CRAWFORD, ANTHONY..............Abbeville, Abbeville Co.....................Self-defense

1917
Aug. 24....SIMS, W. D..................................York, York Co........................Seditious utterance

SOUTH DAKOTA

1891
Nov. 28....*JONES,* ———............................Cherry Creek, Ziebach Co..............Cattle stealing
Dec. 12....*LOVETT, HAND AND UN-*
    KNOWN WHITE MAN.....Deadwood, Lawrence Co.................Stealing horses

1894
Sept. 4....*BOURKE,* ———.............................Watertown, Codington Co............................Rape

1895
Aug. 16....*BIDDERLY BROTHERS*..........Buffalo Co...Cattle stealing

1897
Sept. 18....*TWO CATTLE RUSTLERS*.....Morea River...............................Cattle rustling

1888
July 27....*ELMER, LEE*...............................Wahpeton......................................Murder
Sept. 15....*WISE,* ———.................................Turtle Mountains..........................Horse stealing

1897
Nov. 14....CONDOUT, ALEX. (INDIAN)..Williamsport................................Murder
" 14....TRACK, PAUL HOLY (IN-
    DIAN)...................................Williamsport................................Murder
" 14....*IRELAND, PHILIP*....................Williamsport................................Murder

1902
Jan. 18.... *YELLOWWOLF, JOHN*.............Rosebud, Todd Co...........................Horse stealing

TENNESSEE

1889
Jan. 19....*TWO MEN AND WOMAN*.......Tiptonville, Lake Co.......................Robbery and
    Murder
Apr. 5....*WOLFENBERGER, JOHN*.......Rutledge, Grainger Co...............................Murder
" 7....*BEELER, DANIEL*.....................Rutledge, Grainger Co...............................Murder
June 7....*REYNOLDS, E. R.*.....................Scott Co.......................................Murder
" 7....*LOYD, THOMAS J.*...................Scott Co.......................................Murder
Dec. 12....*CARDEN, WM.*..........................Cleveland, Bradley Co..............................Rape

1890
Feb. 19....STAPLES, JACOB..........................Heiskell's Station, Knox Co.........................Rape
Mar. 16....WILLIAMS, HENRY...................Gadsen, Crockett Co................................Rape
Apr. 5....UNKNOWN MAN.....................Rutledge, Grainger Co..........................Murder
Aug. 18....WOODWARD, THOMAS............Humboldt, Gibson Co............................Robbery
" 21....HENDERSON, FOX....................Trenton, Gibson Co..............................Robbery
Nov. 17....STEVENS, EDWARD...................Savannah, Hardin Co............................Murder

1891
Feb. 16....HAYNIE, FRINCH.......................Hendersonville, Sumner Co.................Rape and
    incendiarism
Mar. 10....SCOTT, BRADFORD..................Pinson, Madison Co...................Unknown offense
" 13....SANDERS, HENRY....................Lavernia, Wilson Co.............................Rape
" 26....HUNTLEY, THOMAS................Cumberland Gap, Claiborne Co.............Murder
Apr. 2....MAYBERRY, MARTIN..............Bryant Station, Maury Co.......................Rape
" 30....TAYLOR, WILLIAM...................Franklin, Williamson Co.............Robbery and
    murder
May 26....WELLS, GREEN..........................Locality undetermined.........................Murder
June 13....CLARK, ROBERT......................Bristol, Sullivan Co.............................Rape
July 5....THOMPSON, ———.....................Dyer, Gibson Co.............................Murder
" 19....WALLING, BEN.........................Decaturville, Decatur Co........................Rape
" 26....BROWN, JOHN.........................Jackson, Madison Co..........................Murder
Aug. 25....LEWIS, WILLIAM.....................Tullahoma, Coffee Co..................Drunkenness
Nov. 13....MITCHELL, JOSEPH................McConnell, Obion Co...........................Rape

TENNESSEE—Continued

1892

Feb. 3	MARTIN, MRS.	Sumner Co.	Race prejudice
Mar. 4	UNKNOWN NEGRO	Waynesboro, Wayne Co.	Robbery
" 8	McDONNELL, CALVIN	Memphis, Shelby Co.	Murder
" 8	MOSS, THOMAS	Memphis, Shelby Co.	Murder
" 8	STUART, WILLIAM	Memphis, Shelby Co.	Murder
Apr. 28	GRIGGARD, HENRY	Goodlettsville, Davidson Co.	Rape
" 30	GROGGARD, EPH.	Nashville, Davidson Co.	Rape
May 5	*MILLER, CHARLES*	Blunt Co.	Murder
" 19	EVERETT, CHARLES	Manchester, Coffee Co.	Attempted robbery
" 31	WILLIS, HECK	Lebanon, Nelson Co.	Rape
June 27	*BATES, THOMAS*	Shelbyville, Bedford Co.	Wife-murder
July 1	LILLARD, THOMAS	Woodbury, Cannon Co.	Rape
" 25	*WYNNE, J. H.*	Burns, Dickson Co.	Murder
" 29	*BESHEARS, ANDY*	Jacksboro, Campbell Co.	Rape
" 29	*WILLIS, JOHN*	Jacksboro, Campbell Co.	Rape
Aug. 1	LANDERS, LOEB	Dresden, Weakley Co.	Attempted rape
" 27	BLACKWELL, DENNIS	Alamo, Crockett Co.	Attempted rape
Oct. 5	BELL, ALEX.	Mt. Pelia	Insulting a woman
Dec. 7	NEGRO TRAMP	Jellico, Campbell Co.	Rape
" 7	*WHITE MAN*	Jellico, Campbell Co.	Rape
" 14	REED, JESSE E.	Locality undetermined	Murder
" 15	A NEGRO	Nashville, Davidson Co.	Rape
" 17	ROBERTS, IRWIN	Shady Valley	Murder

1893

Jan. 3	*DUNCAN, HENRY*	Loudon, Loudon Co.	Murder
Feb. 11	A NEGRO	Forest Hill, Shelby Co.	Rape
" 14	BLOUNT, ANDY	Chattanooga, Hamilton Co.	Suspicion of rape
" 26	HAYNE, JOSEPH	Jellico, Campbell Co.	Rape
Mar. 19	JONES, JESSIE	Jellico, Campbell Co.	Rape
Apr. 24	*TARPLEY,* ——	Verona	By white caps
June 8	DUMAS, L. C.	Gleason, Weakley Co.	Rape
" 21	*HARR, JAMES*	Gleason, Weakley Co.	By mistake
Aug. 21	TAIT, CHARLES	Near Memphis, Shelby Co.	Murder
Sept. 14	WILLIAMS, JOHN	Jackson, Madison Co.	Murder
Oct. 22	GAMBLE, JOHN	Pikeville, Bledsoe Co.	Rape

1894

Feb. 11	McGREEG, HENRY	Pioneer, Campbell Co.	Rape
" 14	*UNKNOWN TRAMP*	Quito, Tipton Co.	Murder
Mar. 6	GREGORY, LAMPSON	Bells Depot	Unknown cause
Apr. 18	MONTGOMERY, HENRY	Lewisburg, Marshall Co.	Larceny
June 1	BALLARD, FRANK	Jackson, Madison Co.	Attempted murder
" 10	PERRY, JAMES	Knoxville, Knox Co.	Introducing small-pox
July 7	BALL, JAMES	Charlotte, Dickson Co.	Murder
" 14	BELL, WILLIAM	Dixon Co.	Barn burning
Aug. 12	NERSHBRED, WILLIAM	Rossville, Fayette Co.	Rape
Sept. 1	HAWKINS, DANIEL	Millington, Shelby Co.	Barn burning
" 1	HAYNES, ROBERT	Millington, Shelby Co.	Barn burning
" 1	WILLIAMS, WARNER	Millington, Shelby Co.	Barn burning
" 1	HALL, EDWARD	Millington, Shelby Co.	Barn burning
" 1	HAYES, JOHN	Millington, Shelby Co.	Barn burning
" 1	WHITE, GRAHAM	Millington, Shelby Co.	Barn burning
" 21	*DARCEY, JAMES*	Near Bristol, Sullivan Co.	Giving information
Nov. 10	SMITH, NEEDHAM	Tipton Co.	Rape

1895

Mar. 20	TALLEY, HARRIET	Petersburg, Lincoln Co.	Suspected arson
Apr. 25	UNKNOWN NEGRO	Parsons, Decatur Co.	Unknown offense
" 28	*GIBSON, THOMAS*	Sevierville, Sevier Co.	Unknown offense, by white caps
Sept. 3	JOHNSON, JERRY	Farmington	Insults
" 6	"DOC." KING	Fayetteville, Lincoln Co.	Attempted rape
" 10	*WOOD, LUM*	Union City, Obion Co.	Giving evidence
Oct. 15	VANCY, EUGENE	Manchester, Coffee Co.	Rape
" 15	ELLIS, JEFF	Braden, Fayette Co.	Murder
Nov. 21	HURD, CHARLES	Wartburg, Morgan Co.	Murder
" 29	ROBINSON, JOSEPH	Fayetteville, Lincoln Co.	Murder
" 29	McGAHEY, OZIAS	Fayetteville, Lincoln Co.	Murder
" 29	*SMITH, CAD*	Near Ootlewah, James Co.	Attempted rape

TENNESSEE—Continued

1896

Jan.	8	SIMPSON, FRANK	Lexington, Henderson Co.	Rape
"	8	FULLER, HARRISON	Lexington, Henderson Co.	Rape
Mar.	22	*MURPHY, WILLIAM*	Huntsville, Scott Co.	Murder
Apr.	17	DOUGLAS, YORK	McMinnville, Warren Co.	Incendiarism
"	18	*SAVAGE, STERLING*	Irving College	By moonshiners
"	26	*HILLIS, WILLIAM*	Shellsford	Murder
"	26	*HILLIS, VICTOR*	Shellsford	Murder
"	27	*GIVENS, O. H.*	Dandridge, Jefferson Co.	Murder
June	12	CLAY, SAMUEL	Martin, Weakley Co.	Attempted rape
"	30	UNKNOWN NEGRO	Near Trenton, Gibson Co.	Rape
July	6	CROSS, NIMROD	Sardis, Henderson Co.	Rape
Nov.	15	ALLEN, CHARLES	McKenzie, Carroll Co.	Rape
"	19	DONALD, SAMUEL M.	Huntingdon, Carroll Co.	Threats

1897

Feb.	17	TWO NEGROES	Webb City	Arson
"	26	BROWN, CHARLES	Soddy, Hamilton Co.	Attempted rape
Mar.	3	*WHALEY, WILLIAM*	Sevierville, Sevier Co.	By white caps
"	3	*WHALEY, MRS. WILLIAM*	Sevierville, Sevier Co.	By white caps
June	23	UNKNOWN NEGRO	Newcastle	Murder
July	15	WILLIAMSON, TONY	West Point, Lawrence Co.	Murder

1898

Mar.	21	COLLAR, JOHN	Godson	Attempted rape
May	27	MITCHELL, JOSEPH	Rives, Obion Co.	Murder
June	23	WASHINGTON, CHARLES	Mine Lick	Rape
Aug.	8	THURMOND, RICHARD	Ripley, Lauderdale Co.	Attempted rape
Sept.	20	WILLIAMS, JOHN	Mountain City, Johnson Co.	Rape
Nov.	19	SMART, JOHN	Chapelton	Race prejudice

1899

Jan.	17	CALL, GEORGE	Lynchburg, Moore Co.	Bad reputation
"	17	SHAW, JOHN	Lynchburg, Moore Co.	Bad reputation
Apr.	18	*LARNE, A. M.*	Henderson, Chester Co.	Murder
Aug.	11	CHAMBERS, WILLIAM	Bellbuckle, Bedford Co.	Rape

1900

Jan.	9	GIVENEY, HENRY	Ripley, Lauderdale Co.	Murder
"	9	GIVENEY, ROGER	Ripley, Lauderdale Co.	Murder
"	16	GANSE, ANDERSON	Henning, Lauderdale Co.	Aiding in escape of murderer
Mar.	23	RICE, LEWIS	Ripley, Lauderdale Co.	Testifying for one of his own race
Sept.	10	REAMS, LOGAN	Duplex	Attempted rape
"	26	UNKNOWN NEGRO	Near South Pittsburg, Marion Co.	Rape
Oct.	3	WILLIAMS, ——	Tiptonville, Lake Co.	Robbery

1901

Feb.	18	KING, FRED	Dyersburg, Dyer Co.	Attempted rape
Mar.	16	CRUTCHFIELD, BALLIE	Rome, Smith Co.	Alleged theft
"	17	*FITZGERALD, ISAAC*	Tiptonville, Lake Co.	Rape
Apr.	29	MALLORY, WYATT	Springfield, Robertson Co.	Murder
"	2	*DAVIS, CHARLES*	Smithville, De Kalb Co.	Rape
"	25	NOLES, HENRY	Near Winchester, Franklin Co.	Murder
Oct.	4	McCLENNON, WALTER	Huntingdon, Carroll Co.	Assaulting white man
"	7	FOUR NEGROES	Caney Springs, Marshall Co.	Theft

1902

Feb.	6	WHITAKER, ENLESS	Lynchburg, Moore Co.	Murder
May	12	UNDERWOOD, JAS.	Decatur, Meigs Co.	Making threats
Oct.	8	BURLEY, GARFIELD	Newburn, Dyer Co.	Murder
"	8	BROWN, CURTIS	Newburn, Dyer Co.	Murder
Nov.	13	DAVIS, JOHN	Lewisburg, Marshall Co.	Murder

1903

June	24	JONES, CHARLES	Elk Valley, Campbell Co.	Rape
Aug.	5	UNKNOWN NEGRO	Lewisburg, Marshall Co.	Unknown offense
"	5	UNKNOWN NEGRO	Lewisburg, Marshall Co.	Unknown offense
Sept.	—	SMALL, ALLEN	Lynchburg, Moore Co.	Attempted rape
Dec.	10	BRAKE, JOSEPH	Ripley, Lauderdale Co.	Murder

TENNESSEE—Continued

1904

Jan.   3....ALEXANDER, ROBERT.............Ripley, Lauderdale Co.................Race prejudice
Apr. 29....SEACEY, THOS.........................Haywood...Rape

1905

Mar. 8....GWYN, RONCE........................Tullahoma, Coffee Co.............. ....Theft
Oct. 10....BILLINGS, LUTHER..............Brunswick, Shelby Co..................Attempted rape

1906

Mar. 19....JOHNSON, ED.......................Chattanooga, Hamilton Co.......................Murder
Oct. 29....ESTES. GEO.........................Hales Point, Lauderdale Co.....................Murder

1907

July 22....TWO NEGROES......................Lake Co.................................Fighting white man

1908

Jan. 21....COLE, WALTER.....................Morgan Co.......................................Murder
May   8....GARVARD, ELMO...................Pulaski, Giles Co.......................Attempted rape
July 14....JONES, HUGH.......................Middleton, Hardeman Co..........Attempted rape
Aug. 28....JOHNSON, GEO......................Murfreesboro, Rutherford Co......Attempted rape
Oct. 19....TAYLOR, R. E......................Walnut Log..........................By night riders
 "   19....RANKIN, QUINTEN...................Walnut Log.........................By night riders
 "   30....*COOK, GEO.*.......................Kingston, Roane Co........................Murder
Nov. 24....STINEBACK, MARSHALL..........Tiptonville, Lake Co........................Murder
 "   24....STINEBACK, EDWARD.............Tiptonville, Lake Co......................Murder
 "   24....STINEBACK, TENNES..............Tiptonville, Lake Co........................Murder

1909

July 20....LAWSON, ALBERT...................Paris, Henry Co..............................Murder
Sept. 11....*SPENCER, JOHN*.................Jonesboro, Washington Co....................Murder

1910

Sept. 13....SHARP, WILLIAM..................Tiptonville, Lake Co..................Attempted rape
 "   13....BRUCE, ROBERT....................Tiptonville, Lake Co..................Attempted rape

1911

May 25....SWEET, JAMES.......................Gallatin, Sumner Co...........................Murder
June 1....CRUMP, PATRICK...................White Haven, Shelby Co...........Attempted rape
 "   8....WINSTON, JOHN.....................Lafayette, Macon Co.........................Murder
Dec.   6....TWO UNNAMED NEGROES.....Near Clifton, Wayne Co............Race prejudice
 "   6....UNNAMED NEGRO...................Near Clifton, Wayne Co.............Race prejudice

1912

Feb. 15....UNNAMED NEGRO..................Memphis, Shelby Co............................Rape
 "   19....GRER, WALTER.....................Shelbyville, Bedford Co......................Murder
 "   19....NEAL, DAVID.......................Shelbyville, Bedford Co.....................Murder
 "   19....BOMAN, GREEN......................Shelbyville, Bedford Co.....................Murder
May 27....SAMUELS, JACOB...................Robertson Co.................................Rape

1913

Mar. 21....GREGSON, JOHN....................Union City, Obion Co........................Murder
Nov. 7....TALLEY, JOHN......................Dyersburg, Dyer Co..................Attempted rape

1915

Apr. 28....BROOKS, THOMAS...................Somerville, Fayette Co......................Murder
Sept. 4....WILSON, ———....................Dresden, Weakley Co..........................Rape

1916

Mar. 1....WHITLEY, WILLIAM...............Lebanon, Wilson Co..........................Murder
 "   19....THOMAS, WM.......................Dyersburg, Dyer Co. ....Shooting officer

1917

May 22....PERSON, ELL.......................Memphis, Shelby Co....................Alleged rape
                                                                                         and murder
Aug. 24....SHEPPARD, LAWRENCE..........Near Memphis, Shelby Co.................Larceny
Dec. 2....SCOTT, LIGON......................Dyersburg, Dyer Co............................Rape

TEXAS

1889

Feb. 19....TWO NEGROES (2)	Liberty, Texas		Murder
" 20....*BROWN, ASA*	San Saba Co.		Unknown offense
" 20....*SMITH, W. L.*	San Saba Co.		Unknown offense
Apr. 15....DRIGGS, GEO.	Hempstead, Waller Co.		Rape
May 17....UNKNOWN NEGRO	Millican, Brazos Co.		Alleged rape
July 14....DAVIS, HENRY	Waco, McLennan Co.		Unknown
" 26....LEWIS, GEORGE	Belen, Paso Co.		Poisoning a well
" 28....LINDLEY, GEO.	Greenville, Hunt Co.		Cause unknown
Aug. 14....BROOKS, JAMES	Orange, Orange Co.		Rape
Dec. 14....*TWO OUTLAWS* (2)	White Rock		Cause unknown
" 28....*O'DELL, ——*	Uvalde, Uvalde Co.		Outlaw
" 28....*O'DELL, WM.*	Uvalde, Uvalde Co.		Outlaw

1890

Mar. 27....UNKNOWN	Hedsville		Murder
Apr. 5....UNKNOWN	Thornton, Limestone Co.		Rape
" 5....WILLIAMS, ——	Kosse, Limestone Co.		Rape
" 20....JACOBS, STEPHEN	Fay		Incendiarism
" ....GARRETTE, SIMEON	San Augustine, San Augustine Co.		Attempt to kill
" 24....TEEL, JERRY	San Augustine, San Augustine Co.		Attempt to kill
" 24....UNKNOWN	Cameron Station, Milam Co.		Rape
May 12....BENNETT, EDWARD	Hearne, Robertson Co.		Rape
June 1....BROWN, THOMAS	Hooks Ferry, Bowie Co.		Murder
" 20....A NEGRO	Livingston, Polk Co.		Murder
" 28....UNKNOWN	Antlers		Cause unknown
July 3....HENRY, PATRICK	Nechesville		Gambling
" 22....YOUNG, ANDY	Red R. Co.		Race prejudice
" 30....HAWKINS, WILLIAM	Cypress, Harris Co.		Theft
Aug. 4....BROWN, JOHN	Navasota, Grimes Co.		Rape
" 8....UNKNOWN NEGRO	Anderson, Grimes Co.		Rape
" 14....TWO UNKNOWN NEGROES (2)	Mexia, Limestone Co.		Rape

1891

Jan. 1....BEALLE, CHARLES	Lang		Rape
Feb. 7....*SALCEDA, JESUS*	Knickerbocker, Tom Greene Co.		Unknown cause
" 17....REBIN, THOMAS	Douglas, Nacogdoches Co.		Desperado
" 24....ROWLAND, THOMAS	Douglas, Nacogdoches Co.		Robbery
" 27....*WILLIAMS, JASPER AND TWO OTHERS*	Sea Junction		By vigilantes
Apr. 1....*FIELD, WILLIAM*	Mineola, Wood Co.		Attempted rape
May 28....*SHEPPARD, MONROE*	Belton, Bell Co.		Unknown cause
June 8....*SHELBY, EVAN E.*	Wickliffe		Murder
" 28....HARTFIELD, WILLIAM	Cass Co.		Being troublesome
" 28....SHEPPARD, MUNN	Cass Co.		Being troublesome
July 22....JOHNSON, WILLIAM	Henderson, Garfield Co.		Rape
Oct. 26....GREEN, LEO	Linden		Murder
Nov. 13....TWO NEGROES (2)	Burnet		Unknown cause
" 22....BLACK, WILLIAM	Moscow, Beaver Co.		Insults

1892

Jan. 29....*SHIELDS, JOSEPH*	Thompsons, Fort Bend Co.		Unknown cause
Apr. 26....A NEGRO	Riesil, McLennan Co.		Murder
June 10....COOK, TOBE	Bastrop, Bastrop Co.		Rape
" 28....WOOD, PRINCE	Spurger, Tyler Co.		Rape
" 28....SMITH, THOMAS	Spurger, Tyler Co.		Rape
" 28....GAINES, HENRY	Spurger, Tyler Co.		Rape
Sept. 6....WALKER, JOHN	Paris, Lamar Co.		Rioting
" 6....ARMOR, WILLIAM	Paris, Lamar Co.		Rioting
" 6....RANSOM, JOHN	Paris, Lamar Co.		Rioting
" 19....A NEGRO	Paris, Lamar Co.		Rape
" 23....SULLIVAN, WILLIAM	Plantersville, Grimes Co.		Rape

1893

Jan. 31....SMITH, HENRY	Paris, Lamar Co.		Murder
Feb. 17....BUTLER, WILLIAM	Hickory Creek		Race prejudice
June 14....WILLIAMS, GEORGE	Near Waco, McLennan Co.		Rape
July 16....*JAZO, M.*	Near El Paso, El Paso Co.		Murder
Aug. 31....UNKNOWN NEGRO	Yarborough, Grimes Co.		Unknown cause

TEXAS—Continued

1894

Jan.	7	*MILLER, JUDAS*	Ft. Reynold	Unknown offense
Feb.	10	DILLINGHAM, JESSIE	Smokeyville	Train wrecking
Apr.	14	*CREWS, JACK*	Gainesville, Cooke Co.	Murder
"	14	BREN, ALFRED	Gatesville, Coryell Co.	Unknown
May	9	UNKNOWN NEGRO	West Texas	Writing letter to white woman
"	17	SCOTT, HENRY	Jefferson, Marion Co.	Murder
June	13	HALL, LON	Sweet Home, Lavaca Co.	Murder
"	13	COOK, BASCOM	Sweet Home, Lavaca Co.	Murder
"	29	WILLIAMS, JOHN	Sulphur Springs, Hopkins Co.	Murder
July	20	GRIFFITH, WILLIAM	Woodville, Tyler Co.	Rape
Oct.	8	GIBSON, HENRY	Fairfield, Freestone Co.	Attempted rape
Dec.	20	ALLEN, JAMES	Brownsville, Cameron Co.	Arson

1895

Jan.	9	*BOYD, THOMAS*	Bowie, Montague Co.	Alleged murder
Mar.	11	MANION, ISAAC	Athens	Murder
Apr.	12	CALHOUN, NELSON	Corsicana, Navarro Co.	Rape
"	30	JONES, GEORGE (INDIAN)	Devers, Liberty Co.	Assault
May	25	*CROCKER, JOHN, WIFE AND SON (3)*	Wharton, Wharton Co.	Murder
June	11	JOHNSON, WILLIAM	Lufkin	Rape
"	11	WHITE, ALEXANDER	Keno	Murder
"	11	CHERRY, JOHN	Keno	Murder
July	20	PHILLIPS, MRS. ABE	Mant, Sanpete Co.	Race prejudice
"	20	PHILLIPS, HANNAH E	Mant, Sanpete Co.	Race prejudice
"	20	PHILLIPS, ABE, Jr.	Mant, Sanpete Co.	Race prejudice
"	20	PHILLIPS, EDWARD	Manr, Sanpete Co.	Race prejudice
"	20	JOHNSON, BENJAMIN	Mant, Sanpete Co.	Race prejudice
"	20	TAYLOR, K. D.	Mant, Sanpete Co.	Race prejudice
"	23	UNKNOWN WOMAN	Brenham, Washington Co.	Race prejudice
"	29	LOFTIN, SQUIRE	Lexington, Lee Co.	Rape
Aug.	2	MASON, JAMES	Daingerfield, Morris Co.	Unknown offense
"	2	MASON, MRS. JAMES	Daingerfield, Morris Co.	Unknown offense
"	12	UNKNOWN NEGRO	Delta Co.	Race prejudice
"	22	UNKNOWN NEGRO	Wharton, Wharton Co.	Murder
"	26	COLE, JEFFERSON	Paris, Lamar Co.	Race prejudice
Oct.	14	*SUITTA, FLOANTINA (F)*	Catula	Murder
"	29	HILLIARD, HENRY	Tyler, Smith Co.	Murder
Nov.	21	A NEGRO	Madison Co.	Guilty of no offense

1896

Feb.	20	*LEWIS, T.*	Wichita Falls, Wichita Co.	Robbery and murder
"	29	*CRAWFORD, FOSTER*	Wichita Falls, Wichita Co.	Robbery and murder
May	3	BENBY, WILLIAM	Beaumont, Jefferson Co.	Murder
June	10	WHITEHEAD, LOUIS	Bryan, Brazos Co.	Rape
"	10	JOHNSON, GEORGE J.	Bryan, Brazos Co.	Rape
Aug.	13	GAY, BENJAMIN	Hopkins Co.	Arson

1897

Jan.	25	WASHINGTON, EUGENE	Bryan, Brazos Co.	Rape
Mar.	5	UNKNOWN NEGRO	Elgin, Bastrop Co.	Burglary
Apr.	27	WRIGHT, HAL	Harrison Co.	Robbery and arson
"	27	WRIGHT, RUSSELL	Harrison Co.	Robbery and arson
"	—	BROWN, ROB.	Harrison Co.	Robbery and arson
"	30	RHONE, FAYETTE	Sunnyside, Waller Co.	Murder
"	30	GATES, WILLIAM	Sunnyside, Waller Co.	Murder
"	30	THOMAS, LEWIS	Sunnyside, Waller Co.	Murder
"	30	THOMAS, JAMES	Sunnyside, Waller Co.	Murder
"	30	THOMAS, BENJAMIN	Sunnyside, Waller Co.	Murder
"	30	WILLIAMS, WILLIAM	Sunnyside, Waller Co.	Murder
"	30	THOMAS, AARON	Sunnyside, Waller Co.	Murder
May	14	COTTON, DAVID	Rosebud, Falls Co.	Attempted rape
"	14	WILLIAMS, HENRY	Rosebud, Falls Co.	Attempted rape
"	14	STEWART, SABE	Rosebud, Falls Co.	Attempted rape
"	18	WHITE, WILLIAM	San Augustine, San Augustine Co.	Murder
"	18	WHITE, WILLIAM	San Augustine, San Augustine Co.	Murder
"	18	WHITE, JOHN	San Augustine, San Augustine Co.	Murder
"	21	*PETER ——*	Brown Co.	Cause unknown
"	23	JONES, WILLIAM	Tyler, Smith Co.	Murder

TEXAS—Continued

Aug. 6....WHITE, ESSECK.............................Nacogdoches, Nacogdoches Co......................Rape
  "   10....*JONES, REV. CAPTAIN*.......Paris, Lamar Co................................Elopement
  "   26....BONNER, ————.................Bellville, Austin Co.............................Rape
  "   26....JOHNSON, WESLY.................Mooreville...Attempted rape
Oct. 11....CARTER, ROBERT.................Brenham, Washington Co.......................Murder
Nov. 18....SWEAT, THOMAS................Bryan, Brazos Co................................Murder

1898

Apr.   5...GUILEN, CARLOS.................Brownsville, Cameron Co......................Murder
June 6....WASHINGTON, GEORGE..........Wemar, Weno....................................Murder
Aug. 8...OGG, DAN.................................Palestine, Anderson Co.........................Rape

1899

May 23....*HUMPHRY AND TWO*
         SONS, JAS. (3)......................Ally..................................Helping murderer
                                           to escape
July   1...THOMPSON, ALLIE.................Waskom, Harrison Co...........................Rape
  "   9...*BRAKE, BUD*.......................Corning..Accomplice in
                                           murder
  " 14...BROWN, ABE.............................Gilead...Rape and murder
  " 14...UNKNOWN NEGRO................Iola, Grimes Co..................................Murder
  " 16...McGEE, HARRY.......................Navasota, Grimes Co...........................Murder
  " 25...HAMILTON, HENRY.................Near Navasota, Grimes Co.............Incendiarism

1900

Feb. 11...*SWEENY, JAMES*.................Port Arthur, Jefferson Co......................Murder
Nov. 15...THREE NEGROES (3)............Jefferson, Marion Co................Attempted murder

1901

Feb. 11...CARTER, GEORGE.................Paris, Lamar Co..................................Rape
Mar. 13...HENDERSON, JOHN.................Corsicana, Navarro Co..........................Rape
Aug.   1...UNKNOWN NEGRO...............Mobile, Tyler Co..........................Insulting white
                                           woman
  " 20...WILDER, ABE.........................Dexter, Cooke Co................................Murder
  " 25...*MARTINEZ, FELIX*.................Kenedy, Karnes Co..............................Unknown
Oct.   3...FIVE NEGROES (5).................Harrison.............................Quarrel over profit
                                           sharing
  " 25...GORDON, GALNER.................Quitman, Wood Co..............................Murder
Dec. 25...McCLINTON, J. H.................Paris, Lamar Co..................Unknown offense

1902

Mar. 11...BIRD, NATHAN.........................Luling, Caldwell Co.................Unknown offense
  " 11...SON OF BIRD.........................Luling, Caldwell Co.................Unknown offense
May 22...MORGAN, DUDLEY.................Long View, Gregg Co.................Criminal assault
Sept. 4...WALKER, JESSE.....................Hempstead, Waller Co...........................Rape
Oct.   4...DUNCAN, UTT.........................Columbus, Colorado Co...............Attempted rape
  " 21...WESLEY, JOS.........................Hempstead, Waller Co...........................Rape
  " 21...BARTON, REDDISH.................Hempstead, Waller Co...........................Rape

1903

Jan. 14...O'NEAL, RANSOM.................Angleton, Brazoria Co..........................Murder
  " 14...TUNSTALL, CHARLES.............Angleton, Brazoria Co..........................Murder
Apr. 26...JOHNSON, HENSLEY.................Carthage, Panola Co...............Attempted rape
May 27...UNKNOWN..............................Kemp, Kaufman Co...............................Murder
July 23...ALLEN, MOONY.....................Beaumont, Jefferson Co........................Murder
July 31...UNKNOWN..............................Near Alto, Cherokee Co..........................Assault
Oct.   1...DAVIS, WALKER.....................Marshall, Harrison Co..........................Murder

1904

July 30...LARREMORE, JNO.................Lockhart, Caldwell Co..................Race prejudice,
                                        by white caps
Aug. 31...TURNER, OSCAR.................Weimar, Colorado Co...............Attempted rape
Sept. 1...TUCKER, OSCAR.................Weimar, Colorado Co...........................Rape

1905

Feb. 16...*MUNOZ, CARLOS*.................Near Dale, Caldwell Co........................Rape
  " 17...JOHNSON, WM.....................Smithville, Bastrop Co..........................Rape
Mar. 14...STEVENS, JULIUS.................Long View, Gregg Co...............Murderous assault
June 20...SIMON, FORD.........................Riverside, Walker Co...........................Rape
July 14...MASON, FRANK.....................Golinda, Goliad Co...............................Rape
  " 20...GREEN, SAM.........................New Braunfels, Comal Co.......................Rape
  " 29...UNKNOWN NEGRO................Avery, Avalon Co.................................Rape

TEXAS—Continued

Aug. 8	MAJORS, SANK	Waco, McLennan Co.	Rape
" 11	*WILLIAMS, THOS.*	Sulphur Springs, Hopkins Co.	Attempted rape
" 14	WILLIAMS, THOS.	Sulphur Springs, Hopkins Co.	Attempted rape
Sept. 7	DAVIS, STEPHEN	Italy, Ellis Co.	Rape
Nov. 11	REESE, JOHN	Henderson, Rusk Co.	Murder
" 11	ASKEW, ROBT.	Henderson, Rusk Co.	Murder
" 11	UNKNOWN NEGRO	Henderson, Rusk Co.	Murder

1906

Jan. 10	HARRIS, BENJ.	Moscow, Polk Co.	Murder
Apr. 24	NEGRO	Groesbeck, Limestone Co.	Rape
" 25	NEGRO	Oakwood, Leon Co.	Rape
Sept. 15	FRAZIER, MITCHELL	Rosebud, Falls Co.	Murderous assault
Oct. 26	PITTS, "SLAB"	Toyah, Reeves Co.	Marrying a white woman

1907

July 14	WILSON, FRED.	Del Rio, Valverde Co.	Murder
Aug. 6	HALL, THOS.	Goliad, Goliad Co.	Attempted assault
Nov. 4	JOHNSON, ALEX.	Cameron, Milam Co.	Attempted rape
Dec. 26	CALLAWAY, ANDERSON	Marquez, Leon Co.	Attempted rape

1908

Feb. 28	SCOTT, CLEM.	Conroe, Montgomery Co.	Attempted rape
Mar. 10	CAMPBELL, JOHN	Navosota, Grimes Co.	Murderous assault
" 24	UNNAMED NEGRO	Conroe, Montgomery Co.	Attempted rape
" 24	TWO UNNAMED NEGROES (2).	Magnolia, Montgomery Co.	Attempted rape
Apr. 9	FIELDS, ALBERT	Long View, Gregg Co.	Rape
" 19	DOUGLAS, JASPER	Atlanta, Cass Co.	Rape
May 7	WILLIAMS, JOHN	Naples Morris Co.	Murder
June 22	EVANS, JERRY	Hemphill, Sabine Co.	Murder
" 22	JOHNSON, WM.	Hemphill, Sabine Co.	Murder
" 22	MANUEL, WM.	Hemphill, Sabine Co.	Murder
" 22	McCOY—"RABBIT BILL"	Hemphill, Sabine Co.	Murder
" 22	SPELLMAN, MOSES	Hemphill, Sabine Co.	Murder
" 22	WILLIAMS, FRANK	Hemphill, Sabine Co.	Murder
" 22	TWO UNIDENTIFIED (2)	Hemphill, Sabine Co.	Murder
" 22	WILLIAMS, CLEVELAND	Hemphill, Sabine Co.	Murder
July 15	UNNAMED NEGRO	Beaumont, Jefferson Co.	Mistaken identity
" 28	SMITH, TAD.	Greenboro.	Rape
Aug. 15	JACKSON, MOSES	Bellville, Austin Co.	Unknown reason
Sept. 13	NEWTON, DANIEL	Brodeshire.	Murder

1909

Mar. 7	ELLIS, ANDERSON	Rockwall, Rockwall Co.	Rape
Apr. 27	HODGES, JAS.	Marshall, Harrison Co.	Rape
" 30	"CREOLE MOSE"	Marshall, Harrison Co.	Murder
" 30	HILL, "PIE".	Marshall, Harrison Co.	Murder
" 30	CHASE, MATTHEW	Marshall, Harrison Co.	Murder
May 28	*BURNETT, THOS.*	Abilene, Taylor Co.	Murder
Sept. 13	UNNAMED NEGRO	Bellamy.	Murder
" 13	UNNAMED NEGROES (2)	Sandy Point, Brazoria Co.	Murder
Dec. 20	MILLS, COPE	Rosebud, Falls Co.	Murder

1910

Feb. 2	UNKNOWN NEGRO	Beaumont, Jefferson Co.	Rape
Mar. 3	BROOKS, HOLLAND	Dallas, Dallas Co.	Rape
Apr. 5	BATES, FRANK	Centerville, Leon Co.	Murder
June 26	JOHNSON, LEONARD	Rusk, Cherokee Co.	Murder
July 5	UNNAMED NEGRO	Rodney.	Attempted rape
" 12	*GENTRY, HENRY*	Belton, Bell Co.	Murder and alleged rape

(There were fifteen victims of race rioting in Texas in July, which are not included as lynchings. Race Riot in Texas growing out of a quarrel between a colored and white man.)

Nov. 8	*RODIGUEZ, ANTONIO*	Rock Springs, Edwards Co	Murder

1911

June 20	MEXICAN BOY	Thorndale, Milan Co.	Murder
Aug. 12	JONES, "COMMODORE"	Farmersville, Collin Co.	Insulting women
Oct. 29	UNNAMED NEGRO	Marshall, Harrison Co.	Attempted rape
Nov. 8	JOHNSON, RILEY	Clarksville, Red River Co.	Attempted rape

TEXAS—Continued

1912

Feb. 13....SAUNDERS, GEO..........................Marshall, Harrison Co.................Complicity in murder
" 13....JACKSON, MARY................Marshall, Harrison Co................Complicity in murder
May 25....DAVIS, DAN................Tyler, Smith Co................Rape

1913

Jan. 17....MONSON, HENRY................Paris, Lamar Co................Murder
" 23....STANLEY, RICHARD................Fullbright, Red River Co................Rape
Feb. 25....ANDERSON, ———................Near Marshall, Harrison Co................Murder
" 25....PERRY, ROBERT................Karnach, Harrison Co................Horse stealing
June 4....UNNAMED NEGRO................Beaumont, Jefferson Co.........Murderous assault
" 5....GALLOWAY, RICHARD................Newton Co................Race trouble
Sept. 21....DAVIS, WILLIAM................Franklin, Robertson Co................Murder

1914

Jan. 8....LEE, DAVID................Jefferson, Marion Co................Murderous assault
Mar. 13....WILLIAMS, WILLIAM................Hearne, Robertson Co................Murder
June 7....ROBERTSON, WILLIAM................Navasota, Grimes Co................Murder
Oct. 17....DURFEE, JOSEPH................Angleton, Brazoria Co................Murder

1915

May 9....UNIDENTIFIED NEGRO................Big Sandy, Upshur Co................Murder
July 29....*MUNZ, ADOLFO*................Brownsville, Cameron Co................Murder
Aug. 20....SIX MEXICANS (6)................San Benito, Cameron Co.......Pillage and murder
" 24....*SLOVAK, JOHN*................Shiner, Lavaca Co................Wife beating
" 29....RICHMOND, KING................Sulphur Springs, Hopkins Co................Murder
Sept. 3....THREE MEXICANS (3)................Murder
" 14....SIX MEXICANS (6)................San Benito and Edenburg, Co................Banditry
Oct. 10....TEN MEXICANS (10)................Near Brownsville, Cameron Co................Train-wrecking and murder

1916

Jan. 24....*MAXFIELD, W. J.*................Boston, Bowie Co................Murder
May 5....DIXON, THOMAS................Hempstead, Waller Co................Rape
" 15....JESS, WASHINGTON................Waco, McLennan Co................Rape and murder
June 20....LERMA, JERONIMO................Brownsville, Cameron Co.......Murderous assault
Aug. 7....BROWN, STEPHEN................Seymour, Baylor Co................Murder
" 19....LANG, EDWARD................Rice, Navarro Co................Murder
Oct. 5....SPENCER, WILLIAM................Graceton, Upshur Co................Alleged murder
Nov. 5....JOHNSON, JOSEPH................Bay City, Matagorda Co................Murder
" 29....THOMAS, BUCK................Clarksville, Red River Co.......Murderous assault

1917

June 22....HARPER, BENJAMIN................Courtney, Grimes Co................Murder
" 23....HAYS, ELIJAH................Reisel................Striking white woman
" 25....SAWYER, CHARLES................Galveston, Galveston Co................Rape
" 29....JEFFERSON, ROBT................Temple................No cause
July 3....GUIDRY, GILBERT................Orange................Attempted rape
" 23....UNNAMED................Elysian Fields................Entering white woman's room
Aug. 22....JONES, CHARLES................Near Marshall, Harrison Co.......Attempted rape
Sept. 3....JENNINGS, CHARLES................Beaumont................Cause unknown
" 21....SMITH, BERT................Goose Creek, Harris Co.............Attempted rape

VIRGINIA

1889

Mar. 14....FLETCHER, MAGRUDER................Tasley, Accomac Co................Rape
Apr. 3....ROLAND, MARTIN................Abingdon, Washington Co................Murder
" 23....BAILEY, SCOTT................Halifax................Rape
June 11....FORBES, JOHN................Petersburg, Dinwiddie Co................Alleged rape
Sept. 16....GARNER, SAMUEL................Bluefield, Mercer Co................Rape
Nov. 8....ANDERSON, OWEN................Leesburg, Loudoun Co................Attempted rape
" 23....BLAND, ROBERT................Petersburg, Dinwiddie Co................Cause unknown

VIRGINIA—Continued

1890

July 10....A NEGRO...Lebanon, Russell Co....................Making threats
Dec. 24....FIVE NEGROES..Mecklenburg Co.....................................Murder

1891

Feb. 23....BISHOP, SCOTT..Blackstone, Nottaway Co.........................Robbery
Mar. 18....*BELA, NOGRADE*....................................Branchville, Southampton Co................Stealing
Apr. 6....*PUMILL, THOMAS*..................................Gladys, Campbell Co.................................Robbery
Oct. 17....SCOTT, JAMES..Clifton Forge, Alleghany Co.....................Rioting

1892

Feb. 12....LAVENDER, WILLIAM..............................Roanoke, Roanoke Co..................Attempted rape
Mar. 18....HEPLIN, LEE...Farquhar Co....... ....Murder
 " 18....DYE, JOSEPH..Farquhar Co......................................Murder
Apr. 9....BRANDON, ISAAC.....................................Charles City, Charles City Co....Attempted rape
July 9....ANDERSON, WILLIAM.............................Louisa Court House, Louisa Co...................Rape
Nov. 1....*TWO BURGESS BROTHERS*..Lebanon, Russell Co........................Murder

1893

Feb. 1....BROWN, JERRY...Richmond, Henrico Co..............................Murder
 " 1....BRANCH, SPENCER....................................Richmond, Henrico Co..............................Murder
 " 1....JOHNSON, JOHN..Richmond, Henrico Co..............................Murder
 " 1....ELLERSON, SAM..Richmond, Henrico Co..............................Murder
Mar. 1....ANTHONY, ABNER.....................................Hot Springs, Bath Co................................Rape
May 12....A NEGRO...Wytheville, Wythe Co................................Rape
June 13....SHORTER, WILLIAM.................................Winchester, Frederick Co.........................Rape
Oct. 2....McFADDEN, GEORGE.................................Moore's Cross Roads.................................Rape
Nov. 1....REDMOND, ABRAHAM.............................Charlotte Co..Desperado
 " 4....WAGNER, EDWARD...................................Lynchburg, Campbell Co............Alleged barn-
                                                                                                    burning
 " 4....WAGNER, WILLIAM...................................Lynchburg, Campbell Co...............Alleged barn-
                                                                                                    burning
 " 4....MOTLOW, SAM...Lynchburg, Campbell Co..................Alleged barn
                                                                                                    burning

1894

Apr. 27....ROBINSON, JAMES..................................Manassas, Prince William Co ....Rape
 " 27....WHITE, BENJAMIN...................................Manassas, Prince William Co...................Rape
May 17....WOOD, SAMUEL.......................................Gate City, Scott Co...........................Without cause
June 8....KEMP, ISAAC..Cape Charles, Northampton Co...............Murder
Nov. 10....YOUNGER, LAWRENCE...........................Lloyds, Essex Co......................................Murder
 " 10....*WILLIAMS, CHARLES*..........................Lloyds, Essex Co......................................Murder

1895

Sept. 10....WINGFIELD, WESLEY,............................Lunenburg, Lunenburg Co.........Attempted rape
Dec. 2....POSS, ———..Fairfax Court House, Fairfax
                                                                     Co..Murder
 " 2....HENRIP, ———...Fairfax Court House, Fairfax
                                                                     Co..Murder

1897

Mar. 14....CLEMENT, WILLIAM................................Lynchburg, Campbell Co...........................Felony
Apr. 2....McCOY, JOS..Alexandria, Alexandria Co.........................Rape
Aug. 20....*NOWHIR, JOHN E.*................................Runneybag..............................Revenue informer
Sept. 6....WALL, HENRY..Friends Mission..Rape
Oct. 2....*FALLS, PEB. (WOMAN)*........Cowans Depot........................Disreputable char-
                                                                                                    acter

1898

Apr. 29....*SMITH, PARIS*..Coeburn, Wise Co....................................Murder
July 12....JAMES, JOHN H.......................................Charlottesville, Albemarle Co....................Rape

1899

Aug. 8....THOMPSON, BENJAMIN...........Alexandria, Alexandria Co...........................Rape

1900

Jan. 5....*WATES, W. W.*......................................Newport News, Warwick Co.......................Rape
Mar. 24....COLTON, WALTER....................................Emporia, Greensville Co...........................Murder
 " 24....O'GRADY, BRANDT.................................Emporia, Greensville Co...........................Murder
Apr. 5....UNKNOWN NEGRO..................................Southampton Co.......................................Arson
 " 22....PETERS, JOHN...Tazewell, Tazewell Co...............................Rape
Sept. 19....UNKNOWN NEGRO..................................Arrington, Nelson Co.................................Rape
Dec. 8....LONG, DANIEL..Wythe Co..Rape

VIRGINIA—Continued

1901

Mar. 22....UNKNOWN NEGRO................Halifax Co..Arson
July   1....WALKER, ———................Lawrenceville, Brunswick Co......................Rape

1902

Apr.   6...CARTER, JAS.............................Amherst, Amherst Co.............Murderous assault
June 6...GAM, WILEY........................Toms Brook, Shenandoah Co......Attempted rape
•   11...UNKNOWN NEGRO..................Near Newport News, War-
                                                      wick Co.................................Unknown offense
July 31...CRAVEN, CHAS...................Leesburg, Loudoun Co..............................Murder

1904

Jan. 14...MOSELEY, ELMER................Sussex Co...Murder
May 19...WHITEHEAD, ———...Rape
Aug. 4...DUDLEY, ANDREW..................Greenfield, Nelson Co.................Attempted rape
Oct. 24...*BLUNT, GEO. W*...................Berkely, Norfolk Co...............Assaulting police-
                                                                                                                   man

1905

Feb. 20...HENDERSON, HENRY................Ingram, Halifax Co....................Race prejudice

1908

Mar. 10...*JACKSON, PRESLER*...........Bristol, Washington Co...........................Murder

1909

Dec. 26...*REMINGTON, HENRY*..........Menley...Murder

1910

Nov. 30...NEAL, MACH...............................Warren, Albemarle Co..............................Murder

1912

Aug. 8...UNNAMED......................................Richmond, Henrico Co..............................Rape

1915

Dec. 9...UNNAMED NEGRO....................Hopeful, Louisa Co....................................Theft

1917

Aug. 17...PAGE, WILLIAM.............................Lilian, Northumberland Co.........Attempted rape
Oct. 13...CLARK, WALTER...................Danville, Pittsylvania Co...........................Murder

WASHINGTON

1890

Jan. 7...*SHAFFORD, ALFRED*.............Klichitat Co...Murder

1891

Apr. 12...*ROSE, JOHN*.................................Seabury, Whitman Co................................Murder

1892

June 16...*FOUR ITALIANS*...................Near Seattle, King Co..............................Murder

1893

Oct. 17...*HIGHWAYMAN*......................Pullman, Whitman Co...................................

1894

June 2...*HILL, ———*...............................Colfax, Whitman Co...................................Murder
"   2...*PARKER, ———*.........................Colfax, Whitman Co...................................Murder

1895

Aug. 14...*VINSON, SAMUEL*.................Ellensburg, Kittitas Co..............................Murder
"   14...*VINSON, CHARLES*...............Ellensburg, Kittitas Co..............................Murder

1897

Dec. 23...*MARSHALL, CHADWICK*.....Colfax, Whitman Co...................................Murder
"   23...*McDONALD, JOSEPH*...............Colfax, Whitman Co...................................Murder

1898

Jan. 8...*CHADWICK, MARSHALL*......Colfax, Whitman Co...................................Murder

1903

Aug. 5...*HAMILTON, WM*.....................Asolo..Murder

WASHINGTON TERRITORY

1889
Jan.　7....*SHAFFORD, ALFRED*............Gilman,..Murder

WEST VIRGINIA

1889
July 24....*CARTER, JOHN*........................Hinton, Summers Co................................Murder
Aug. 30....TURNER, JOHN........................Fayetteville, Fayette Co........................Murder
Sept. 10....*THE HALL BROTHERS*................................Rape and murder
Oct. 25....*McCOY, GREEN*....................Hamlin, Lincoln Co.....................Murder
"　27....*HALEY, MILTON*.................Hamlin, Linclon Co......................Murder

1891
Apr. 13....FOOTE, ALEXANDER..............Princeton, Mercer Co........................Murder

1892
May 13...LUTHER, MILLS.................Mercer Co.................................Murder
"　15..."RED" SMITH................Naugatuck, Mingo Co.........................Murder
"　27...SMITH, JAMES.................Logan Co.................................Murder
July　6...JONES, EDGAR.................Weston, Lewis Co.............................Murder
Dec.　5...COFFEE, CORNELIUS................Keystone, McDowell·Co...........................Murder

1894
Aug.　2...HOLLIDAY, ANDERSON.............Elkhorn, McDowell Co.................Murder
Dec.　5...*ARTHUR, MRS. T*...............Lincoln Co........................Cause unknown,
by white caps

1896
Jan. 28...JONES, ALEXANDER.................Bluefield, Mercer Co.......................Murder
Feb.　1...UNKNOWN NEGRO.................Bramwell, Mercer Co......................Murder

1900
May 11...LEE, WILLIAM...........................Hinton, Summers Co....................Attempted rape

1901
July 22...BROOKS, WILLIAM................Elkins, Randolph Co........................Murder

1902
Feb.　7...WILLIAMS, T...................Glen Jean, Fayette Co..............Alleged conjuring
July 25...JACKSON, PETER...................Elkins, Randolph Co..............Mistaken identity
"　25...CLEMENTS, RUDOLPH...........Wanelsdorf.........................Murder
"　25...CARROLL, WM...................Wanelsdorf........................Murder
"　25...TWO NEGROES.................Wanelsdorf.......................Murder

1903
Feb.　4...BROWN, FRANK..................Madison................................Murder

1909
Mar. 19....*BROWN, JOS.*............................Whitmore........................Murder
Nov.　3...LEWIS, CHAS...................Near Sutton, Braxton Co...............................Rape

1910
Oct. 14....NEGRO...................Huntington, Cabell Co.....................Murder

1912
Sept.　5....JOHNSON, WALTER................Bluefield, Mercer Co.......................Rape

1917
Nov. 22....UNIDENTIFIED NEGRO.............Welch, McDowell Co. ....Attempted rape

WISCONSIN

1889
Nov. 25....*OLSEN, HANS JACOB*...........Preston, Grant Co........................Cause unknown

1891
Sept. 21....*SIEBOLT, ANTON*...................Darlington, Lafayette Co...................Murder

1894
Feb.　6....*PIKKARIEN, A.*........................Ewen,..Rape

WISCONSIN—Continued

1903

J**a**n. 30....*MITCHELL, EDWARD*............Madison, Dane Co...Murder

WYOMING

1889

July 22....*AVERILL, JAMES*...................Sweetwater...................................Cattle stealing
    22....*WATSON, ELLA*................Sweetwater...................................Cattle stealing
Dec. 11....*ELEVEN OUTLAWS*.............Big Horn Basin, Sheridan Co....................Murder

1890

Aug. 15....*LASHMAN, P.*.............................Roslyn..Murder

1891

June 18....*WAGGONER, JAMES*................Cook Co..Stealing horse

1892

Aug. 16....*THREE HIGHWAYMEN*.......Nassau Creek..
Oct. 12....*TWO HORSE-THIEVES*...........Casper, Natrona Co...
    16....**BEDFORD, J. S.**.....................Big Horn, Sheridan Co........................Horse-thief
Nov. 16....*TWO HORSE-THIEVES*..........Fremont Co., Wyoming Territory...................

1898

Mar. 7....*JOHNSON, LOUIS P.*............Near Cheyenne, Laramie Co....................Murder
    7....*BANVRET, J.*..................Near Cheyenne, Laramie Co....................Murder

1902

Mar. 28....*WOODWARD, CHAS.*................Casper, Natrona Co..................................Murder

1903

May 27....*CLIFTON, W. C.*..................Newcastle, Weston Co...............................Murder
July 19....*GORMAN, JAMES*...............Basin, Big Horn Co.................................Murder
    19....*WALTERS, J. P.*...................Basin, Big Horn Co.................................Murder

1904

Aug. 30....**MARTIN, JOHN**.............Laramie, Albany Co....................................Assault
Oct. 2....**WIGFALL, FRANK**................Rawlins, Carbon Co..................................Murder

1917

Dec. 14....**HAMPTON, WADE**....................Rock Springs, Sweetwater Co......Annoying white
    women

PLACE UNKNOWN

1889

Mar. 5....*THREE HORSE-THIEVES*......"No Man's Land."...

1890

— —....INDIAN...

1891

May 22....*LUPERSKY, F.*...Rape

1893

Feb. 7....*GONZALEZ, IRENO L.*...Desperado
Nov. 21....*JOHNSON, F. O.*...Rape

1894

Mar. 6....*RODGERS, JOHN*...Larceny

1897

May 15....**ALIVATE (INDIAN)**..Murder

1902

Aug. 12....*SALYERS, CHARLES*..Murder

1908

Dec. 19....*FRANKLIN, CLEVELAND*...Murderous assault

List of Persons Lynched in 1918, by States

ALABAMA

May 22....WOMACK, JOHN........................Redlevel, Covington Co............Assault on white woman
Nov. 11...BIRD, WILLIAM.........................Sheffield, Colbert Co............Creating disturbance
" 12...WHITESIDE, GEORGE...............Sheffield, Colbert Co............Murdering policeman

ARKANSAS

June 13...MITCHELL, ALLEN.....................Earle, Crittenden Co...................Wounding white woman
Aug. 28....*WAGNER, FREDERICK*..........(near Hot Springs) Garland Co...Disloyal remarks
Dec. 18....ROBINSON, WILLIS...............Newport, Jackson Co..........Murdering policeman

CALIFORNIA

Sept. 3....*CZERICH, MARION*...................San Pedro, Los Angeles Co........................Murder

FLORIDA

May 22....JACKSON, HENRY....................Miami, Dade Co.............Throwing white man under train
Aug. —....UNIDENTIFIED NEGRO...........Quincy, Gadsden Co.......Throwing white man under train

GEORGIA

Feb. 7....COSBY, "BUD".......................Fayetteville, Fayette Co............Intent to rob and kidnapping
" 7...DANSY, ED................................Willacoochee, Coffee Co..........Killed two officers, wounded two
Mar. 22...EVANS, SPENCER.....................Crawfordville, Taliaferro Co.....Assault on colored woman

May 17 { HEAD, WILL
THOMPSON, WILL
TURNER, HAYES
RILEY, CHIME
TURNER, MARY
JOHNSON, SYDNEY
RICE, EUGENE
SCHUMAN, SIMON
THREE UNIDENTIFIED NEGROES } Brooks and Lowndes Cos...Murdering white man

May 23...COBB, JAMES.................................Cordele, Dooly Co.................Murdering white woman
" 25...CALHOUN, JOHN..................Barnesville, Pike Co...................Murdering white man
Aug. 11...RADNEY, IKE....................Colquitt, Miller Co............Killing officer, wounding one
Sept. 3...GILHAM, JOHN............................Macon, Bibb Co.................Attacking white woman
" 24...REEVES, SANDY..................Way Cross, Ware Co...............Assaulting white girl

ILLINOIS

April 4...*PRAEGER, ROBERT P.* ....Collinsville, Madison Co.........Making disloyal remarks

KENTUCKY

Dec. 16...LEWIS, CHARLES..................Hickman, Fulton Co...................Beating sheriff

LOUISIANA

Jan. 26...HUDSON, JIM (NELSON)..........Benton, Bossier Parish.............Living with white woman
Feb. 26 { LEWIS, JIM
JONES, JIM
POWELL, WILL } Rayville, Richland Parish................Stealing hogs
Mar. 16...RICHARDS, JOHN.....................Monroe, Ouachita Parish..........Attack on white woman
" 16...McNEEL, GEORGE..................Monroe, Ouachita Parish..........Attack on white woman

April 22....WILLIAMS, CLYDE...................Monroe, Ouachita Parish........Shooting white man
June 18....CLAYTON, GEORGE...................Mangham, Richland Parish..Murdering white man
Aug. 7....HALL, BUBBER...................Bastrop, Morehouse Parish.........Attacking white
woman

MISSISSIPPI

Jan. 17....EDWARDS, SAM...................Hazlehurst, Copiah Co.....Murdering 17-year old
girl
April 20....SINGLETON, CLAUD...................Poplarville, Pearl River Co.......Murdering white
man
Aug. 15....DUKES, BILL...................Natchez, Adams Co....................
Dec. 21 { CLARK, MAJOR...................
CLARK, ANDREW................... } Shubuta, Clarke Co..........Murdering white man
HOUSE, MAGGIE...................
HOUSE, ALMA................... }

NORTH CAROLINA

Mar. 26....BAZEMORE, PETER...................Lewiston, Bertie Co...................Attack on white
woman
Nov. 5....TAYLOR, GEORGE...................Rolesville, Wake Co...................Rape

OKLAHOMA

June 29....MAGILL, L...................Madill, Marshall Co...................Assaulting white
woman

SOUTH CAROLINA

Feb. 23....BEST, WALTER...................Fairfax, Barnwell Co...................Murder

TENNESSEE

Feb. 10....LYCH, G. W...................Estill Springs, Franklin Co....Aiding colored man
(McIlheron) in es-
cape
" 12...McILHERON, JIM...................Estill Springs, Franklin Co.....Shooting two white
men
April 22...NOYES, BERRY...................Lexington, Henderson Co........ Murdering sheriff
May 20....DEVERT, THOMAS...................Erwin, Unicoi Co.............Murdering white girl

TEXAS

May 27....GOOLSIE, KIRBY...................Beaumont, Jefferson Co........Attacking white girl
June 4....CABANISS, SARAH................... }
" 4....CABANISS, PETE................... | { Alleged threat by
" 4....CABANISS, CUTE................... | Huntsville, Walker Co....{ Geo. Cabaniss to
" 4....CABANISS, TENOLA................... } { white man
" 4....CABANISS, THOMAS ....
" 4....CABANISS, BESSIE ....
" 4...*VALENTINE, EDW.*...................Sanderson, Terrell Co...................Murder
July 27....BROWN, GENE...................Benhur, Terrell Co...................Assault on white
woman
Sept. 18...O'NEAL, ABE...................Buff Lake, Terrell Co...........Shooting white man
Nov. 14....SHIPMAN, CHARLES...................Ft. Bend Co...................Disagreement with
white man

VIRGINIA

Nov. 24....THOMPSON, ALLIE...................Culpepper Co...................Assaulting white
woman

WYOMING

Dec. 10....WOODSON, EDWARD...................Green River, Sweetwater
Co.   Killing R.R. switch-
man

www.ingramcontent.com/pod-product-compliance
Lightning Source LLC
Chambersburg PA
CBHW030309100426
42812CB00002B/635